UNIVERSITY OF MAINE
AT FARMINGTON

UNIVERSITY OF MAINE AT FARMINGTON

A STUDY IN EDUCATIONAL CHANGE (1864-1974)

by

Richard P. Mallett

The Bond Wheelwright Company
Publishers · Freeport, Maine

To W. G. Mallett

PREFACE AND ACKNOWLEDGMENT

My original intention was to confine this history to the Farmington State Normal School. Upon my completion of its eighty-one-year story (1864–1945), there were those who expressed a strong interest in my bringing the history up to date. I finally agreed to do so, but only with the greatest reluctance. This was because of the difficulties and hazards that are involved in writing about the immediate past. There was a plethora of information about the normal school years, for I had access to diaries, letters, scrapbooks, a brief history of the school by George C. Purington, and the folksy and quaint news releases of the ever-present *Chronicle* and *Franklin Journal* reporters.

In addition to the advantage of copious sources, the normal school story represented a much simpler task than that of the burgeoning college of more recent times. Emerson's well-known dictum about an institution being the lengthened shadow of an individual had applicability to Farmington Normal. On the other hand, during the past decade Farmington developments have been the lengthened shadows of not only the heads of the college but also of committees, faculty, deans, department heads, and vice-presidents. Such a dispersion of authority made it difficult at times to identify the movers and shakers. There is a good possibility that some of them have been overlooked or, if they have been mentioned, their contributions to the college have not been evaluated correctly. My apologies are hereby extended to them.

Some may wonder why anyone should feel an urge to write about such an outmoded institution as the normal school. My two main motives were filial devotion and the conviction that throughout most of its history the local normal school did heroic work in raising the teaching standards of Maine. Farmington Normal had its weaknesses, but these were at least partially caused by a pathetically small budget. Throughout the years, the school always had at least two or three teachers whose influence on mind and character was of a lifetime durability. My witnesses are unanimous in expressing this opinion. In its formative years, Farmington was also fortunate in having a scholar such as C. C. Rounds. Although normal schools did show an occasional anti-intellectual tendency, this was not the result of anything written or said by Rounds. He agreed with his distinguished friend, William T. Harris, that the first priority of a normal school was to strengthen its academic program. It was his belief that when this was combined with an appreciation of child development, a normal school would justify its existence. He wanted all teachers, at whatever levels, to be instructed in the best ways to provoke thought in the classroom. By saying that this was being neglected in the academies and liberal arts colleges, he antagonized many of their supporters. He lost out in his attempt to strengthen the Farmington Normal curriculum, at least to the extent he thought it should be strengthened, but he has triumphed posthumously. The present-day offerings of the state college are closer to Rounds's conception of the ideal curriculum than anything he or his successors were able to achieve in their lifetimes.

Dr. Einar Olsen and Professor Gwilym Roberts were the two who finally convinced me that I should bring this history up to date. Not only did they expend time and energy in changing my mind, but they then helped to make the task much easier than it otherwise would have been. Dr. Olsen has thrown the financial and moral support of UMF into the publishing of this book, while Dean Roberts has been indispensable in both ferreting out facts and preventing the presentation of nonfacts.

John Burnham allowed me to investigate every nook and cranny of the library, including the archives room. My ardent hope is that librarians will be able to find the things that I may have misplaced. Shirley Martin was consistently successful in finding material for me that I had given up hope of ever locating. Ben and Natalie Butler responded with speed and thoroughness when I called on their expertise to fill in some gaps. Myron Starbird has represented a one-

man cheering section in encouraging me to go on after he had read
the first draft of this opus. Mrs. Hughes, in charge of the Abbott
Collection in the Bowdoin library, has allowed me to examine all the
material pertaining to the involvement of the Abbotts in Farmington Normal history. Dr. Dearborn and Miss Emma Mahoney have
saved me from several errors as a result of their willingness to read
the manuscript. Allen Flint has read much of the history and I have
eagerly adopted his suggestions. Dr. Carlene Hillman allowed me
to read her excellent history of the home economics department.
Roger Wing has contributed much of the recent athletic history.
Mrs. Dee McCormick and Eileen Adams have been indispensable
in typing sections of the manuscript. Mrs. McCormick has also made
insurance copies for me so that a manuscript-consuming fire would
not put me out of business. Anne Mullin did nobly in producing
pictures on short notice; Mickey Maguire opened his photographic
files for use in the history, and there have been countless others
whose help has been appreciated even though my infirm memory
prevents me from giving them proper credit.

Richard Mallett

CONTENTS

LIST OF ILLUSTRATIONS

PART ONE

AN EARLY GATHERING OF FARMINGTON NORMAL SCHOOL STU-DENTS: This building and ell (the latter the old Farmington Academy) served the FSNS from 1865 to 1888. In the latter year, the ell was moved to Middle Street, and in 1895 the remainder was torn down to be replaced by the present front part of the Administrative Building of the University.

I. THE FOUNDING OF THE WESTERN STATE NORMAL SCHOOL *

There is a wide divergence of opinion among even the better historians as to the performance of colonial schools and their contribution to the general welfare. A rather long period that found New England historians praising the early schools extravagantly was succeeded by the inevitable critical reaction. Such distinguished historians as Charles M. Andrews and Charles Beard have either belittled or attacked the colonial school, whereas the no less distinguished Samuel Eliot Morison has praised the educational developments of puritan days.

All of these historians, however, would certainly agree that the better schools of the colonial period were made possible by the concentrated and compact village. Because of it, the resources of the early citizens of New England supported only one school in the community. Subsequently, when many former villagers settled on farms in outlying districts, the village school was reduced in numbers of students and quality of teaching. Itinerant teachers and district schools were the inevitable result of this hegira to the rural areas. Along with them came the school agent. This official did the

---

* The Farmington State Normal School was called the Western State Normal School, and in 1867, the Eastern State Normal School was established in Castine. With the founding in 1878 of Gorham Normal, Farmington's designation was changed to the Northern State Normal, and Gorham became the Western Normal. With the founding of the Aroostook State Normal School in Presque Isle, the local normal school lost its northern designation and had to settle in its title for the name of the town.

hiring of the teachers for his district, even though he may have been abysmally ignorant of school problems. Moreover, the agent was sometimes known to submit to pressure to employ the dull-witted daughter of some local and prominent farmer. State legislatures passed laws that were designed to keep the ignorant teacher out of the classroom, but unfortunately more than laws were needed to uphold teaching standards. Prospective teachers of quality veered away from the classroom when offered wages that were about those of a hired hand on an average farm.

The post-revolutionary dispersal of the population, such as took place on the Maine frontier between 1780 and 1820, contributed to the range and complexity of educational problems. Rural and frontier life helped to bring about short school terms, irregular attendance, ungraded schools, and most deplorable of all, untrained teachers. Add to all this the multiplication of school districts, the payment of mere subsistence wages, the absence of a systematic course of study, the want of general interest in the schools, and even the most optimistic educational reformers must have blanched at the amount of work that lay ahead for those who realized the importance of an educated citizenry.

The majority of Maine's more famous academies were founded during the post-revolutionary settlement of the State. They had a private and semi-private status that was not challenged or resented during the early days of the republic. They were primarily designed to prepare boys for college. Later, girls were allowed to attend, and the curriculum was expanded and modified for those not headed for college. Eventually, however, the private school, with its tuition fees, began to give way to free high schools. This was hastened by the missionary zeal of such people as Horace Mann who traveled up and down the land preaching the gospel of equal educational opportunity for all. Included in his remarks was a plea for the establishment of normal schools. He told his audiences that he considered them "a new instrument of progress for the improvement of the human race." Mann did not believe that acceptable public schools were possible without normal schools. He sharply attacked those who defended the status quo by saying that if the academies and colleges were capable of producing the necessary number of teachers it was strange they had not done so.

In the 1830s a few voices in Maine began to harmonize with Horace Mann. These included Governor Fairfield who, in his 1839 inaugural address, expressed his hopes for educational reforms. In this year, while Horace Mann was helping to establish the first normal school in the country, the Governor of Maine was urging that the State establish a board of education. Such a group, Governor Fairfield asserted, should have, as Massachusetts had, an active and efficient secretary. He went on in his address to propose the establishment of a teachers' seminary.

In 1846 a convention of Maine teachers and friends of education appointed a committee to "carefully consider defects in our school system and to suggest measures for improvement." This same convention recommended the establishment of a state board of education, and shortly thereafter, a legislative act in 1846 provided for such a board. Before it expired from political causes in 1852, it was to perform many valuable services for the advancement of Maine education.

William G. Crosby,* as the first secretary of the State Board of Education, proved to be energetic, efficient, and highly articulate. Although he realized that popular support was lacking in 1847 for the establishment of a normal school, he anticipated the time when the people of the State would more fully appreciate the benefits of such an institution. As a stopgap measure he proposed, the Board recommended, and the legislature established, teachers' institutes to assist teachers in acquiring some knowledge of their profession. These meetings were to be convened in preparation for the school year and at such a place in each county as would afford maximum attendance. They were to be no longer than ten working days and were to feature the advice and wisdom of some of the leading educators of the New England region. Such organizations marked the beginning of teacher training in Maine. Their value and need were recognized at once; during 1847 thirteen institutes were attended by 1,686 teachers.

---

* In 1853 and 1854 Crosby was governor of Maine. Later he was connected in Boston with the Littell publications. He early demonstrated his writing ability as an undergraduate at Bowdoin. A native of Belfast, he wrote a history of his home town. In 1870 he received an LL. D. from Bowdoin, and for many years was on its Board of Overseers.

Despite the benefits derived from these gatherings, the normal school idea continued to gain ground in Maine during the 1850s. In 1854 the State established the position of State Superintendent of the Common Schools. Each superintendent from 1854 to 1863 pushed hard for a normal school system. The ablest of this group may have been Mark H. Dunnell.* Certainly he was one of the heroes in the battle for improved schools. In addition to his super-intending duties, he was editor and publisher of an educational monthly, *The Maine Teacher*. In 1858 he wrote: "Many regrets have been expressed to me, in various parts of the State, that the higher branch of the last legislature should have failed to act in concert with the popular branch in the establishment of a State Normal School." His articles in praise of the normal school system were well written and persuasive. They must have had considerable effect in advancing the cause they espoused.

By 1857 the teachers of Franklin County needed no oratory nor cogent arguments to convince them that the establishment of a state normal school was overdue. They expressed their distress and frustration in the form of the following resolution passed during their 1857 convention:

> Resolved: That the interests of our common schools and the teachers having them in charge, not only require the fostering care of the State, but most imperatively demand the immediate establishment of that long neglected source of improvement, a State Normal School; but that in its endowment no partisan or political interest should be observed, and that no locality should be the object of favor, unless a disposition be manifested to re-turn ample equivalent for all.

---

* Born in Buxton, and a Colby graduate, State Superintendent Dunnell in each of his reports recommended the establishing of state normal schools. *The Maine Teacher* was the first publication of its kind in the State, and its influence was thought to have been considerable. After serving in the Civil War, Dunnell became a lawyer in Owatonna, Minnesota. In 1867 he became Minnesota State Superintendent of Schools, and in 1871 he was elected to Congress and served there until 1885 and from 1889 to 1891. The twenty-two Farmington Normal School graduates who went to Minnesota in the 1860s and '70s were lured there either directly or indirectly by Dunnell. He prevailed upon George M. Gage, second principal of Farmington Normal, to become the first principal of Mankato Normal.

In this way the local teachers prodded the legislature and went on record not only in urging the immediate establishment of a normal school, but in stating their opposition to making the normal school issue a political football with the winning goal being scored through the connivance of a partisan referee.

In the days before there were many free high schools, the academies oftentimes had strong local support. Farmington was no exception. In 1860 the Maine legislature saw the possibility of satisfying everyone by establishing teacher-training departments in eighteen academies in the State. The academies in Franklin and Piscataquis counties declined to institute these departments, and two others were released from the arrangement. The remaining fourteen academies started their new teacher-training departments with a substantial number of students. It was soon apparent, however, that the regular academy work and teacher education made a poor mixture. State Superintendent Edward P. Weston,* in his report for 1861, resumed the campaign that was destined to result in the formation of separate normal schools in Maine. He expressed his regret and chagrin that during the 1860-61 academic year, thirty students from Maine were attending four normal schools in Massachusetts. Such an exodus of prospective teachers had taken place, he went on to note, despite the 1860 legislative act that had set up normal departments in some of the better known academies. By 1862 the legislature was ready to admit the impracticability of normal departments and requested the State Superintendent to make inquiries concerning the possibility of a more efficient and satisfactory system for the training of teachers.

This seemed to mean that the legislature, after a long period of listening to the proponents of normal schools, was getting closer to passing an act establishing the normal school system. The loss

---

* Edward P. Weston was born in Cumberland and graduated from Bowdoin in 1839. For seven years he was in charge of the Lewiston Falls Academy and then became head of Gorham Academy. Appointed State Superintendent in 1860, he served in that position for five years. In 1865 he became the headmaster of the Abbott School, where he was for four years. He played an important role in establishing the normal school system in Maine. At the time of his death, he was running a school near Chicago called Highland College for Women. Like Crosby, he was a man of literary tastes, was a contributor to the *Portland Transcript,* and in the '60s was editor of *The Maine Teacher.*

of prospective teachers to Massachusetts was regarded as regrettable and preventable. Several methods for teacher training had been tried and found wanting. Certainly it had been proved that state boundaries could not contain the ambitious teacher, so a legislative committee on education was assigned the task of evaluating the need for a teacher-training institution. The supporters of the normal school idea felt greatly encouraged, but the traditionalists, who looked askance at any kind of educational innovation, were still a force to be reckoned with.

In March 1863, the legislature was in the concluding stages of a discussion concerned with a report of the Committee on Education. This contained a strong recommendation for the establishment of normal schools in the State. It maintained that despite all the recognized virtues of the state academies and private colleges, there was need for the kind of institution that had for its main objective the training of teachers. Pro-normal school legislators said that just as a student in law, medicine, or divinity needed special training, so did the prospective teacher. Furthermore, it was pointed out that normal schools had proved successful in Europe, the British Provinces, and the United States. The more reluctant and timid of the legislature were assured that the introduction of a normal school would not constitute a venture into the unknown and experimental.

Accompanying the Committee's report was a bill that outlined the steps that were to be taken in preparation for the establishment of normal schools. Three persons were to constitute a commission to make investigations and to locate, subject to the approval of the Governor and his executive council, two normal schools, one in the eastern and one in the western part of the State. The Commissioners were to be guided in their selection by such considerations as: the size and condition of the buildings, the character of the community, the means of access by railroad or water, facilities for obtaining board, extent and quality of the library and other equipment, and opportunity for experimental or model schools.

The bill also set August 1863 as the time for the opening of the two normal schools. It was recognized, however, that such a goal might be unrealistic in view of all the arrangements that had to be made before it would be possible to open them. For one thing, one of the traditional and slow methods of raising money for institutions of higher learning was to be used. This involved the sale of four half-townships of public lands that could be sold in whole or in part. The proceeds of such sales were considered essential to defray the anticipated expenses of the new institutions. A principal and his assistants must be signed up and the time that would be involved in this procedure was problematical. The State Superintendent was given the responsibility of hiring the principal and his assistants, as well as of making sure the right equipment was available for conducting the operations of the school. Every move made by the State Superintendent was subject to the approval of the governor and his council. (This latter group adopted the perplexing title of The Board of Trust and Oversight.) All of this might well take longer than the time allotted before the target date of August 1863.

After a series of somewhat heated discussions, the Normal School Act was passed by a vote of thirteen to seven in the Senate and sixty-three to twenty-nine in the House. Governor Abner Coburn* of Skowhegan signed it on March 25, 1863. The Act established the normal schools by prescribing that they "shall be thoroughly devoted to the work of training teachers for their professional labors"; that "the course of study shall include the common English branches in thorough reviews, and such of the higher branches as are especially adapted to prepare teachers to conduct the mental, moral, and physical education of their pupils"; that "the art of school management, including the best methods of government and instruction, shall have a prominent place in the daily exercises of said schools"; and that "while teaching the fundamental truths of Christianity, and the great principles of morality, recognized by statute, they shall be free from all denominational teachings, and open to persons of different religious connections on terms of perfect equality."

The investigating Commission was invited after the passage of the bill to visit Paris Academy, Gorham Seminary, Farmington Academy, and Litchfield Academy. These institutions had tentatively offered to furnish the necessary accommodations for the Western State Normal School. After carefully considering the various offers

---

* It was appropriate for Governor Abner Coburn to sign the Normal School Act because of his interest in and contributions to Maine education. At a later period, his donations to Colby College and the University of Maine were significant both from the point of view of services rendered and financial generosity. His assistance to the old Waterville Academy resulted in it being renamed Coburn Classical Institute.

from this part of the State, the Commission decided to locate the new educational institution in Farmington. This was to be subject to the approval of the governor and his council and the willingness of the trustees of Farmington Academy to fulfill, in a manner satisfactory to the State Superintendent, the terms of the property conversion that had been previously agreed upon.

The Commission's statement in regard to the Farmington offer was as follows:

> The trustees of Farmington Academy offer their present Academy building, which is fifty by thirty feet, and two stories high, to be divided into recitation rooms, with settees, blackboards, etc.
>
> They propose to erect an additional building about sixty by forty-five feet, and to finish upon the first floor a schoolroom with permanent seats, with desks for two hundred persons; upon the second floor a hall for lectures and other uses, to be furnished with movable settees. Also, other suitable rooms for library, apparatus, dressing rooms, etc. They have also an available cash fund of $4,000 all of which they will appropriate for erecting, altering and furnishing the buildings, and for such other objects as may be deemed necessary.
>
> We are assured that board for two hundred students may be had in respectable private families, within three-quarters of a mile from the Academy, at from $1.75 to $2.50 per week, according to the accommodations required; and that an arrangement will be made with the Androscoggin Railroad to transport students from abroad to and from the school for one fare.
>
> All of which is respectfully submitted.
>
> Philip Eastman
Henry Williamson
Ephraim Flint
>
> *Augusta, June 19, 1863*

Despite this pro-Farmington description of the advantages to be derived from locating in the shire town, there is reason to believe that after June 19, a mighty effort was made to have the Western State Normal School located in some other community. On June 24, the Executive Council passed an order "that the Commissioners should deposit in the office of the Secretary of State, the several propositions submitted to them by citizens or trustees, with all the facts within their knowledge or possession relating to the establishment of said schools." In George C. Purington's history of the school from 1864 to 1889, he mentioned the long delay that followed this request.[1] The facts and papers asked for were submitted on August 7, and after a long debate, the governor and his council, on October 9, 1863, confirmed the action of the Commissioners in deciding upon Farmington as the site for the first normal school.

No known vote was taken to indicate how the local citizens felt about having Farmington Academy replaced by a normal school. There is reason to believe that some were sad and others were irate. Letters written to D. C. Heath before an Academy reunion in 1902 prove that even at that late date some graduates had never become reconciled to the loss of their beloved school. *The Somerset Reporter* in 1880 reported that many Farmington citizens had never recovered from the conversion that deprived them of their Academy. This was understandable in view of the quality of the preceptors. One was Oren B. Cheney, the first president of Bates College. From 1841 to 1849 the preceptor was Alexander H. Abbott, who was later to become the head of the Abbott School as well as a trustee of the normal schools. The preceptor from 1849 to 1859 was Jonas Burnham. His Latin professor at Bowdoin, Alpheus S. Packard, singled him out in a history of the college as having been a particularly promising classical scholar.[2] The last preceptor of the Academy was Ambrose P. Kelsey, who was to become the first principal of the Western State Normal School.

There was another side to the Farmington Academy ledger, and that was the debit side. The institution from its beginning had been in financial trouble. The trustees were unable to collect a portion of the original pledges, and were unfortunate in the selection of the half-townships that were granted them for an endowment fund. In its earliest days of insolvency, the Academy had hoped to combine with the forerunner of Colby College, the Maine Literary and Theological Institution. Such a union failed to take place, possibly because the first preceptor of the Academy, the Reverend James Hall (1812–14), advised the Waterville trustees not to tie up with Farmington. Such a warning was understandable because Hall had repeatedly been unsuccessful in collecting the full pay that was due him for serving as the local preceptor.

Chronically short of funds as they were, the trustees of the Academy had been unable to keep their physical plant in repair. A letter to the local paper, *The Patriot*, dated the twenty-sixth of December, 1862, complained about the condition of the Academy's building. The hope was expressed that the trustees would remove the old building and replace it "with a structure such as the times required." There was no question in the writer's mind that the Academy would have to rebuild or go into oblivion. After describing its site as "the most beautiful in our village" the letter went on to say that without thorough repairs the building "would be unsuitable for a shop and hardly an answer for a stable." After reading such a description of the Academy, and realizing the perennial insolvency of the institution, there can be little doubt that the local trustees were greatly relieved to unload their building onto the State.

There were some in Farmington who thought that the normal school site was most unfortunate. A letter to *The Farmington Chronicle* in the spring of 1864 expressed acute displeasure at the prospects of keeping an educational center on Academy Street. Furthermore, the writer ventured the opinion that he was expressing the general dissatisfaction of the townspeople in having the school on the principal business street. Looking into a crystal ball, the writer foresaw the time when the business expansion of the town would be blocked by the presence of the Normal School. In ten years he thought the people of the town would curse the day when they had allowed the Normal School to take up such precious land. A plea was made to locate the institution in some secluded spot such as Powder House Hill or even farther out on Perham Street Hill. The letter concluded by recommending the selling of the entire Academy area for building lots.

There is reason to believe that the townspeople were not so generally averse to the Academy lot for the Normal School as this letter indicated. When C. C. Rounds resigned as principal of the Normal School in 1883, he went on record in his annual report to the State Superintendent as still regretting the failure of the town to accept the recommendation of the building committee for the removal of the Normal School to a five-acre lot on Middle Street. He bemoaned the fact that the opportunity was turned down because of "the popular clamor" for the Normal School to stay on Academy Street. As late as 1869, he believed it was both feasible and reasonable to move the school. This was because he had such contempt for the school's facilities when he became its principal in 1868. The old Academy building that had been judged in 1862 hopeless and obsolete was, until 1888, used as the ell to the new building. Furthermore, the new structure, in its first four years, was too rough and crude to fulfill its educational mission satisfactorily.

In view of the inadequacies of the plant, the question naturally arises as to the reasons for selecting Farmington as the site for the first normal school in the State. Certainly there were many towns which could have furnished the State with better educational facilities. The Commissioners were instructed to be partly guided in locating the normal schools "by the character of the community and healthfulness of the location." Farmington could well qualify within such terms. Its reputation was state-wide for physical beauty, social attractiveness, and lack of contamination from industrialism. The tendency throughout the country was for normal schools to be located in towns rather than in the larger cities. Whether deserved or not, Farmington had a reputation for being devoid at least of the grosser temptations. There were no fleshpots or saloons to entice plastic youth, and the physical attractiveness of the village was beyond questioning. The day Jonas Burnham arrived in town in 1849, he wrote his daughter that Farmington was the prettiest village he had ever seen.

The Commissioners were also instructed to look for a town that had access by "railroad or otherwise." The "otherwise" transportation referred to stagecoaches and ships. (Accessibility by water certainly played a role in the selection of Castine as the Eastern State Normal School). Farmington was connected in 1859 by railroad with the outer world. More accurately, it was almost connected, because until 1870 the train went no farther than West Farmington. Getting that far, however, was a sufficient advantage in fast transportation to assist in making Farmington eligible for the normal school. Certainly the students could be depended upon to negotiate the last mile by foot or buggy. Moreover, the Androscoggin Railroad sweetened Farmington as a normal school site by promising all prospective students half fare. Here again the importance of the railroads to nineteenth century towns was demonstrated.

The difficulties in getting the building program started were finally overcome in the spring of 1864. *The Farmington Chronicle* noted in August that "the majestic brick walls" of the new building were looming ever higher as the days went by. This may have been taking liberties with the word "majestic," but compared with the old Farmington Academy structure, the walls might very well have justified such an adjective. The opening day of the Western State Normal School was August 24, 1864. Unfortunately the new building was not ready for occupancy, but the trustees of the old Academy proved their resourcefulness by renting an attic room which was part of a business block in town known as Beal's Hall. Consequently, on this historic day, thirty-one young ladies and gentlemen were called to order and initiated a new development in normal school history. During the winter term the new building became usable. It was rough, crude, and plenty humble, but at last the Western State Normal School had a place to call home.

II. THE KELSEY, GAGE, AND ROUNDS ADMINISTRATIONS

At the time of the founding of Farmington Normal, teacher-training institutions in the United States were just starting to proliferate and become well attended. The first normal school in Lexington, Massachusetts, opened its doors in 1839 to three students, who shared one instructor. Subsequent normal schools, founded in the 1840s and 1850s, experienced similar difficulty in enrolling enough students to justify their existence. State legislatures were constantly threatening to cut off support for such poorly attended institutions. Consequently it was particularly encouraging when thirty-one students were present as the Farmington Normal School began its operations. This number changed to fifty-nine before the close of the term, and during the academic year, one hundred and thirty pupils entered the school. In later years there would be occasional slumps in registration, but the initial enthusiasm for the normal school movement was important in that the state legislature could not charge the new institution with a lack of student support.

Friends of the local normal school emphasized the fact that such an institution was no longer an experiment. However, despite the increase in popularity of teacher-training institutions, there were many who insisted that any replacement of the old academies by the normal school would be a grave mistake. Doubt concerning the desirability of teacher training was reflected in the absurdly meager appropriations meted out to Farmington Normal in its first years. Governor Joshua L. Chamberlain, hero of Little Round Top and Petersburg, had just such penurious opposition in mind when he delivered his 1866 inaugural address and said this:

BEAL HALL: The third floor of the second building from the left, located in the middle of the business section of Farmington, was the home of the FSNS from August 24, 1864, to January 1865.

What these schools most need is competent teachers, those who know and can impart. There is probably no means by which we can more benefit our schools, and excite a more intelligent interest in them than by encouraging an institution you have already founded for this purpose—the Normal School. The report of the principal shows this to be in a very flourishing condition. As it is, however, regarded by many as still an experiment, there is naturally much wanting to enable it to fulfill perfectly the important ends for which it was established. It would be well, it seems to me, since we have undertaken this experiment, to make the trial a fair and thorough one. That would include an early opening of Castine as provided by law.

Governor Chamberlain's expression, "flourishing condition," had reference to the enthusiasm and booming attendance of the new school and not to its financial condition. The "wanting" that he referred to was to persist for a long time.

The primary purpose of a normal school was to improve elementary education by producing a professionally trained teacher. The new breed who were beginning to get such training in the 1860s were instructed to avoid imposing upon their pupils the mere memorization of dull textbooks. Furthermore, the new teacher was encouraged to acquire enough knowledge to free himself from a complete dependence on one book, including the answers in the back of the text. Before the advent of normal schools, and even long after their appearance, the requirements for teaching in the lower grades were minimal. Elementary teaching was considered a temporary job, notorious for its poor pay and available to anyone who could read and look menacing enough to keep order in the classroom.

The normal school movement, in its early stages, was championed by men who had been nurtured in the liberal arts tradition. Of the five principals who directed Farmington Normal School from 1864 to 1940, only George M. Gage had failed to graduate from a liberal arts college. By the twentieth century, a feud had developed between the liberal arts supporter and the professional educator. The latter emphasized "the whole child," whereas the liberal arts man maintained that such an objective had led to an alarming downgrading of mental discipline and development. Although the early normal schools emphasized in nearly every subject how to teach, the courses of present-day professional education had not as yet developed to represent a challenge to the liberal arts curriculum.

An example of one who combined the liberal arts training with an enthusiasm for the normal school movement was A. P. Kelsey, first principal of the Farmington Normal School. He was born in the State of New York and graduated from Hamilton College in 1856. From 1859 to 1861, he was a professor in the Albany State Normal School, which was the first institution of its kind in New York, having been established in 1844. A. P. Kelsey's career highlights the ease with which, in a less complicated era, the educator could slip from one level of education to another. From 1861 to 1863 he was the preceptor of the Farmington Academy. For a year he was principal of Farmington Normal. In the seventies he served as headmaster of the Abbott School and then became principal of the New Hampshire State Normal. In 1879 he went back to his alma mater, Hamilton, as professor of natural history, the position he held at his death in 1891.

The evidence seems to indicate that A. P. Kelsey, more than any other person, was responsible for the first Maine normal school being located in Farmington. State Superintendent Edward Ballard, in his report for 1865, paid tribute to both A. P. Kelsey and Edward P. Weston for their successful efforts in establishing the normal school in Farmington. *The Farmington Chronicle*, in its July 15, 1869 issue, announced with great regret the resignation of Weston as head of the Abbott School, a position he had held since his resignation from the state superintendency in 1865. The newspaper expressed the belief that Weston, more than anyone else, was responsible for the normal school being in Farmington. In the July 22 issue, however, *The Chronicle* made this unqualified correction: "We were in error last week in stating that we were indebted to the Hon. E. P. Weston, more than to any other man in the State, for the establishing of the Normal School. A. P. Kelsey should have been named for that honor."

The local paper never told its readers what evidence had been presented to take away from Weston the laurels bestowed upon him in the July 15 issue. Despite the retraction, Weston deserved and received some recognition for the founding of the State's first normal school. As State Superintendent he pushed hard in all his reports for a teacher-training institution. In the Cleaveland-Packard history of Bowdoin College appears this statement about Weston: "After a service of thirteen years he received the appointment of

State Superintendent of schools, and a reappointment three years later. While in office he was largely instrumental in the establishment of the normal school system, and opened the first institution of the kind in Farmington."[3]

Despite the undeniable contributions of Weston, it may very well be that A. P. Kelsey deserved the accolade bestowed upon him by *The Chronicle*. It was Kelsey who convinced the Academy trustees that they should relinquish their building to the State. Because of Kelsey's prodding, the trustees expended more than eight thousand dollars in erecting and furnishing a new brick schoolhouse as well as providing the disreputable old wooden structure that had served so many years as the Farmington Academy.[4] In Edward Ballard's 1866 report appears the following concerning Kelsey's contribution: " . . . it is due to Mr. A. P. Kelsey, the first principal, to say that he devoted a year's time in laboring for the establishment of the school and superintending the building operations without compensation."

The Maine legislature in 1863 passed a law empowering Weston, as State Superintendent, to act for the normal schools:

> It shall be the duty of the Superintendent of Common Schools to act as Superintendent of Normal Schools, to employ teachers and lecturers for the same, and with the consent of the Governor and Council to provide such apparatus and other facilities for conducting the operations of the schools as may be deemed necessary; the whole arrangement to be approved by the Governor and Council who shall audit all accounts for the expenditures in this behalf; and draw their warrant for payment of the same when approved.[5]

Acting in accordance with the law, Weston selected not only Kelsey as principal but also his assistants, George M. Gage and Annie E. Johnson. Walter Wells, M.A., was taken on as a lecturer. Before coming to Farmington, Gage had been principal of the Adams School in Quincy, Massachusetts. Annie E. Johnson, a native of Maine, had been one of the teachers at the Framingham Normal School. The credentials of Walter Wells are unknown except for the M.A. degree. Both George Gage and Annie E. Johnson were to have distinguished careers after they left Farmington. Miss Johnson became principal of Framingham Normal and then headmistress of

Bradford Seminary. Gage, after the initial year of the school, would become Kelsey's successor.

The 1860s constituted an important decade in the rapid growth of normal schools. Of all those which were founded in this period, the most influential was without any question the Oswego Normal School, headed by Edward A. Sheldon. Oswego championed the educational principles of the Swiss educator, Pestalozzi. So did Farmington. A few weeks before the opening of the local normal school an article appeared in *The Chronicle* in which the ideas of Pestalozzi were presented.

Readers of the local paper were told that in many parts of the country the Pestalozzian method was superseding the old mechanical teaching which had made so many "book teachers and parrot scholars." Its main purpose was to communicate instruction by direct appeal to the senses, using objects of nature as well as man-made constructions such as pictures, toys, and puzzles. According to the normal school idea, the student was not to be a passive recipient in the learning process. Pestalozzi, and others who influenced the normal schools, believed that one cause of the teacher's inability to govern his school was his inability to interest his pupils in their work. The normal method was designed to awaken the children's interest by presenting things and ideas that their young minds could comprehend. The method was also designed to show them the objective for which they were studying, thus giving them a motive for attending school.

One of the most widely read and influential works in the field of pedagogy during this time was David P. Page's *Theory and Practice of Teaching.*[6] The author was the first principal of the Albany State Normal School where, as we have noted, Kelsey had taught for two years. According to Page, fitness to teach involved three main qualifications: scholarship, skill and method in teaching, and understanding the science of teaching. Page inveighed against the rote method of recitation and deplored the lack of mental challenge represented by the textbook-tied teacher of the times.

Although Page emphasized the importance of teaching skills, it should be noted that he put scholarship first in judging the fitness of those who wanted to teach. Years later liberal arts partisans would accuse his successors in the twentieth-century teachers colleges of putting scholarship last on the priority list.

AMBROSE P. KELSEY, first principal (1863–64) of the Farmington normal school, known as the Western State Normal School.

One of the early textbooks at Farmington Normal was James P. Wickersham's *Method of Instruction.* This was published in 1865 and attained instant popularity.[7] (Wickersham later became State Superintendent of Pennsylvania and wrote a history of education in his state.) Many of his comments on the teaching of history and geography seem as up to date as yesterday's teachers convention. Wickersham helped to popularize the Pestalozzian practice of preparing lessons according to the stages in children's mental growth. Like Pestalozzi, he said that in naming the qualities of objects, pupils were helped in their accuracy of perception, reasoning power, and written and spoken expression. A substantial part of the book is hard going now because of its extensive use of terms of the old psychology.

Exit Kelsey

Although Kelsey labored mightily to get Farmington Normal started, he lasted only one year as its principal. The reasons for this quick exit are not too clear, but his departure probably could be explained primarily in economic terms. Kelsey received a salary of $1,200 a year. This was by far the lowest of all the salaries paid normal school principals. Albany paid $2,100, Salem and Bridgewater $2,500 and Illinois Normal $3,000. The highest salary paid to assistants at Farmington was $500. The average for assistants at other normal schools was $1,400 to $1,500. The new building that Kelsey saw take shape, brick by brick, was rough and crude, without even a minimum of school equipment. (In a few years the "minimum" would be available as the result of private generosity.) This situation would remain unsatisfactory for years to come. For almost the first nine years of the school's existence only $25 was appropriated for the library and scientific apparatus, according to Rounds's statement at the Farmington State Normal School Decennial.[8]

Kelsey must have enjoyed Farmington as a place to live, especially when he could get his mind off the inadequacies of the brick building. He married a local girl whose father, Robert Goodenow, had served in Congress and was a prominent and scholarly lawyer and banker. Kelsey was recognized as a superior scholar (his Ph. D. from Bowdoin in 1881 was recognition of his scholarly attainments) and he also seemed to be the kind of individual who enjoyed the personal relationships that are an important part of town life. Some of his

Academy students remembered him as not only a fine teacher but one who took a personal interest in their welfare.[9] He indicated his fondness for Farmington by returning in 1874 to head the Abbott School.*

---

* Samuel P. Abbott founded the Abbott School in 1844 after discovering that his pastoral labors in "one of the outposts of Zion," alias Houlton, were overtaxing his limited physical resources. He turned to Farmington as the location for his private school for two major reasons. The first was that Jacob, one of his brothers, had some attractive real estate in Farmington and part of this could be converted into a school. The second reason was that Samuel, as a graduate of the Farmington Academy, thought of the town as providing an ideal environment for educating young men. (Asa Gray, the eminent Harvard botanist and champion of the Darwinian theory, helped recruit the first students for the school. He had been impressed with its prospects during a visit with Samuel Abbott. On this same northern trip he went on a botanical excursion to Mt. Blue, and the results of this were included in his monumental work, *The Flora of North America.*[10])

The Farmington Academy, Abbott School, and Farmington Normal were to have an inter-related history. After the early death of Samuel Abbott in 1849, Alexander H. Abbott, a Farmington native, resigned as preceptor of Farmington Academy and took over the direction of the Abbott School. Shortly thereafter he became its owner as well as its headmaster. (A. H. Abbott belonged to a different branch of the clan from Jacob and Samuel.) In 1865 A. H. Abbott leased the Abbott School (sometimes known as the Little Blue School) to Edward P. Weston, and then from 1874 to 1876 to A. P. Kelsey. This meant that the two men most responsible for the founding of the Farmington Normal School were to serve later as headmasters of the Abbott School. Furthermore both A. H. Abbott and A. P. Kelsey had been preceptors of the Farmington Academy. In 1876 A. H. Abbott resumed direction of the Little Blue School after serving as a Normal School trustee and finding himself unable to make his fortune in developing a slate quarry.

Abbott School enrollment reached its peak during the time of the Weston and Kelsey stewardship. There were about 80 students and all of them were boarders, for no day students were allowed. (One of the boarders was a Farmington boy, Warren Johnson, who, as State Superintendent in 1869, would play an important part in Farmington Normal developments.) Abbott School students came not only from many states of the Union, but also from several foreign countries. They paid $150 for 46 weeks; this included all expenses except those for travel and clothing.

Gage Takes Over

In 1865 George M. Gage became the second principal of the Western State Normal School. (And, up to this point, the last to sport sideburns.) He was born in Waterford, Maine, August 22, 1834. Two years younger than Kelsey, he was thirty-one when he took on his new duties. His career represented one of the many examples of an ambitious and plucky lad whose life was to be filled with obstacles overcome. When George was eight, his father died, leaving a widow with eight small children. His mother was a good scholar, and Latin was studied in the Gage household almost as early as English. From the age of fourteen to sixteen, George lived on a farm with a court-appointed guardian. Farming had no lure for him so at sixteen he started out on his own. He worked his way through North Bridgton Academy, and in 1858, graduated from the State Normal School at Bridgewater, Massachusetts. His employment as a young man included teaching in the schools of six different Maine towns, working on farms in haying season, and serving one year as a brakeman on a railroad.

From 1858 to 1864 Gage taught successfully in Massachusetts public schools. He was principal of the Adams School, Quincy, Massachusetts, when Edward P. Weston, knowing that Gage had been enthusiastically urging teacher-training institutions for Maine, hired him as one of Kelsey's assistants.

Gage's reports emphasize Maine's low salaries and the inadequacies of the Farmington facilities. In 1866, however, Gage managed to get enough money to found *The Maine Normal*, which he edited and published until he went to Minnesota two years later. The journal advocated the revival of the Maine State Teachers' Association, and according to George Purington, was mainly responsible for the formation in 1867 of a new organization of the teachers of the State.[11] Jacob Abbott lent his prestige to the periodical by writing the feature article for each issue.[12] One of his best articles, and one of the few that was not too heavy in moralizing, had to do with the most effective methods to be employed for the arousal of scholastic activity. Jacob Abbott thought it was important to expect big things of one's students and have that distinctly understood. Another suggestion was to praise whatever was worthy in a student's efforts and strictly limit the critical comments. Babies learned to walk and do other things through encouragement. But

GEORGE M. GAGE, second principal (1865–67) of Western State Normal.

some teachers did not adopt this positive approach and became nothing but carping critics. This, according to Jacob Abbott, was completely discouraging to many students.*

On May 25, 1866, George Gage presided at the graduating exercises of the first graduating class at Farmington Normal. (The program referred to the school as the Maine State Normal School in Farmington. This was because it was the only normal school in the State until the following year, when Castine, or the Eastern State Normal, opened its doors after a long delay because of opposition based upon its location.) The exercises had been preceded by a general examination of the entire school. The senior class started off at 9:00 A.M. by submitting to questions in geology, astronomy, and the theory and art of teaching. The remaining groups then answered questions in geometry, the U.S. Constitution, algebra, reading, and arithmetic. There were also exercises in singing, mental arithmetic, calisthenics, and declamations.

In the afternoon, a three-hour program was devoted for the most part to hearing the ten seniors (all women) deliver graduation speeches. (The lone male of the class, George F. Stackpole, was teaching out of town at the time of the first graduation, so he failed to get his diploma at the 1866 ceremony. In 1890 George Purington urged the board of trustees to grant Stackpole a delayed diploma. The board complied with the request but, by 1890, Stackpole had an A. B. and A. M. from Dartmouth. He was present at the school's 50th anniversary and spoke at that time). Two

---

* As a classical scholar, Jacob Abbott may have been influenced by the writings of Quintilian. Rousseau and Pestalozzi were not the only writers who felt tender about childhood. Quintilian, in the first century A.D., was expressing such thoughts as must have influenced many Latin scholars of later days. Typical of his solicitude for childhood is this passage:

I am not so blind to differences of age as to think that the very young should be forced on prematurely or even given real work to do. Above all things we must take care that the child, who is not yet old enough to love his studies, does not come to hate them. . . . . . His studies must be made an amusement: he must be questioned and praised and taught to rejoice when he has done well; sometimes, too, when he refuses instruction, it should be given to some other to excite his envy, at times also he must be engaged in competition and should be allowed to believe himself successful more often than not, while he should be encouraged to do his best by rewards as may appeal to his tender years.

undergraduate males provided a patriotic mood with their declamations. One was called: "One Nation, One Destiny"; the other was "Patriotism." The seniors had a variety of subjects that ranged from "Progress in Astronomy" to the "Life and Assassination of Thomas A. Beckett" to "Footprints of the Departed." The parting song led the audience from the assembly hall on a hopeful note. The last stanza was:

> Our footsteps oft may faltering be,
> Walking the narrow road,
> That pathway, still, we soon shall see,
> Leads home to Heaven and God.
> Beyond the river, we shall view
> Our Father's house on high:
> We'll greet each other there anew
> And never say good-bye.

During the nineteenth century more than two-thirds of all who entered Farmington Normal failed to graduate. This meant that a majority of the students spent from one to five terms on Academy Street before they departed, usually to accept teaching jobs. Many students found even the modest expenses of attending the school a heavy burden; others, especially those twenty or over, found the rules too restrictive; still others were repelled by the necessity of taking a course of study which had no options, and some felt that a normal school was not worth the necessary effort.

For those who attended the school from 1864 to 1869 the following course of study was presented:

First year: Spelling: oral, phonetic, written; Reading: with careful training in the analysis of sounds, enunciation, and expression; Arithmetic: mental and written, analytic and formulary; Geography: physical and political, with map drawing and use of globes; History: American and foreign, "so far as is consistent with other studies"; English grammar: including the analysis and composition of the language; Natural philosophy and physiology; Constitution of Maine; School laws; Good manners.

Second year: Algebra, Bookkeeping, English Literature, Chemistry, Astronomy, Geometry, Rhetoric, Intellectual and Moral Philosophy,

Theory and Art of Teaching, U. S. Constitution, Latin and French (the latter two were optional). General exercises were given in gymnastics, singing, public speaking, and composition.

The conditions of admission in the early years stipulated that females must be sixteen years old and males seventeen. All applicants had to pass tests in reading, spelling, writing, grammar, geography, and arithmetic. In addition to the mental requirements, each applicant had to present a certificate of good moral character from some responsible person. The course of study required for its completion two years of three terms each. It was this program that two-thirds of the entering classes found too exacting, or unrewarding, or too expensive to complete.

In the beginning, the school year consisted of thirty-eight weeks. The fall and spring terms had fourteen weeks each and the winter term ten weeks. In 1872 a system of two graduations each year was introduced. This arrangement lasted until 1885 when the original one-graduation system was re-adopted. The classes of 1867 and 1868 numbered thirty-two and thirty-five. Such numbers were not exceeded consistently until the 1890s, and before that decade there were substantial slumps in registration.

The first meeting of the Farmington alumni was called to order in Normal Hall on June 5, 1867. The officers selected were all males who belonged to the class of 1867. Whereas there had been only one non-graduating male in the 1866 class, eleven males were in the 1867 group.

The first president of the Farmington Alumni Association was Roliston Woodbury. Born in Sweden, Maine, in 1840, he died in Castine, in November 1888. After preparing for college at Bridgton Academy, he entered Bowdoin, but soon after volunteered for the Union army. For almost four years, he participated in some of the bloodiest battles of the war, including Fredericksburg, Gettysburg, and Chancellorsville. Woodbury did not return to Bowdoin, but entered Farmington Normal shortly after he was mustered out of the army. After his graduation he accepted an offer to join the faculty of the school. He remained in Farmington for twelve years despite an offer from Red Wing, Minnesota, the State that was proving so attractive to so many Farmington graduates. Appointed principal of the Castine Normal School in 1879, he held this position until his death in 1888.

During all but one of the twelve years that he served in Farmington, Woodbury was Principal Rounds's first assistant, and a heartfelt tribute to his memory was prepared and read by Rounds at a meeting of the Maine Pedagogical Society. "To his faithful assistance I owed much, and he came by right to fill to me a place which has never since been filled, which will, most likely, remain unfilled. In more than eleven years of daily intercourse there was never a word of difference between us, and yet by nature from our training, and our diverse experiences in life, we differed in many ways." [13]

The first vice-president of the Alumni Association, Charles A. Boston, came from Avon, Maine. In 1868–69, he taught in the Mankato State Normal School. Later he was appointed superintendent of schools of Watonwan county, Minnesota. Like so many others in the early days of the normal school, he settled permanently in Minnesota. In 1875 he married a Farmington classmate, Electa W. Bixby.

The secretary of the first Alumni Association, John Allen Sweet, taught one term in Farmington and then went West. Eventually he became manager of Carson, Pirie, Scott & Co. of Chicago, one of the largest dry goods houses in America. Years later Farmington was fortunate to have his son, John Allen Jr., settle in town with his family.

Edmund Hayes was the first treasurer of the Alumni Association. After leaving Farmington Normal he studied at both Dartmouth and M.I.T. In 1873 he became one of the four members of the Union Bridge Company, which built the famous cantilever bridge over the Niagara River, the first bridge of its kind ever constructed.

This quick look at officers of the first Alumni Association of Farmington Normal is sufficient to underline the quality of the early leaders of the school.*

---

* In subsequent years branch associations of the alumni were formed. For some time the largest and most enthusiastic of these was the Massachusetts Association, founded October 10, 1891. The New York branch, with George Stackpole as its first president, was founded in March 1915. The Hartford branch was formed on January 31, 1936; the Eastern Maine on June 9, 1937, and Southwestern Maine on April 13, 1938. My evidence indicates that the New York and Hartford branches expired during the Second World War.

Social and Recreational Notes of the 1860s and 1870s

In this day of television, transistor radio, movies, sports for spectators as well as participants, not to mention campus riots and fast private transportation, it may seem incredible that in the nineteenth century so many students throughout the land could abide by the typical normal school rules without a serious protest. The average age of the normal school student of a hundred years ago was about two years older than that of today's crop, because most of the students stayed out of school for a year or two to teach before they enrolled at Farmington. The statement of the catalogue and circular of the Western Maine Normal concerning rules and regulations was a masterpiece of brevity. "Students," it stated, "are presumed to be ladies and gentlemen, and can remain with the school only so long as this presumption holds true." Certainly this did not sound too restrictive; however, there was more to come. A printed sheet of instructions was distributed, in August 1868, that gave specific rules to be followed for the preservation or attainment of correct behavior:

Regulations for the Western State Normal School

I. Study hours begin at 7:00 A.M., end at 9:30 P.M.

Students are required to be in their rooms during study hours, and engaged in silent study. No communication is allowed. Every student is expected to spend at least one hour in the morning at silent study hour. The morning hour may be kept in two periods of one half hour each.

II. Retiring and rising hour—Rooms are to be closed, lights are to be extinguished, and students are to retire for the night at 10 P.M. Students are not to arise before 5:00 A.M.

III. Visiting—Gentlemen are in no case allowed to visit or call at the rooms of ladies; nor will ladies be permitted to visit the rooms of gentlemen.

IV. Attendance—All students are required to be prompt and regular in attendance and no unexcused absence or tardiness will be allowed.

V. Church attendance—Students are required to attend church twice every Sabbath. They may attend Sabbath School or meeting for social prayer once in the day instead of hearing a sermon. But they are expected to hear one pulpit service.

VI. Students are allowed to attend either of the five churches in which divine service is held, Unitarian and Universalist, Free

Will Baptist, Baptist, Methodist, or Congregationalist. But having chosen a place of worship, they are expected to make it their home.

Any interference on the part of any person connected with the school with the religious prerogatives of the students should be at once reported to the Principal. It is desired that students who have not formed opinions differing from those to which they have been trained at home, attend church with the denomination with which their parents have been accustomed to worship.

There was no dormitory at Farmington Normal until 1914, so the students had to board with private families. Occasionally, an entire house would be available for students to rent. A matron would be sought to supervise the house and see to the enforcement of existing regulations. It is doubtful that the private families with Normal School boarders were always on guard to prevent all infractions of the rules. It is also difficult to believe that the regulations concerning church attendance were enforceable. The magnitude of the task involved would appear to be too much for the troops available.

The records do not indicate any material difference in the rules and regulations during the Kelsey, Gage, or Rounds administrations. Moreover, there seemed to be little difference between the restrictions in Farmington, or Oswego, or Albany, or any other normal school in the land. All the students, at least on paper, were held to the same strict standards, for the schools strove conscientiously to act *in loco parentis*.

In the early years of Farmington Normal, baseball was becoming popular. Soldiers in the Civil War spent a great deal of their spare time playing this new game and popularized it when they went back home. Intelligent and constant changes in the rules of the sport improved it for participants and spectators alike. The first accounts of local ball playing involving students appeared in 1867 in *The Chronicle*. Farmington Normal boys played a game that started at 2:33 P.M. and closed at 7:15 P.M. Although the reporter was careful in his timekeeping, it was very likely he failed to get the exact score. Possibly there was an unresolved discussion as to what the score was. *The Chronicle* contained this rather perplexing statement: "On account of pressure of other matters, we omit the score which showed good playing on both sides."

Another game in 1867 was between the Eaton School of Norridgewock and Farmington Normal. The Normals won. *The Chronicle* reporter was there: "The game was witnessed by a large number of persons from the village, and by some who came from as far as New Sharon to see what ball playing was. The clubs after cheering each other, the umpire and scorer left the field wishing they could try it again."

Accounts of the ball games always emphasized their friendliness. The reporter seemed to be impressed time and again that the Normals could play so many games without any fights breaking out. The names of the umpire and scorer were always given, but not those of the players. On May 30, 1867, there was a game between the Normals and a local outfit known as the Friendship Base Ball Club. Again the local sports reporter noticed some features that might not be included in any modern account of a ball game: "The game was noted for fly catches and heavy batting but there were no home runs. The decisions of the umpire were very satisfactory. Play was called at 1:55 and closed at 5:30." John Allen Sweet was the umpire who proved to be so satisfactory; all the others involved were unidentified.

The Normal Lyceum provided another release from the routine imposed by the classroom and evening study. Two of the speakers in 1866 were General O. O. Howard and Governor Joshua L. Chamberlain. Not only were these two genuine war heroes, but they were also excellent speakers. (General O. O. Howard was probably easily talked into coming to Farmington because, at that time, his brother Rowland was the local Congregational minister.) Another favorite of the Lyceum circuit was the Reverend J. S. C. Abbott. A brother of Jacob and Samuel, he was a popular speaker and the author of sixty-two books on history. (Unfortunately his ability as a historian did not equal his zeal for florid and didactic writing.)

Nearly all the entertainers who came to town in the 1860s performed in Beal's Hall, the building that provided shelter for the Normal School before the completion of the brick building on Academy Street. The Swiss Bell Ringers came several times to Farmington in the early days of the school, and presumably, many students were allowed to attend the concert. Certainly it would have been unreasonable for the school authorities to deny permission for their charges to hear Georgie Dean Spaulding, "the greatest harpist in the world, and the only lady that performs three tunes at one time."

In the early days of Farmington Normal, with its heavy emphasis on strict standards for correct behavior, there was a great deal of social life in the school and church. The students frequently furnished their own entertainment by presenting vocal and instrumental music, select reading, and pantomimes. C. A. Allen was for many years the leader of the Normal School chorus, and his singing schools were always popular. Prayer meetings, held in the middle of the week, were always popular among the religious and among some who were not.[14]

The inevitable series of lectures for 1874 featured, among others, Lyman Abbott,* our old friend A. P. Kelsey, and C. C. Rounds. Kelsey had returned to town as the head of the Abbott School. For the 1874 program he spoke on "The Unsocial Element." (The element proved to be nitrogen, which was described as so unsocial that when it was wedded to other gases it obtained a divorce at the earliest possible moment.)

Readings, as well as lectures, were staple fare in Normal Hall. *The Chronicle* reported in April 1875, that C. D. Robinson had been his usual sparkling self in his readings. The reporter, however, sorrowfully wrote about some rude young people who had been noisy in the back of the hall. In fairness to the youngsters, it should be noted that C. D. Robinson gave so many readings in Farmington it was possible that the less attentive part of the audience had already heard renditions of "Darius Green and His Flying Machine" as well as selections from "The Pickwick Papers."

The most important social events at the Normal School in the 1870s were the two graduations, one in the winter and the other in the summer. Many of Maine's leading officials and officeholders, including the governor, showed up for the latter academic finale. In addition to the chief executive, a special delegation was usually

---

* As a youngster, Lyman Abbott attended the Little Blue School and later on became an eloquent Congregational preacher. He was one of the sons of Jacob Abbott, author of the Rollo books, whom we have met before as a contributor to *The Maine Journal*. After resigning from the ministry, Lyman Abbott became editor of the influential magazine of opinion, *The Outlook*. His contributing editor for several years was Theodore Roosevelt.

C. C. ROUNDS, left, third principal (1868–83) of FSNS, and his assistant, Roliston Woodbury, first president of the Farmington Alumni Association (1867), and a member of the faculty from 1867 to 1879.

chosen by the legislature to attend. In this group were the State Superintendent, a member of the governor's council, three or four senators, and ten or so representatives. Sometimes the representation from the legislature would be limited to the committee on education.

Administration of C. C. Rounds

In 1868 Mark H. Dunnell enticed George M. Gage to become the first principal of the Mankato State Normal School of Minnesota. It was the second institution of its kind in Minnesota, and Dunnell not only captured the second principal of Farmington Normal, but for several years made successful raids on the Farmington graduating classes in order to staff his faculty. He was familiar with the quality of Maine teachers and he was also well informed from personal experience concerning comparative pay scales. As State Superintendent in Maine his salary was $1,000. (It had been $1,200 but the legislature in 1860 decided that was too much.) In Minnesota he received $2,500 a year, plus $500 for traveling expenses. Mainly through Dunnell's efforts, twenty-two graduates of Farmington Normal accepted permanent teaching jobs in Minnesota during the 1860s and 1870s. In addition, others taught for a short time there and then returned to the East.

C. C. Rounds, the successor of George M. Gage, was born in 1831 in Waterford, Maine. From the ages of eighteen to twenty-two, he was a printer in Portland, Boston, and Cambridge. He entered Dartmouth College after his printing days were over and graduated in the class of 1857. From 1857 to 1859, he was principal of the South Paris Academy; from 1859 to 1865, of a public school in Cleveland. Just before arriving at Farmington, he had been principal of the Edward Little Institute in Auburn. From 1868 to 1883 he served at Farmington; after that, he was for thirteen years principal of the State Normal in Plymouth, New Hampshire. Resigning from Plymouth in 1896, he moved to New York and became a lecturer on educational subjects. For the last two or three years of his life, he moved back to Farmington and died here in 1901.

C. C. Rounds garnered the B. S. and M. S. degrees from Dartmouth, an M. A. from Colby, another one from Bowdoin, and a Ph. D. from Bates. The Dartmouth degrees were probably both earned, the others honorary. Rounds was honored by his colleagues in being elected to many prestigious educational offices. He was president of the Maine State Teachers' Association, twice president of the National Normal Association, president of the New England Normal Association, and three successive times elected by the National Education Association as a member of the National Council of Education.

It did not take Rounds any appreciable time to establish a reputation for scholarship and affability. On November 26, 1868, *The Chronicle* ran this item: "The Normal levee, Friday evening, was a very pleasant affair. Mr. Rounds, the principal, is evidently an excellent instructor, and has gained an enviable popularity among the scholars." As far as the records indicate, he was always to retain that popularity with the students, even after he ran afoul of three members of his faculty.

A series of lectures was given at Farmington Normal during the first winter Rounds was principal. Such lectures were not uncommon in the larger cities, but without the Normal School, Farmington might not have benefited from this kind of adult education. In the winter of 1868–69, Dr. N. T. True gave four lectures on natural history and geology; Dr. J. B. Severy talked on physiology; Edward P. Weston, completing his last year as head of the Abbott School, gave a pre-Freudian talk on dreams; the Rev. Howard Life consented to speak on the life and character of Robert Burns; and the local legal scholar, Robert Goodenow, described and discussed the judiciary system of the United States.[15]

Despite the admirable series of lectures and the instant popularity of the new principal, all was not well in 1869 on Academy Street. The school's physical plant had had no improvements since the completion of the crude brick building in 1865.

We have noted that the wooden ell (the old Academy building) had been described in a local paper in 1862 as not fit to be a stable. Seven years later nothing had been done inside or out to improve this ramshackle structure. It was likely that at this time State Superintendent Warren Johnson, despite having been born and brought up in Farmington, despaired of ever getting a suitable physical plant for Farmington Normal.

The Chronicle indicated in the winter and spring issues the possibility of Farmington losing its new institution. On February 25, 1869, only a few months after Rounds took over the school, *The Chronicle* ran the following item: "The legislature have introduced an order of inquiry into the expediency of removing the Normal School from this village. An inquiry into the expediency of a coat of paint for the inside and a fence around the grounds would be more pertinent."

In the March 18, 1869, issue of *The Chronicle*, Dr. Russell, the representative to the legislature from this district, was being singled out for praise "for his prompt and efficient efforts to defeat the proposition submitted to the legislature—to remove the Normal School from this place." Finally, on June 10, *The Chronicle* gave the all-clear signal with this statement: "Workmen are engaged in renovating completely the old Academy building now forming the ell of the main edifice. Everybody seems to have settled down with satisfaction on the fact that the school is a fixture in our pleasant village." This certainty about the permant location of the Normal School was to last fourteen years.

One of the important achievements of the Rounds regime was to establish in 1869 a model school. In the beginning, it included only the first three grades; it was not until 1893 that all the pre-secondary grades were represented. In the early years, the course of study followed that of many training schools throughout the land, especially the one in Oswego. The program provided for a carefully graduated course of elementary instruction in reading, spelling, writing, drawing; the correct use of English both in speaking and writing; singing, numbers, and geography. The Pestalozzi influence was apparent in the emphasis on oral object lessons on color, form, plants, and animals. All of this led eventually to the Normal School emphasis on nature study.

The Model School received high marks from the local press. *The Chronicle* praised the instruction available on Academy Street and strongly urged that the Model School be converted into a public primary and graded school.[16]

The local papers were, for the most part, strong supporters of the Normal School. Consequently, if one were to read only the newspapers, one would get the impression that the town was united in backing Farmington Normal. Other sources of information about the early years of the institution indicated considerable indifference on the part of local citizens. Rounds, for example, often complained that there were never very many students at the school from Farmington. Other evidence for this indifference was provided in a report written by D. C. Heath in 1874, after he had served as the Farmington superintendent of schools. Here was how teacher training and the local attitude toward it looked to him:

> Our best educators are now a unit in the belief that the teacher needs a special training as much as those, nay more than those, of any other profession. Until teaching is recognized as a profession to be prepared for and followed as any other profession, our scholars will not receive the culture that they may and ought to receive. And here let me say that, in my opinion—and this opinion has been strengthened by the experience of the past year—we make a mistake in not employing more teachers who have fitted themselves for the work by a course in the Normal School. Of the 39 teachers employed during the year only 8 were students or graduates of the Normal School. Other towns draw largely upon this school for teachers and seem delighted at the results.

Rounds must have been pleased to learn in 1873 that the legislature had passed an act establishing a board of trustees who were given charge of the general interests of the normal schools. For ten years the governor and his council, with help from the State Superintendent, had looked after the new institution. The results seemed to indicate that they were too busy with other matters to be of much help. Certainly it could not be worse with new trustees, and the chances were good it would be better. The law that set up the Board stated:

> Said schools are under the direction of a board of seven trustees, five of whom shall be appointed by the governor, with the advice and consent of the Council, for not more than three years under one appointment; and the Governor and Superintendent of Common Schools are, by virtue of their office, members of the Board. Each of the trustees appointed by the Governor shall receive ten cents a mile for actual travel each way, and two dollars a day for his service when employed. Said Board has charge of the general interests of said schools; shall see that the affairs there are conducted by law and by such by-laws as the Board adopt; employ teachers and lecturers for the same; and, annually, on the first day of December lay before the Governor and Council for the information of the legislature, a financial statement, furnishing an accurate detailed account of the receipts and expenditures for the school year preceding.[17]

(In 1905 the number of members was changed from seven to five. The State Superintendent was to be one of the five and the governor was no longer included. The Board continued to have "charge of the general interests" of the normal schools and then teachers colleges until 1949 when it was superseded by the State Board of Education.)

In the nineteenth century there was always a local citizen on the Board of Trustees, presumably to make sure that local interests were adequately presented and protected. Alexander H. Abbott was the first person from this area to be appointed to the Board. This was in 1873, and it was generally agreed that he was an excellent choice. He was not only a trustee of Farmington Normal, but a lecturer on physics at the institution. In one of Rounds's reports to the Board, he singled out Abbott for thanks, because during the first twelve years of normal school history the only scientific apparatus available besides what he himself supplied was that provided by the personal generosity of Abbott. Like Kelsey, Abbott played an important part in the history of the Farmington Academy, Farmington Normal, and the Abbott School.

David H. Knowlton succeeded Abbott on the Board in 1876, and here was another excellent choice. Co-founder of Knowlton & McLeary Printing Co., he contributed to the education of many youngsters by publishing paperback classics which were a valuable addition in classrooms that would otherwise have been devoid of interesting reading material.

In 1880 Judge J. B. Severy became a member of the Board and served until 1882 when he left town for Colorado.

In March 1883, I. Warren Merrill succeeded J. B. Severy. A popular citizen and treasurer of the Franklin County Savings Bank, Merrill was the father of two future teachers at the school, and one of his sons would serve on the Board throughout most of the first half of the twentieth century. Unlike many others, Warren Merrill did not seek this appointment to the Board, nor did he allow his name to be used as a candidate for the position. The office sought the man, and the years were to prove how wise the selection was. After Merrill's death, George C. Purington, with perhaps some degree of modest exaggeration, wrote that whatever success the Normal School had had from 1883 to 1893 was largely attributable to I. Warren Merrill.[18] His value to the school was subsequently recognized in the naming of Merrill Hall auditorium. Later the administration building would be named Merrill Hall in recognition of the services of this remarkable family.

Rounds came to Farmington at a time when the school was still regarded by most people as an experiment. As previously indicated, the original opposition to the normal school idea was only gradually disarmed. In 1869 the condition of the old Academy building made it unacceptable as any part of a school facility. By dint of heroic efforts on the part of Farmington-born Warren Johnson, this ancient edifice was at least considered usable after the renovation of 1869. This was hardly enough, however, to provide a satisfactory physical plant for Farmington Normal students. The rooms in the main building were much too cold in the winter, the roof leaked badly, the furniture was grossly inadequate, and satisfactory lighting arrangements belonged to the future.

In 1870 the classrooms became semi-comfortable after $2,000 was spent on a steam-heating apparatus. Adequate furniture and lighting fixtures were obtained and installed in 1875, and a slate roof was added in 1876. Not the least of the improvements came in 1874 when a fence was finally constructed that discouraged foraging cattle from using Academy Street as bovine headquarters.

The hardships engendered by a rough and crude school building could have been more easily tolerated if the all-important library had been anything but pathetically small. In the winter of 1873 a legislative committee visited the school and spent a whole day listening to recitations in both the school proper and the training department. One of the reporters for *The Chronicle*, in reporting that they had also visited the library, went on to have his say about that: "They also inspected the thing called a library and, we are glad to know, were surprised to find so few books upon its shelves that can be of any earthly use to the pupils of the school, for it is hardly possible that their astonishment upon learning the fact will result in anything less, when they return to Augusta, than united efforts to secure a liberal appropriation for the library, so that the congressional reports and other public documents which have been placed in it simply to keep up appearances, may be displaced by other and more useful works."

During Rounds's administration, he repeatedly attempted to get greater prestige and rewards for those who obtained a Farmington diploma. He never succeeded in this, but he may have made it easier for his successors to do so. His favorite complaint was that in establishing normal schools the law of the State declared training and special study necessary for the teacher, but then refused to follow up on it by making this admittedly desirable preparation for teaching a condition for employment. He was convinced that the Maine legislature was remiss in its refusal to pass a law which would permit the diploma to serve as a teaching certificate.

School committees, according to Rounds, were chosen for their supposed fitness to pass judgment on the qualifications of teachers. The school agent was seldom regarded as fit for selecting teachers; unfortunately, however, it was usually the school agent who employed them. Rounds thought that this was reason enough to account for some of the low quality of Maine teaching, especially in the rural areas. Any person looking for a teaching job had a better chance for employment if he became friendly with a school agent rather than spending time and money in the Normal School. Rounds was firmly convinced that this mainly accounted for the fact that of the more than seven hundred pupils who registered in the early days of the school, only one in six graduated.

The Early Normal School Graduates

One of the most impressive features of early normal school history was the quality of the students, particularly those who stayed long enough to graduate. In those days many graduates, after fulfilling their teaching requirements, would transfer to other occupations, and an impressive number would attain eminence in engineering or manufacturing or the law or religion. In the first twenty-five years of Farmington Normal history, more graduates became lawyers than school superintendents. There were also more clergymen than school superintendents.

This should by no means be interpreted as downgrading those who did stay in education. Not only did many Farmington alumni have a marked impact on education within the State, but others attracted national attention. One of these was Lucilla E. Smith from the class of 1869.

The first principal of the Model School, Miss Smith remained in Farmington one year before accepting a position in the public school system of Washington, D.C. In 1873 she was asked to organize a white normal school to provide the nation's capital with much needed primary grade teachers. She stayed on as principal for twelve years. During this time over two hundred teachers were trained for the Washington schools.

Leading Negroes like the Douglasses,* father and son, believed that school integration was essential for their race's progress so they championed mixed schools.[19] They were opposed to the all-white school such as Lucilla Smith was heading. Philanthropists raised money for the so-called Miner Fund, which was used to enable Howard University to open a teacher-training institution. It was patronized only by blacks, but it did not have a segregated faculty. One of the instructors was Mary B. Smith, a graduate of Salem Normal, who taught in Farmington during the Gage administration. So these two ex-members of the Farmington Normal faculty played an important role in the post Civil War history of Washington, D.C.

Frederick E. Whitney was a Farmington alumnus who had two careers. Born in Farmington, he graduated from the Normal School in 1868. After receiving an A. B. degree from Bowdoin in 1873, he was for several years a teacher in the Boston public schools. In 1878 he received an appointment as professor of English literature in the government school in Tokyo, Japan. He remained in Tokyo for three years and then studied law at Washington University in St. Louis. In the latter part of his life, he was a very successful lawyer in Oakland, California.

Two of the most famous alumni of Farmington Normal were the Stanley twins, Francis E. and Freelan O. Born and brought up in neighboring Kingfield, they entered the Normal School in 1869. Over the years they were to become two of the most famous practitioners of Yankee ingenuity in the land. Francis did not attend the institution for the full two years, but his later accomplishments were to be recognized with an honorary diploma. Freelan O. not only graduated in the class of 1871, but went on to do considerable teaching.**

---

* The father, Frederick Douglass, was an ex-slave, lecturer, and editor of *The New National Era*.

** "For the first year after graduation he taught district schools in Andover, Farmington, and Lisbon. In the summer of 1872 he began to fit for college at Hebron Academy and entered Bowdoin in the fall

Soon after leaving FSNS, Francis set up a studio in Lewiston where he was to do portrait work both in crayons and in photography. By 1885 the Stanley brothers were partners and had patented a machine for coating dry plates, the first of their kind on record. They then proceeded to establish the Stanley Dry Plate Co. In 1889 they moved to Newton, Massachusetts, where the dry plate business flourished until it was sold in 1905 to the Eastman Kodak Company. The Stanley brothers also invented a process for manufacturing illuminating gas from gasoline; this was known as the Stanley gas machine. But such scientific achievements did not catch the public fancy as did the world-famous Stanley Steamer. In 1897 the brothers visited the Brockton Fair, where a Frenchman displayed a steam-driven car. He claimed that he could drive it completely around the track; however, a quarter of the way around, the car stalled, and the Frenchman could not start it up again. This prompted the Stanley brothers to think they could make a better machine than this unreliable import. The Stanley Steamer made its first appearance soon after this, a product of the newly-formed Stanley Motor Carriage Company.

In this age of accelerating air pollution, there has been a revival of interest in the feasibility of the steam car. The emission of harmless steam rather than noxious fumes of carbon monoxide has taken on new meaning in recent days. But in its early years the Stanley Steamer had much to offer in addition to a clean exhaust. Its pioneering achievements made it the most wonderful car on the road, regardless of environmental considerations. *The Farmington Chronicle* kept a constant watch on the progress of what the press called "The Flying Teapot"; in 1899 the vigilant local paper noted with

---

of 1873 where he remained one year. Was Principal of the Mechanic Falls High School for several terms and then taught in Columbia, Penn. In 1880 he accepted a position in the Farmington Normal where he remained one year, resigning on account of failing health to go into some less sedentary occupation. For two or three years he was a manufacturer of school supplies and apparatus, some of which he invented at Mechanic Falls and Boston, Mass. In connection with his twin brother Frank E., at one time a member of the school, he discovered and perfected a superior process of coating photographic dry plates by which, current rumor says, they have made a handsome manufactory and a constantly growing business. He married April 18, 1876, Flora J. R. Tileston of Mechanic Falls."[20]

FREELAN O. STANLEY (class of 1871), in his Steamer, about 1909.

JOHN F. STEVENS (class of 1872), engineer, at his desk.

great satisfaction that F. O. Stanley, with his wife along, drove his steamer to the top of Mt. Washington in two hours and ten minutes. In its glowing account of this spectacular achievement, *The Chronicle* asserted that F. O. Stanley would have made the ascent even more quickly if he had been able to avoid stopping at a spring for much-needed water. Three years later, *The Chronicle* was happy and proud to announce that F. O. Stanley had taken his steamer up the Washington trail in twenty-seven minutes. (The Stanley brothers may have concluded that the local reporter was following their activities with excessive ardor; it was occasionally printed under *Local Items* that one of the brothers, or both, had been arrested and fined for speeding on Boston streets.)

Two of the outstanding drivers of the early racing cars were Fred Marriott and Barney Oldfield. The Stanleys employed the former to race their cars and supervise the maintenance department; Barney Oldfield was an employee of Henry Ford. Their competition highlighted the struggle between the proponents of steam and gasoline. In 1906, at Ormond Beach, Marriott drove a streamlined steamer to a new world's record—128 miles an hour. The following year the competition remained red-hot between Oldfield and Marriott when the latter brought back his cut-down steamer to Ormond Beach in a try for a new record. The Flying Teapot was clocked at 197 miles an hour before it hit a slight bump. Whereupon it took off like an airplane and traveled some one hundred feet in the air before it struck the ground. The result of this was that both the car and driver were badly smashed up. Miraculously, the driver mended, not only to tell the tale but to live well into his eighties.

A few years later, Francis E. Stanley was not to be so fortunate. In 1918, coming to the top of a Massachusetts hill, he found the road blocked by two wagons. In order to avoid smashing into them he turned off the road. Some say he crashed into a ditch, others maintain that he hit a woodpile. All agree, however, that he was killed instantly. By 1918 it had been demonstrated that gasoline was to win out over steam. Freelan recognized this and spent his later years in making high-grade stringed instruments. At the same time he attained fame in Maine as the chief benefactor of Hebron Academy. In the 1930s he was a regular attendant at Farmington Normal commencements and Massachusetts Alumni gatherings. He presented in those days a striking appearance with his erect bearing and luxurious white beard.[21]

For many years the best-known of all FSNS alumni was John F. Stevens, who graduated on June 28, 1872. (The other part of the so-called 1872 class had received their diplomas on December 29, 1871).

The personality of John F. Stevens clearly reflected his early family and educational background. He was a genuine Maine Yankee in every respect, and those who knew him best never failed to mention this. A former farm boy from West Gardiner, Stevens was never to go beyond FSNS in his formal education. After teaching ten weeks in Westport and ten in Manchester in recognition of his free tuition, Stevens obtained a surveying job in the then fast-growing city of Lewiston. (The normal schools were inclined to stress useful knowledge. It took Stevens little time to prove the usefulness of his surveying course.) In 1873 he followed the examples of some other New England youth by seeking his fortune in Minnesota. He became a rodman on a team operating out of Minneapolis. Pictures of him reveal a powerfully built and handsome man. John F. was known to some as "The Big Smoke" because of an ever-present cigar that he held in his mouth at a jaunty angle. His assets included such intangibles as personal charm, a gift for mathematics, an enormous capacity for hard work, and a spirit of adventure. Before his career was over, Stevens would build bridges, tunnels, and many miles of track for James J. Hill, whose Great Northern railroads, thanks to Stevens, would gain recognition as the best-built in the land. In addition to his engineering feats, Stevens would become a railroad executive, serving at one time as vice-president of the New York, New Haven & Hartford Railroad; after that he was to become the president of the Oregon Trunk Railway Company.

Stevens's life was a personification of the continental expansion that produced so many romantic and arduous feats relating to the winning of the West. It seems unlikely that any one person outdid him in contributing to railroad transportation, so important in the nation's expansion and economic growth. Starting from Maine, his work was to take him over the Great Plains and through the Rockies; eventually his iron tracks extended to the shores of the Pacific. One of his most spectacular exploits while working for the Great Northern consisted in his establishing the practicability of building a railroad through the Marias Pass in Montana. This was to provide the main route across the continental divide, and over the years, it has proved to be the lowest and best pass through the Rockies in the northern part of the United States.

In an 1889 exploration of this area, Stevens was accompanied by a half-breed Indian who was noted for his endurance. This was essential, for the two of them were to hike over the rugged country near Helena, Montana, in the severest part of the winter. However, the Indian became exhausted and Stevens had to leave him beside a fire while he plodded on. Within the next few hours he was to determine the railroad route that was to shorten the trip to the coast by over a hundred miles and make possible much easier grades. He tramped back and forth the rest of the night to keep from freezing to death. The next day he found his Indian helper half-frozen, for the fire had gone out during the night.

In 1925, in recognition of his service to Great Northern and the country, the railroad company had a heroic bronze statue of Stevens erected at the Marias Pass.

In 1905 the lagging construction on the Panama Canal threatened to become a national disgrace. (When Stevens arrived in Panama he said that the only busy ones were the ants and typists.) Americans seemed about to match the French failure in Panama Canal construction. Many difficulties had developed; probably the worst one was an unnerving number of casualties from yellow fever and malaria. This threat brought on resignations of key figures, among them Wallace, the chief engineer. President Roosevelt, after conferring with James J. Hill, named Stevens to assume control of the canal construction. (Shortly before this, William H. Taft, the Secretary of War, had asked Stevens to develop a railroad system in the Philippines.) After arriving on the Panama scene, Stevens said: "There are three diseases here: malaria, yellow fever, and cold feet."

For the next eighteen months, he was to become a familiar and popular figure as he walked in hip boots the entire length of the Canal. His workers liked him from the first. He did not try to impress by pretensions, or condescension, or airs of authority. Unlike his predecessors, he never used the train previously reserved for the brass. He also turned down a proposal that an expensive residence be constructed for him. He described native labor as "slow as the wrath of God," but he was enough of a realist to appreciate the dangers of trying to speed them much beyond their traditional pace. He did try to increase the output of all by setting a good example in working harder than anyone else. His employees continued to like him even though he was often blunt in answering their questions. A carpenter, told to build some sheds, found old French equipment in the way. He wrote to Stevens asking him what he should do. Stevens replied: "Wait till I have a free Sunday, and I'll come down and move it for you." A young engineer complained about the difficulty of a job that had been assigned him. Stevens assured him he was equal to the task and then ended the letter with this sentence: "There is only one mistake you can make that will be absolutely fatal with me, and that is to do nothing." When someone told him there had been a few collisions on the supply railroad he said: "A collision has its good points as well as bad ones—it indicates that there is something moving." A complete reorganization and development of supply lines produced greater activity, and existing housing was improved. Stevens threw his full support behind Col. William Gorgas in implementing sanitary and health measures. A U. S. Senate committee voted in favor of a sea-level canal, which caused Stevens to hotfoot it to Washington to push successfully for a lock canal. After eighteen months of bringing order out of chaos, Stevens, for personal reasons never made clear, resigned from his dual responsibilities as chief engineer and chairman of the Canal Commission. In view of his increasingly sarcastic remarks to President Roosevelt about bureaucratic interference, he may have tired more from this harassment than from tropical heat, or the other demands of his Panama job.

President Roosevelt would never forgive him this decision; he was always thereafter to give the Canal credit to others, primarily to General Goethals. But fully appreciating the importance of his predecessor's months in Panama, General Goethals said of Stevens: "The Canal is his monument."

For many years history textbooks gave all the credit for the Panama Canal to General Goethals and William C. Gorgas. Within the past ten years, however, several historians have re-discovered the accomplishment of John F. Stevens. Apparently the Army, which had been given most of the credit for the construction of the Canal, felt embarrassed or guilty about monopolizing the spotlight for this accomplishment. In an attempt to make amends, Stephen Ailes, Secretary of the Army in 1963, unveiled in Balboa in that year a monument and circle to the memory of John F. Stevens. A reappraisal of Canal accomplishments resulted in Stevens receiving credit for the design of the canal, the plan for digging it, and the decision to build locks rather than a sea-level waterway.

In 1917 the Provisional Government of Kerensky badly needed help in Russia if it were to continue in World War I as one of the Allies. Hence, President Wilson appointed an advisory commission of railroad experts who were enjoined to keep the Russian railroads operating. Stevens was chairman of the group and was supported by about two hundred engineers, the more important ones selected by Stevens himself. After landing in Russia in June 1917, these experts began to reorganize the Trans-Siberian and Chinese Eastern railways. Much of this work in the beginning was to forestall a German takeover in Siberia. This included making it possible for the Czech legion to use the Trans-Siberian railroad to avoid both the Bolsheviks and the Germans. During the Russian Civil War, Stevens took the position that he was not there to take political sides, but should confine his energies and efforts to his engineering tasks. Partly as a result of this attitude, he stayed on after the Bolsheviks had won the Civil War, returning to the United States in 1923.

In 1925 John F. Stevens was the recipient of the prestigious John Fritz Medal. Others who had received it were Lord Kelvin, George Westinghouse, Alexander Graham Bell, Thomas A. Edison, General George Goethals, Orville Wright, and Guglielmo Marconi. In accepting the award, Stevens made a few remarks, among them that whatever success he had had was primarily attributable to a natural aptitude for mathematics combined with wanderlust.

In 1927 Stevens served as the president of the American Society of Engineers. In addition to his signal honor in receiving the John Fritz Medal, he received honorary degrees from Bates College, the University of North Carolina, the University of Michigan, and Brooklyn Polytechnic Institute. Decorations came from the United States, France, China, Japan, and Czechoslovakia. Stevens was active in engineering until 1931. In 1943 he died at the age of ninety, and was buried near his wife in Mount Hope Cemetery, Boston, Mass.[22]

There were other members of the 1872 class who had more than

Left: Hortense Merrill, later Hortense M. Keith (class of 1881), language teacher from 1885 to 1901, and from 1903 to 1921 teacher of English literature and history.
Right: Nellie Skinner (class of 1887), teacher of rhetoric from 1893 to 1902.

ordinary influence in their time. Among these was Fred E. C. Robbins, who became principal of Deering High School in Portland, Maine. Along with his teaching and administrative duties, Robbins was for many years an editorial writer for the *Portland Evening Express*. Dora M. Norton was a teacher of drawing at the Pratt Institute in New York City. Ezra Elliot was for many years superintendent of schools in Polk county, Minnesota. Lewis A. Thomas of the same class became superintendent of schools in Illinois.

The salutatorian of the 1873 class was Enos F. Floyd. Because of his health he went to Murphys, California, where he taught for twelve years. There he was an Associated Press agent and for several years president of the board of education of Calaveras county. (He was a grandfather of Dr. Paul Floyd of Farmington, Maine).

In the class of 1874 was James O. Bradbury, who became a successful lawyer and served at one time as the Somerset County attorney. He took a great deal of interest in Farmington Normal events even after his graduation and was to play a prominent role in the crisis of 1883. In 1888 Governor Marble appointed him a trustee of Maine normal schools.

One of the most successful of the alumni, especially from a worldly point of view, was A. Arthur Greene of the 1876 class. After his graduation he taught in the Abbott School and was principal for two years of the Farmington High School. Later, he became a New York lawyer and still later co-owner of a successful publishing house. He married Clara Allen, who was for many years a popular teacher at the Normal School.

Advanced Course Introduced

On July 27, 1880, Rounds sent to the graduates and friends of the Normal School an announcement of an advanced course which was to be offered the following September. It would add one full year to a teacher's preparation, and its main purpose would be to train teachers for work in the burgeoning high schools. For foreign languages, Latin, French, and German were to be taught; other additions to the curriculum included English literature, advanced math, physics, chemistry, history, and philosophy of education.

This advanced program lasted some twenty-four years with from two to seven students receiving annually the special diploma that signified the completion of the course. A total of 55 students received

LILLIAN I. LINCOLN, graduate of regular course in 1885
and advanced course in 1890, teacher of history from 1885 to
1894 and 1896 to 1924. Miss Lincoln wrote the words to the
FSNS "Alma Mater."

the third-year diploma; 38 women and 17 men. Rounds was justly proud of the additional year of study. For many years he had been of the opinion that Farmington Normal students should have the opportunity for advanced work of this kind. Although a comparatively small number took advantage of it, the quality of the students was always high. Nearly all those who attended for a third year went on to distinguished teaching careers. Included in this list were Hortense Merrill Keith, for thirty-seven years a prominent teacher at the Normal School, and Lillian I. Lincoln, for twenty-eight years the brilliant head of the Model School.

Another Rounds accomplishment in 1880 was the establishment of the Maine Pedagogical Society. George C. Purington thought of it as unique among the educational associations of the land. Those who were invited to join held scheduled meetings where they read papers on educational problems. This opportunity for exchanging views was highly enough regarded to keep the organization going until 1901.

1883—*Town vs. Gown and the Resignation of Rounds*

In the spring of 1883, rumors began to get louder and more frequent concerning the alleged unfriendliness of the townspeople toward the Normal School. This was resented by many citizens who thought of it as a base canard that had its origin on Academy Street. Finally, on March 28, a special town meeting was held in the courthouse. J. C. Holman Esq. presided, and a committee was appointed to draw up and present a resolution. At the second meeting, the committee presented the following preamble and resolutions:

> Whereas, there was at one time an attempt made to secure the removal of the Normal School of this place to some other locality, and
>
> Whereas, it is understood that desires have been expressed and efforts made from time to time tending toward that end, and
>
> Whereas, the continuance of the school here and its prosperity are matters of great importance to this town and section of the state, and
>
> Whereas, the right of petition and resolve on the part of the people is sacredly guaranteed by the Constitution under which we live, therefore

A determined looking basketball team, posing with their mascot in the basement gym of Merrill Hall. Does anyone recognize them?

Resolved, that we, the citizens of Farmington, in mass meeting assembled, disapprove of any action on the part of any person or persons with a view to the removal of the School from this place, and that any such act is unjust to the people.

Resolved, that the claim that the citizens of Farmington are unfriendly to the School is not warranted by the facts, and is a great injustice to this community.

Resolved, that we most respectfully ask the Governor and Board of Trustees of the Normal School, to institute an investigation, that it may be ascertained, if possible, the cause of the decline of the school located here.

Resolved, that a copy of this preamble and resolutions be placed in the hands of the Governor and Board of Normal Trustees.

A member of the resolutions committee was Charles W. Keyes, editor of *The Farmington Chronicle*. One day, during this tempestuous spring of 1883, he went to New Sharon where he interviewed Judge H. B. Prescott, a former member of Governor Chamberlain's council. The Judge told Keyes that in 1869 he had talked with Farmington-born Warren Johnson, who was then State Superintendent of Schools. Keyes learned that in 1869 Johnson and Rounds had tried to get the Normal School moved to Gorham. The Judge told Keyes that after learning of this proposed move he had called upon Dr. Edmund Russell, the representative from Farmington to the legislature, and by the prompt and effective efforts of Prescott and Russell the scheme to move the school was thwarted and the institution saved for Farmington. Such information had a decided influence on the editorial policy of *The Chronicle*. Its editor was from then on anti-Rounds.

There were two major developments in the Normal School story of 1883. The first had to do with a misunderstanding between the townspeople and the Normal School administration; the second development involved a split within the Normal School faculty. The loss in the number of Normal School students from 1879 to 1883 convinced many of the local citizens that not all was well on Academy Street. In 1878 there were 254 students; in 1879, 202; in 1880, 141; 1881, 143; 1882, 104; 1883, 139. Three members of the Normal School faculty charged that Rounds was overbearing, changeable, and uncertain in making arrangements for studies, and that his teachers did not know from one day to the other what to expect. The revelation of dissension within the institution was conclusive proof to many that the place was headed for oblivion.

Soon after these accusations were made, an investigating committee was appointed. This consisted of two Normal School trustees, Amos Plummer, of Bangor, and I. Warren Merrill; the third member was N. A. Luce, State Superintendent of Schools. Their first move was to pour all the available oil on the troubled waters. This took the form of encouraging all who were involved in the dispute to keep their cool and continue their work until the end of the term. After that a complete investigation might be made if it still seemed advisable.

This attempt at conciliation was aborted because of developments that soon followed. One Monday morning, at a meeting of the students and faculty, a poem was read that some thought reflected upon two teachers, Miss Perley and W. C. Philbrook. Partly because these two had brought charges against Rounds, they suspected that he had approved of the reading of the poem. Whether he had or not, the incident caused three Farmington Normal teachers to withdraw. Miss Perley and W. C. Philbrook were joined in their exit by William Harper, who had been the Normal School science teacher for several years. The three teachers insisted that their withdrawal did not mean they were resigning, but that they were merely refusing to work any longer under the existing management. Whatever such a move was to be called, the fact remained that the Normal School management was faced with the necessity of filling three faculty spots in the middle of the spring term.

By this time it was obvious that drastic action was essential in order to settle this increasingly unhappy situation. *The Farmington Chronicle* was reminding local citizens that talk was cheap and, in this case, was being engaged in "by men and women who have about as much right to pass judgment in the conduct of the investigation as a cow has to give sour milk." Charles W. Keyes was getting more anti-Rounds by the minute. One of his editorials stated: "The credit of a large and prosperous Normal School here belongs to the principal; the humiliation of a small and distracted school belongs to him also."

Rounds seems to have handled himself throughout this unpleasantness with dignity and decorum. There is no evidence that he ever made countercharges, and he seems to have maintained a complete and discreet silence. He may have antagonized irretrievably three members of his faculty, but the students and alumni gave him strong support. In *The Portland Times* a dozen Farmington alumni sponsored the following statement: "We the undersigned, graduates of the Farmington Normal School, wish to express the high esteem in which we hold the principal, Dr. C. C. Rounds, and our appreciation of his judicious, untiring, and unselfish work. We also wish to express the indignation with which we have learned of the charges made against him, and to declare that from personal knowledge we believe them to be utterly false."

After a while, the three disaffected members of the faculty withdrew their original charges. The reason given for this *détente* was that an investigation such as they had asked for was being conducted, and furthermore, they wanted it understood that they were not being actuated by animosity toward Rounds. The influence of student and alumni opinion, recognized as such or not, may have played a role in the retraction. It is also possible that the three dissidents had had time to cool off and regretted their previous strong language.

Despite the dropping of the original charges against Rounds, investigation of the local difficulties continued. Moreover, it was being carried on at a high level with the governor and his council participating as well as the Normal School trustees.

The governor at this time was Frederick Robie. Here was a man who really cared about the normal school movement. In 1878 he had been partly responsible for the establishment of the Gorham Normal, and his public speeches almost always showed a concern about the teaching situation in Maine. In his inaugural address of January 1883, he bemoaned the fact that one-third of Maine's 6,500 teachers entered their schools without experience or previous training. Governor Robie was happy to note an increasing enthusiasm for normal schools throughout the land. A few weeks after this address, he would be playing an unforeseen part in a normal school squabble.

When Governor Robie was in town for the investigation, some of the local citizens expressed a desire to participate in a full airing of the situation. They invited the Governor to be the moderator at a special town meeting, an invitation he readily accepted. Consequently one May evening in 1883 a well-filled Normal Hall heard the Governor call the meeting to order. He expressed his appreciation for the interest shown by the local citizens and said he believed they had a right, and even the duty, to discuss the activities of their state institution.

Despite this expression of good will, the meeting soon became overheated after Governor Robie "gracefully set forth the objects for which the citizens were invited to be present." Set at ease and soothed by the Governor's gracious words, the citizenry became agitated as a result of listening to the first speaker, James O. Bradbury. This gentleman as previously noted, was county attorney of Somerset and a graduate of the Farmington Normal School. His opening remarks were considered insulting and many at the meeting found it difficult to maintain their composure. The trouble was that Bradbury asked that the people at the meeting be put under oath. He thought this was reasonable, and for purposes of getting at the truth, necessary. He based this on his conviction that the townspeople, for the most part, were anti-Normal. The feelings between the students and townspeople were worsened when Bradbury's suggestion received a loud cheer from the students. It was certainly an inflammatory remark, because this so-called anti-Normal sentiment was what had been so vehemently denied in a previous town meeting. The Governor recognized the Bradbury motion as a serious gaffe and denied its applicability. It had served only to infuriate the local citizens.

One of the severest critics of Farmington Normal management was Jonas Burnham, who for a decade (1849-1859) had been the preceptor of the Farmington Academy. He spoke of the dwindling number of students who enrolled and expressed the belief that this proved that the institution was under the wrong management. He attributed it to a rigidity of school government and its lack of interest in the pupils. Burnham stated that throughout his days at the Academy there were never less than a hundred students. T. W. Vose of Bangor, counsel for Rounds, said that such comparisons were unfair and then proceeded to read the appropriate statutes that had a bearing on admission to normal schools. This was partly for the purpose of showing that a teacher's institution would inevitably have considerable fluctuations in attendance and could not be compared with Farmington Academy. All males, for example, had to be at least seventeen before being allowed to enter the Normal School. In the old Academy the ages ranged from nine to thirty. Moreover, the Normal student was required to commit himself to teaching two years in Maine in order to compensate the State for free tuition. No such commitment was required in the old Academy.

The two men who seemed to remain the calmest and apparently spoke the most judiciously were a former Normal School trustee, David H. Knowlton, and the newly appointed trustee, I. Warren Merrill. Both of them expressed their deep interest in the welfare of the Normal School and their heartfelt regret over the unhappy state of affairs. Merrill, as well as others, reminded the more critical of the citizenry that Gorham Normal had been established in 1878, so it was inevitable that Farmington registration would drop as a consequence. David H. Knowlton thought the length of study required for a Normal School diploma discouraged many from registering. He did not propose to change the requirements; he merely recognized it as a possible reason for the low attendance figures. He assured Rounds that the community was not bent on persecuting him. Both Knowlton and Merrill were the constant champions of good will and a cool climate of opinion.

Now that the smoke of battle has long since cleared away, it is impossible to divide the participants into the innocent and guilty parties. Even during the 1883 days, with their overcharged atmosphere, there was no pinning of charges by the investigating committee. C. C. Rounds was completely exonerated of any reprehensible conduct. Miss Perley, W. C. Philbrook, and William Harper were described as honorable people who at least thought they were justified in withdrawing from the institution. Considering their later records of achievement it is easy to accept such a conclusion.

No one accused the three dissidents of maliciousness or willfulness. All three were consistently popular and successful teachers. Whether right or wrong, they felt put upon by the administration and it is possible they had good reasons for this belief. In those days a principal had dictatorial powers. He needed to give the impression that he was using these powers with great restraint and reluctance. Rounds may have become distraught and harassed at this time because of the critical comments that were inevitable since the school registration had been dropping for several years.

Miss Perley earned an M.A. degree and was a high school principal in Iowa after leaving Farmington. Before she came to Farmington she was the preceptress at Kents Hill. William Harper was the

popular Normal School science teacher for six years before he became embroiled in the 1883 incident. In the fall of 1883 he became
the principal of the Farmington High School, where he stayed for
two years.[23] The other disaffected member of the faculty, W. C.
Philbrook, became a distinguished lawyer and then was appointed
to the Maine Supreme Court. His accomplishments were recognized
by his alma mater, Colby, when it bestowed upon him an honorary
LL.D.

Did Rounds and Johnson want to move the Normal School from
Farmington to Gorham? Probably, but that was in 1869 and not
1883. The future of Farmington Normal had looked bleak to Rounds
in 1869. No progress had been made on the pathetically inadequate
physical plant since the first class in 1865 had moved into the building. However, as we have seen, with the help of Warren Johnson,
things got rolling in the summer of 1869 and by 1876 the building
and grounds were much improved. Among his valedictory remarks,
Rounds wrote the following to the Board of Trustees before he assumed his new duties as principal of the Plymouth Normal School
in New Hampshire:

> Closing at this time my connection with this school to enter
> upon another field of labor, in this my last report to your honor-
> able body some comparative statements may not be out of place.
> I became principal of the school at the beginning of its fifth
> year. I found no records to assist me in my work. I believe the
> records are complete for the past fifteen years. The building com-
> mittee, after selecting a beautiful lot of five acres, where the pub-
> lic school-house now stands, gave way to popular clamor and
> located the building where it now stands, down on the main
> street on the old Academy lot, and kept the Academy, a worth-
> less wooden building some sixty years old, as an ell to the new
> structure. The new part was very much in the rough, the Aca-
> demic ell unsightly within and without. By the energy of Supt.
> Johnson, money was found for the completion of the building
> in its present style. There were not books enough belonging to
> the school to deserve the name of library. Instruction in the
> physical sciences was required by the course of study; the appar-
> atus of the school consisted of a pair of globes, Madeburg hemi-
> spheres, a small microscope, an air pump, a spirit lamp, and
> two or three test tubes. A chemical apparatus, which I took to
> the school, the State never paid for. Subsequently, by a special

appropriation, apparatus and books were purchased. The school is now furnished with good apparatus for instruction in physics and chemistry, and a convenient laboratory. It has a library of more than thirteen hundred volumes, exclusive of textbooks, carefully selected, classified and catalogued.

Concerning the criticism within the community about diminished attendance, Rounds had this to say: "The work of the normal school is to form teachers, and it is to be tested, like other professional schools, by the number of its graduates rather than by its aggregate attendance. The standard required for graduation from this school has not been lowered for these fifteen years. The facts show that notwithstanding fluctuations in attendance, the number of graduates in each period, and the ratio of graduates to numbers in attendance has steadily increased."

In the 1870s, as one of the editors of *The Maine Journal of Education*, Rounds advanced his educational theories with clarity, fervor, and frankness. He was appalled by the inaccuracies and inanities of the average textbook and deplored the teachers' ignorance which required bondage to them.[24] He urged teachers to go to original sources, and wrote that he wanted only those who plainly showed that they were anxious to learn while they taught. After recognizing and commenting on the shortcomings of textbooks, he recommended what he called oral teaching. This would have to come from a lively and living teacher and not from a dead and unfit book:

A few words then, with you, fellow-teachers, on the necessity, the subjects, the methods, of oral teaching. The work now carried on in our common schools is fragmentary and incomplete. It starts the pupil on the road to scholarship and culture, but he has a long road to travel before reaching the goal. It commences the work of preparing him for the responsible and honorable duties of American citizenship, but it does not prepare him. He is taught to read: is he fired with an eager desire for reading the best books, and told where to find them? He studies grammar that he may know how to speak and write the English correctly: does he learn to use the language with propriety, elegance, and force, and does he have in his own mind a standard of pure and idiomatic English by which he may judge the written and spoken word of others? He ciphers: does his mathematical study show him the true place and scope of the science of numbers in the scheme of education, or lead him to suspect that it is susceptible of applications nobler than those to the fluctuations of stock? And what else than these is the average boy or girl now learning in the common school? Not much. Of our noble literature; of our history, and its relations to the history of other nations and of other times; of the fundamental principles of our governmental polity; of the results of that scientific research which is the especial characteristic of our age, and of which modern civilization is a growth,—of these, and of other things as important as these, the common school takes little note. Nearly all the instruction in the common school must, for a long time to come, be oral mainly, from the living teacher, not from a dead book; for the fit book cannot be found, nor time for its use.[25]

Rounds came to Farmington at a time when many people in the State were not convinced that the normal school idea was a good one. In the December 1872 *Maine Journal of Education*, he answered some of the questions of those who were skeptical about the advantages of the new teaching methods. To the first question, whether or not one needed special training for the work of teaching, Rounds's reply was:

> Yes. However it may have been in former times, teachers now can hardly expect to achieve the highest success without special preparation. The growth of this conviction among us is shown by the following contrast: Some thirty years ago the first normal school in America opened with three pupils. There are now in the United States about one hundred and fifty of these institutions, and their pupils are numbered by thousands. Teaching is now recognized as a science, based upon principles which can be taught; as an art, the methods of which can be practically illustrated. The principles of this science, the methods of this art, have been slowly evolved, classified, organized, through successive centuries, by the earnest thought and labors of the wisest and best of the human race; they have been embodied in school systems, and enacted into laws, which have shaped the civilization of nations. Will you refuse to be illumined by these lights, to avail yourself of results so patiently and laboriously achieved?

The skeptic and critic of normal schools contended that he thought it enough to copy the teaching methods of the best teachers without spending so much time on elementary school training. Rounds replied to that:

Methods well adapted to advanced pupils become increasingly inappropriate as we approach the lower grades. The methods of the teacher of children depend upon the nature of the child's mind and the laws of its natural development. As the mind matures, these considerations recede and the subject-matter of the various branches of study becomes of increasing importance, until in the highest grades of instruction, with mature minds, a thorough, clear, scientific treatment of the respective subjects becomes the only consideration. The most disastrous failures arise from the teacher's ignorance of psychological principles, his neglect to take into account the interval which separates his own mind from the mind of the pupil, and the consequent attempt to use in the education of the child methods appropriate only to the adult.[26]

In 1869, when there were few primary training schools in the land, Rounds had the courage and vision to realize their importance and talked the authorities into organizing one in Farmington. As his successor wrote, "Such a school proved to be the strong right arm of the institution." It is difficult to believe that anyone fought a more valiant fight than did C. C. Rounds for his educational program. His efforts were held in the highest regard, not only by Maine and New England educators, but by such national leaders as W. T. Harris, distinguished philosopher, superintendent of schools at St. Louis, and for some years after that, U.S. Commissioner of Education. For years Rounds fought for a school building that would provide essential educational facilities as well as properly lighted and heated rooms. Year after year he fought for a reasonably good library and resisted temptation to lower his standards in order to combat the sagging registration. In his 1882 report to the State Superintendent, he rejected the proposal of some educators to reduce the number and quality of the academic studies and of still others to offer in normal schools only professional subjects. He recognized the importance of professional studies, but at the same time, realized the importance of teachers learning the subject matter they were to teach. Two of his successors, George C. Purington and W. G. Mallett, appreciated the educational legacy left them by C. C. Rounds and never were reluctant to say so.

GEORGE C. PURINGTON, principal of the FSNS from 1883 to 1909.

III. EXIT ROUNDS: ENTER PURINGTON

The Farmington town meeting of May 4, 1883, at which the Governor presided, did little to clear the air or reconcile the warring elements of school and town. In some respects the situation after this notable meeting deteriorated. In the May 24 issue of *The Chronicle*, appeared an article clipped from the *Portland Press* that took Rounds to task for claiming too much credit for the normal schools. Rounds was reported to have implied, in speaking to a meeting of the Maine Pedogogical Society, that a normal school diploma was not only desirable but a necessity for a successful career in teaching. Furthermore, he supposedly had said that a law should be passed denying a teaching certificate to anyone who did not have such a diploma. As an ardent defender of the academies and colleges, the writer for the *Portland Press* thought this was a narrow and arrogant attitude. The editor of *The Chronicle* thought so too.

It is doubtful that the hostility of a section of the press, or the resentment of some of the local citizens, would have been sufficient to prevent Rounds from continuing his work in Farmington, if he had been so inclined. Other factors, in addition to the unfortunate spring events, probably had at least as much influence in contributing to his decision to leave Farmington. Three of his four children were ready to move on after they received their third-year diplomas from the Normal School in 1883; Rounds continued to be frustrated in his attempts to increase the prestige of the Normal diploma; and the Plymouth Normal offered him a raise in salary. Rounds had had trouble with his faculty, but he still had the support of those who could hire or fire.

Rounds's fellow educators, the Normal School trustees, and the Normal alumni said in no uncertain terms what they thought about the departing principal's contributions and qualifications. The State Superintendent of Schools, N. A. Luce, bestowed an unqualified encomium upon Rounds and his Farmington record. Among other compliments he wrote: "He has won a place in our (State) educational history second to that of no other man. Such men deserve better of the State than they are wont to receive."

The following resolution was passed unanimously by the Normal School trustees:

> Whereas, Dr. C. C. Rounds, Principal of the Farmington Normal School has accepted the principalship of the State Normal School at Plymouth, New Hampshire,
>
> Therefore, resolved, that we the trustees of the State Normal Schools, recognizing as we do the scholarly and professional ability of Dr. Rounds and the great work that he has done for the cause of education in this State, feel that the Farmington Normal School, as does the State of Maine, loses one of its ablest and most efficient teachers and educators.

The Alumni Association was to pass two resolutions, one in 1883 and another in 1886, in which it expressed its admiration and affection for Dr. C. C. Rounds.[27]

The resolution of the Normal School trustees was passed on July 5, 1883, and the town of Farmington, for the greater part of the summer, was filled with rumors as to who would be the new principal. The trustees offered the position to the Reverend A. W. Burr, principal of the Hallowell Classical and Scientific Academy, but Burr declined to be considered.[28] By the middle of August it was revealed that the Normal School trustees had gone again to Edward Little High for their principal. This time it was George C. Purington who left Auburn for Farmington, as Rounds had done in 1868.

George Colby Purington was born in 1848 in Embden, Maine. He received his early education in his home town, and at the age of eighteen began teaching in the district schools. Some time later he took a course in a business college which was designed to prepare him for commercial life. He did keep the books at a country store for several years, but then deserted the marketplace for education. He was for one year assistant at the North Yarmouth Academy, and then became assistant principal of Hebron Academy. There he stayed for two years before entering Bowdoin College in 1874 and graduating in 1878. For two years of his college course he was principal of the Topsham High School. For the last term of his college senior year, he was principal of the Brunswick High School. Although George C. Purington graduated from college at thirty, he was a vigorous and young thirty-five when he became the principal of the Farmington Normal School.

Course of Study at Farmington (1883)

In academic respects Farmington Normal was in sound condition when G. C. Purington took over its management. Certainly it had been a convulsive spring, but the curriculum and quality of instruction were on a par with the better normal schools. This included, as we have seen, an advanced course designed to fit teachers for positions in the fast expanding high schools.[29] Rounds had helped establish normal school policies and standards throughout the country, but the greatest challenge to his educational ideals came from the habits of some of his own students. Many were too prone to take the courses in a desultory and unsystematic way or, worse still, drop out after a term or two. Rounds's remarks in the last circular he wrote at Farmington were typical of his response to the situation:

> Those pupils whose previous education has been gained in the country schools, with their frequent changes of teachers, and their lack of systematic instruction and management, need at least two years of orderly school life and earnest study to acquire such culture, and to form in themselves such habits, as are necessary to assure the teacher's success; and those who have taken a graded course of study, passed over most of the branches which they will be called upon to teach at so early an age that they cannot recall their processes of acquisition, and hence cannot understand the difficulties of their pupils, nor successfully teach them, except after a careful review, conducted with special reference to methods of instruction. Consideration of the course of study will show a very full two years' work. Those who come with the best previous preparation are our most successful and enthusiastic students; and those who have shortened their course, usually express afterwards, deep regret at having done so.

In 1883 the course of study in both the Model School and FSNS was quite similar to what could be found at such normal schools as those in Oswego or Bridgewater or Salem. Like Farmington all these institutions were under the influence of ideas such as championed by Quintilian, Comenius, Froebel, Rousseau, Pestalozzi, Col. Parker, and Horace Mann. (After about 1890, G. Stanley Hall, J. F. Herbart, John Dewey, and William Kilpatrick would become members of the normal school pantheon.) In 1883 Pestalozzi was, apparently, as influential as he had been when Farmington Normal was founded. This meant, among other things, that many of the primary lessons were to encourage and promote vocabulary growth and skill in describing objects both orally and in writing. Converting observations into words was regarded as the basis of all knowledge.

Two of the subjects that Pestalozzi delighted in and championed were music and home geography. The Model School from its beginning included these subjects. In the second year, there was a review of all the letter sounds, and then students spelled the easy words in the reading lesson by sound and letter; they counted to 100, combined to 20, did simple fractions, and added short columns of figures; learned pint, quart, pound, inch, and foot. Pupils continued the work of the first year in object lessons; they also had oral lessons from a geography book called *Our World*. The purpose of this was to acquaint the pupils with their immediate environment in the belief that knowledge of distant lands could be better taught in the more advanced grades.

In the third year the Model School pupils learned about colors and plants. In geography they drew plans of the school room, schoolhouse, and yard. In the third and fourth years, they wrote a reproduction of their object lessons with particular attention to capitalizing and punctuation. In the fourth year they wrote out simple narratives based upon pictures and did some letter writing. In the third and fourth years they also learned to read music. Some songs and hymns were taught by rote.[30]

By 1883 the third-year course at FSNS for those aiming at high school teaching had taken form. In the first term of the third year, a study was made of Chaucer, Shakespeare, and Milton, with special reference to the development of the language. In mathematics, the student studied algebra and plane and solid geometry the first term; in the second term, he took trigonometry and surveying, with field work concentrating on the use of the transit. Chemistry was taught in the second and third years; geology came in the second term of the third year, and it included local geology with excursions for the collection of specimens and the observation of geological features of the locality. Latin and French were offered in the third year, with such reading in Latin as Caesar's *Gallic War* and two books of the *Aeneid*. The course in rhetoric was similar to a course in English composition, and the general history course began with the creation of the world and ended with the present. The only professional subject was the history of education. This reviewed the life and principles of eminent educational reformers.

At first glance, this third year seemed close to the courses offered in the liberal arts colleges. Actually it was quite different with nowhere near the emphasis on the classics at FSNS that was found in the colleges. At FSNS there was a greater emphasis on what Horace Mann called useful knowledge. (The present jargon would refer to such courses as relevant.) Pestalozzi and his followers would have applauded the teaching outdoors of so much of the surveying and geology courses.

Reconciliation of Town and Gown

The Purington administration had at the top of its priority list the bettering of relations between townspeople and school authorities. Along with this priority was a determination to increase the school registration. A comparison of the annual catalogue and circular under the Rounds and Purington managements indicated a new approach, which was designed to heal the recent wounds. In Rounds's circulars he paid his respects to Farmington by commenting favorably on the natural scenery and the pure mountain air. Purington trumpeted the natural advantages, too, but he went on to placate any and all of the Farmington citizens who believed their attitude toward the Normal School had been misrepresented:

> In addition to these natural advantages it is the home of a highly intelligent and enterprising people, who, from its establishment, have been justly proud of their Normal School and ever zealous to promote its welfare. Scholars coming here may be sure of a hearty welcome awaiting them by the citizens of the town. There is but little to draw the student from the work for which he comes here, and the social and religious influences within and surrounding the school are of inestimable value.[31]

Purington's effort at reconciliation was backed up by action. The new principal quickly made himself an important part of community life, and as the years went by, continued to contribute to the more worthy of local enterprises. He became a member of the local grange, chief of the fire department, an active Mason, Sunday School superintendent, a member of the Old South Church business committee, leader of the church choir and regional choral group of the Maine music festival, and founder and president of the public library association. It did not take him long to win over most of the citizens of Farmington, and that included Rounds's severest critic, Charles W. Keyes, editor of *The Farmington Chronicle*.

George C. Purington had a natural bent for public relations work. He had as much missionary zeal in promoting the normal school idea as his wife, Sarah Bailey, had for her missionary work in the church. Purington flooded the State with his promotional bulletins and gave throughout the State innumerable speeches on various subjects. (All of this was accomplished without secretarial help, but the victim was not uncomplaining. In his last years as principal he was still asking in vain for secretarial assistance.) The effectiveness of Purington's writings and speeches was reflected in the increase in Normal School registration. His state-wide activities brought him to the favorable attention of Maine legislators, and this stood him in good stead when he sought appropriations for the school. Eventually he became an overseer of Bowdoin College, president of the Christian Civic League, and grand commander of the Knights Templars of Maine.

In the first year of the Purington administration, there was a complete turnabout in the attitude of the townspeople toward the Normal School. In 1883 many of the local citizens thought the institution was on its way out. But in 1884 the Normal School was regarded as a fixture with its prospects exceedingly bright. In the summer of 1884 the local papers were rejoicing at the rejuvenation which had produced a sharp increase in registration. Whatever acrimony there was between town and gown in the spring of 1883 had given way to an era of good feeling. This was underlined by the headlines in *The Franklin Journal* in June, 1884:

GRADUATED!

From the Northern State Normal School

The Second Class of 1884 Step Out

The Most Successful Exercises Ever Held
A Large Audience Give an Ovation
23 Young Ladies and Gentlemen

In November 1884, *The Franklin Journal* continued to help spread the happy news that a new spirit prevailed between the townspeople and school. On the twenty-second of the month, a fancy dress sociable marked the close of the fall term. Not only was the school out in full force, but many of the townspeople were invited guests. Before the year was over, the winter term was to start with the principal tendering a reception to his pupils, who numbered an encouraging 100. The students, in turn, indicated their enthusiasm for the principal by giving him a silver fruit dish.

Early Purington Faculty

In his first year at FSNS, Purington had support from four assistants and the head of the Model School. His first assistant, Charles F. Warner, was a young graduate of Colby (1879) who had taken a year of work at the Bridgewater Normal School. After he had been on the Farmington Faculty for three years, he married Marion A. Luce, a Normal School graduate who was for two years (1885–87) the head of the Model School. Warner was primarily a science teacher and received a good local press, partly at least in recognition of the intellectual interest he aroused in his students. Here was a typical item about him as carried in a local paper: "Mr. Warner gave his astronomy class another magic lantern exhibition. The lantern used is a very good one and of Mr. Warner's own construction."[32] Principal Purington appreciated his young assistant and was greatly disappointed when he realized that Warner, after serving in Farmington for five years, was about to move on to Cambridge, Massachusetts. The principal used the occasion to deplore the salary scale of the State.

Another teacher in the early years of the Purington regime was Helen B. Coffin. A graduate of Bridgewater Normal, she taught in Farmington from 1866 to 1869. In the latter year, she went to Castine Normal where she taught until her career was interrupted by marriage to Daniel Beedy, of Farmington. Her credentials in the area of morality were impeccable, and they included being the Sunday School teacher for Normal students at the Methodist church as well as president of the Franklin County W. C. T. U. Her return to teaching lasted from 1883 to 1885. She followed Pestalozzian principles in conducting a physiology class as described in *The Franklin Journal*: "Mrs. Beedy delighted and instructed her physiology class, Thursday, by dissecting the heart and lung of an ox. This study of the thing itself instead of textbooks is one of the most prominent features of the Normal School and is carried into all branches of study."

The language teacher in 1883 was Elizabeth G. Bell. She had spent two years in Germany and France to improve her competence. She became "first lady assistant" to Purington when both were at Edward Little and then accompanied her principal to Farmington. Unfortunately her health began to fail during her second year at Farmington, and in a few years she was dead from tuberculosis.

Annie Pinkham, from East Wilton, of the 1878 class, taught English composition. *The Franklin Journal* had nothing but praise for her teaching exercises in letter-writing as she conducted them at a teacher's institute in Strong.

Viola A. Johnson, from Industry, of the 1883 class, was the head of the Model School in 1883–84. The tireless reporter for *The Franklin Journal* visited one of her primary classes: "Taking the number 9, each member of the class was called upon to name some combination of figures making 9. Order was maintained by the kindest of words and utmost patience." Part of the normal school idea was that the strap had been overused by impatient, if not sadistic, teachers.

FSNS Social Life in the 1880s

All the available evidence would lead to the conclusion that the arrival of George C. Purington in Farmington increased the social life of the school. Even the prayer meetings were never so well attended as they were in the early days of his administration. A typical party under the school's new management was reported in *The Franklin Journal* for June 6, 1885:

> Prof. and Mrs. Purington received members of school Friday evening, the occasion being a lawn party and a jolly evening was spent. The party enjoyed themselves with tête à tête, soap bubbles, croquet, etc., till lunch was served, after which they listened to singing and a flute solo by Prof. Purington. Lovers of science reveled in Jupiter and his moons, Saturn and his rings, and valleys of the moon, as seen through the large telescope ad-

justed by Mr. Warner. At an early hour the company went home. If any man on earth knows better than Prof. Purington how to make company happy and contented, it has not been our lot to meet him.

Even the Normal School building was to catch the new spirit. In January 1885, it was announced that the main hall would be warm and lighted until six o'clock. This would afford another hour for study or social enjoyment. It was reported that the students were enthusiastic about the extra hour. To keep the record straight, however, it must be added that the brick building whose "majestic walls" arose so auspiciously in 1864 left something to be desired in the way of providing creature comforts. The severe cold in the first week of February 1885, caused the suspension of school on Monday and Tuesday. This was another reminder that the old Academy building and the crude structure of 1864–65 were in need of attention.

At this same time, developments were taking place in town that added to the opportunities for youthful recreation. A roller skating rink, a gallant reporter stated, was used by many pretty Farmington Normal girls. A new auditorium for shows of all kinds was completed in 1883; it was named Music Hall. In the middle 1880s, thirty-five male students were enrolled at the FSNS, and the baseball season not only started in April but was carried over into the fall. Walks were taken to the Cascades and Powder House Hill; early in some of the milder spring mornings, groups of students walked to Titcomb Hill where they saw the making of maple syrup and candy. Horse-back riding became very popular at this time, and spelling bees were so numerous the local papers described the enthusiasm for them as "spellomania."

A reporter for *The Franklin Journal* outdid himself in the way of rustic humor in describing a memorable ride to New Sharon: "Saturday evening students of the Normal School had a leap ride to New Sharon and out in the direction of Starks. Two of the young ladies invited one of the gentlemen teachers and very nearly talked him to death; another young man froze his face, and a third said his arms ached dreadfully. We have not been able to learn whether his arms were used in holding the horse or the young lady. It was a fine time, nevertheless, and was much enjoyed."

In April 1885, the school lyceum, sometimes referred to as the debating and literary society, was revived. Meetings were held twice a month, and some lively discussions took place over such subjects as: "Resolved, that the use of dynamite by the Irish is justifiable; Resolved, that suffrage should be extended to women; Resolved, that the pen is mightier than the sword; Resolved, that the grading system should be abolished." (W. G. Mallett argued it should be abolished.)

Sometimes the society would push aside their debates to make way for a sociable. Such an occasion was likely to feature a reading, or a flute solo, or a vocal solo by the principal. Sometimes five-minute speeches were delivered. One evening Mallett spoke on botanizing, Miss Adams on chewing gum, and Miss Whitney on baseball. Games and marches followed and Room Two of the old building "echoed with the enlivening strains of Tucker and quaked with the violent exercise of 'chase the squirrel.' At ten good nights were said."

The Relationship of the FSNS to National Trends or Movements

The FSNS, naturally enough, was affected by national trends or movements. One of these was conservation. Another was the prohibition movement, which successfully enlisted the support of normal schools throughout the land. Another was the Chautauqua movement with its adult education. A fourth was the missionary enthusiasm that was to affect several Farmington Normal School students.

Arbor Day, with its emphasis on conservation, was first observed at Farmington Normal in May 1886. This observance started in the Western States and was deemed worthy of being introduced into Maine in order to awaken in the minds of the people the desirability of replenishing our natural resources, especially the disappearing forests. On the first Arbor Day, Philip E. Stanley* of the 1886 class gave the main oration. The program also included a vocal solo by the principal, with more music being rendered by a quartette consisting of Annie M. Fellows, Grace L. Douglass, George H. Winter, and Bert G. Mallett.

---

* Philip Stanley, a few years after this oration, received an A.B. and A.M. from Dartmouth. Eventually he became a writer for *The Boston Herald*. Tuberculosis caused his death in 1901. His widow married Sumner Moulton, who was for many years assistant headmaster of the Abbott School. His son, Philip Jr., was a graduate of the Model School and for many years the head of the philosophy department at Union College, Schenectady, New York.

During the late 1880s George C. Purington compiled a variety of statistics concerning the educational progress and activities of the Normal School and its graduates. The results were based upon a questionnaire the principal sent out to check on the postgraduate interests of those who had attended Farmington Normal during the first twenty-five years of its existence. In answering these questionnaires, over eighty graduates in the 1880 decade stated that they either were, or had been, involved with the C.L.S.C. These letters stood for the Chautauqua Literary and Scientific Circle, possibly the most successful of all experiments in the field of adult education.

In 1878 John H. Vincent, a Methodist minister, instituted as part of the Chautauqua movement a four-year home reading course. From a course describing the chief civilizations of the world, the program was enlarged to include readings in history, literature, and the sciences. A typical reading list for one year, such as a normal school graduate would read, consisted of Green's *Short History of the English People*, Brook's *Primer of English Literature*, two books on the Bible, one on astronomy, and one on physiology.

In addition to the Chautauqua course, many Normal School graduates subscribed to the *Chautauquan*. This was a monthly magazine established for the C.L.S.C. in 1880, the year in which Rounds was helping local scholarship by introducing the third-year course at Farmington Normal. The *Chautauquan* had a very large circulation.

On March 30, 1883, the New York legislature recognized Chautauqua University and granted it the right to confer degrees. This gave greater prestige to the most important of all native-grown correspondence courses of the last century. By 1888, thirty-one Farmington Normal graduates had received their Chautauqua diplomas for four years' work that extended their education well beyond the Normal School level.

Normal schools, as well as nearly all other educational institutions, championed the prohibition movement.* Physiology was a

---

* An exception to this was contained in some of the talks delivered by Franklin C. Robinson, chemistry professor at Bowdoin. He was in the habit of telling the women in the audience that it was better for them to drink gin than load up on Lydia Pinkham's compound. He told the men that if they wanted to partake of alcohol, straight whiskey was better for them than the popular patent medicines.

Photo courtesy Natalie Butler

TENNIS ANYONE? A glimpse backward. The Tarbox House on the right was purchased in 1972 by FSNS to become the present Alumni House, center for Public Information and Alumni Relations.

course which appeared in all normal school courses of study. Some of the texts seemed to be built around an attempt to prove the deleterious effects of tobacco and alcohol, and Charles F. Warner made his contribution to such education. A month after the first Arbor Day exercises were held in Farmington, *The Franklin Journal* announced that the Normal School science teacher had published a pamphlet which contained an account of experiments relating to the use of alcohol and its effects. The local paper assured its readers that Warner's experiments and observations were the best arguments for total abstinence. This meant that the principal and his first assistant were in agreement about the consumption of alcoholic beverages, for George C. Purington was about to become the founder and president of the Maine Civic League.

In the nineteenth century the missionary movement was important beyond the ability of the present younger generation to imagine. Time and money were spent in comparative abundance on missionary projects, and some of the best-known heroes and heroines of the period were missionaries. Of this group Farmington Normal, in its first three decades, had six. The best-known of these was Mary S. Morrill, of the class of 1884, who became a missionary to North China under an appointment by the American Board of Foreign Missions. During the Boxer Rebellion of 1900 she was killed at Pao-Ting-fu, North China. The Normal School had a memorial service for her shortly after her death. In 1908 her portrait was presented to the School and it was hung at that time in what was then Merrill Hall, where it remained for many years.

Graduates in the Early Years of the Purington Regime

The Farmington State Normal School continued to graduate in the 1880s, as it had in the 1860s and 1870s, many who would distinguish themselves in teaching, while others would be no less distinguished in professions outside the classroom. Alumni statistics were collected in 1895 showing occupational data: superintendents of schools, 18; reform school superintendent, 1; normal school teachers, 20; college professors, 6; college students, 13; lawyers, 17; missinaries, 6; medical doctors, 15; medical students, 4; civil engineers, 6; contractors, 3; manufacturers, 7; bank cashiers, 3; farmers, 18; merchants, 3; real estate agents, 2; clergymen, 11; salesmen, 2; druggists, 3; photographers, 1. Among the college professors was Henry Arthur

STUDENT LIFE about 1900.

Sanders, class of 1885, who earned an M.A. from the University of Michigan and a Ph.D. from the University of Munich. For most of his adult life he was professor of Latin and Greek at the University of Michigan. His international reputation for scholarship was evident when he was asked to translate several Greek manuscripts which were uncovered in nineteenth century Egypt.

Among those to receive a degree from medical school was Annie M. Stevens, of the 1885 class. She was one of the first of her sex to receive an M.D. from the University of Michigan.

Among those graduates who went into law was Frank W. Butler, who became one of Farmington's leading citizens. For many years he was the head of the successful Forster Manufacturing Company.

In education the principal of FSNS was able to talk many of his better students into returning to Farmington as members of the faculty. Included in this list were Ella and Hortense Merrill, Lillian I. Lincoln, Ella J. Longfellow and W. G. Mallett.

The Class of 1890

Almost any list designed to include the ablest and most successful graduates of the institution would fail to do justice to many because of a lack of space in a history of this kind. It would be an avoidable injustice, however, to disregard the class of 1890, and its perennially ardent school spirit, a quality that at least in former years was highly rated. The class of 1890 not only produced capable teachers and community leaders, but its loyalty to Farmington Normal has probably never been equaled.

Among its leaders were its president, Carleton P. Merrill, son of I. Warren Merrill, and for many years chairman of the Maine Normal School trustees; Herbert S. Wing, one of Kingfield's all-time greats; Henry H. Randall, a Farmington native, Bowdoin graduate, and successor to Payson Smith as superintendent of schools in Auburn; Amos Butler, lawyer in Skowhegan for many years, and brother of Frank W. Butler; Alice E. Smith, who married Frank Butler, and Edith Clifford. The last named taught most of her years in West Springfield, Massachusetts, and left on her death in 1944 in excess of $50,000 to what was about to become Farmington State Teachers College. The money was to be used primarily for books.

In a ceremony that year in Merrill Hall, Carleton P. Merrill, as chairman of the Normal School trustees, made known the terms of the will to the college. Filled with pride that a member of the 1890 class had made this gift, he became rather expansive and did a little boasting. He stated that his class was the first to unfurl the Stars and Stripes over the Normal building, the first to present a civilized graduation program by excluding twenty or more essays, the only class to plant an oak tree, and by far the leading class in percentage attendance at the five-year reunions. He was too modest to say it, but this record was, at least partly, the reflection of his own personality, loyalty, and leadership. (In addition to his sober virtues, Carl Merrill was an irrepressible prankster.)

The flag ceremony and graduation exercises of the class of 1890 were so typical of similar exercises and subsequent graduations that this seems an appropriate time to describe them in some detail. Moreover, these two 1890 Normal School events featured three members of the Merrill family for whom the administration building was recently named.

On February 27, 1890, the Farmington State Normal School became the first of the three normal schools in the State to display from a tower the national flag. Purchased as it was by the class of 1886, this gift owed its place in the school's history to the co-operative efforts of two classes, trustee I. Warren Merrill, and the Normal School principal.

Here is the flag-raising program in all of its formidable detail:

2:30 P.M. PROGRAM FOR FLAG RAISING
Singing Keller's "American Hymn" – School
Declamation, "The American Flag"
Reading, "Barbara Frietche"
Singing, "Flag of the Free"—School
Class Exercise – Facts about the Flag
Singing, "Star Spangled Banner" – School
Reading, "Old Battle Flags"
Singing, "Freedom's Flag"—School
Reading, Origin of the Flag
Reading, Hymn of Moravian Nuns
Singing, "Columbia Gem of the Ocean" – School

Declamation, American Flag
Singing, "Our Flag is There"
Presentation and Acceptance of Flag
Singing, "America"
Raising of Flag*

After the declamations, readings, and singings, Trustee I. Warren Merrill presented the flag to George C. Purington, who accepted for the school. Following this, "America" was sung by the school and audience, with Principal Purington conducting and Ella Merrill at the piano. The focus of attention then shifted to the tower, where the challenging and arduous part of the program took place. There, through a joint effort, George C. Purington and Carl Merrill hoisted the flag upon the tower despite a heavy gale and bitter cold, an event that was greeted with three hearty cheers.

Whenever exercises involved only the members of the school, they could be held, as was the flag ceremony, in the main hall of the old building. Graduation, with its influx of parents and friends, demanded more room, and in those days, it usually meant reserving the Music Hall. The reporter for *The Chronicle* was on hand to see the class of 1890 receive their diplomas:

Long before the exercises commenced Music Hall was packed to overflowing, chairs being placed in the aisles. Among the audience was Prof. McKeen of Phillips High School, with about 60 of his pupils including the graduating class. They came down on a special train returning home at the close of the exercises.

We have never seen before such a mass of flowers together as was on and about the stage that evening. It was a beautiful sight. The class looked very pretty as they marched up the main aisle behind their President, Carl P. Merrill. Nearly all the ladies were in white, the gentlemen in black. The faculty, State Superintendent Luce, and Trustees occupied seats on the platform.

In the class there are 35 Republicans, 2 Democrats, 1 Pro-

---

* The pledge to the flag was not given because it had not been written in 1890; it first appeared in *The Youth's Companion* in 1892. It was not until 1931 that "The Star Spangled Banner" became the national anthem. In the nineteenth century, Kellers "American Hymn" and "America" outranked it.

hibitionist, and 3 who are on the fence. 12 prefer the Congregational church, 9 the Baptist, 4 Universalist, 3 Episcopal, 2 Roman Catholic, Methodist and Unitarian 1 each, while 7 have no preference. The tallest is 6 ft. 1 (a lady), the heaviest is Mr. Butler at 183 pounds.[33]

Carl Merrill was certainly justified in boasting about the decision of his class to reduce drastically the number of graduation parts. The retention of so many spoken essays for so long probably attested to parental desires to see their offspring perform. Inertia and love of tradition may also have had their part in keeping the programs excruciatingly long. The change of format in 1890 gave the principal an opportunity to spend a longer time giving advice to the departing students. George Purington was never one to avoid taking advantage of such an opening.

Although the principal went on record as believing his era the best the world had ever seen, he nevertheless thought there had never been an age as good as it should have been. His age he described as one of intense unrest and abnormal activity. He thought of discontent as world-wide, much of it reasonable, more of it unreasonable. He warned that almost everyone was living too fast, rushing through life as if it were a chariot race—even express trains were thought to be too slow, ocean greyhounds raced at the risk of many lives to reduce the time a paltry hour in crossing the Atlantic; business was transacted by telephone and telegraph. All, he lamented, had joined in the John Gilpin race and cry, "Hurry, hurry, rest not," no matter if heads or hearts fail. All of this meant a regrettable amount of business for doctors and undertakers. The principal lamented that insufficient time was spent for a thorough education; sham, superficiality, and pretense were the order of the day. The country minister was unable to concentrate on his rural parish, for he was desirous of a city church, and the district school teacher neglected his duties while he sighed for a teaching position in the city. The haste for wealth and honors fostered trusts, gambling, and embezzlement, selfishness, and the breaking of ties of friendship. His peroration included this advice: "Strive not for fame. It is as fleeting as a summer cloud, selfish, seeketh only its own, its temples are built on men's graves.

"Strive not for honors but for honor."

The Building Program (1887–1898)

After the 1883 crisis had passed, and there was no longer any doubt that the institution was a going concern, the increase in attendance helped to remind even the indifferent about the pathetically limited facilities of Farmington Normal. It was ridiculous, but a fact to be faced, that the old moth-eaten and ramshackle Academy building was still serving Maine education as the ell to a brick structure which was already showing alarming and increasing weaknesses.

In 1885 the entire building had been supplied with electric bells, but they represented no adequate solution to the problem of space and efficiency.

In the fall of 1886, an event occurred that almost eliminated the need to dwell on the problem of what to do with the old building. A fire swept down Main Street and burned nearly everything on both sides of the thoroughfare, including the Baptist, Congregational, and Methodist churches. *The Phillips Phonograph* reported that I. Warren Merrill and four students saved the Normal School building. The principal was, apparently, involved in saving his own house, for the newspaper noted that he incurred a $500 loss. The Normal School girls formed a bucket brigade in a vain attempt to save the Baptist church.* They were highly commended for this, and for their later work in rescuing valuables from threatened or doomed houses.

By the spring of 1886, the number of students had increased to absolute classroom capacity. The principal swung into action and told the legislature in urgent terms of his immediate needs. He did not have to wait long for approval. One result of this favorable response was that the old Farmington Academy building, which had listened to so many conjunctions of Latin verbs, was removed to Middle Street. In its place arose a brick ell, larger than the 1864 front part. In his 1888 report to the Normal School trustees, Principal Purington was able to state that the school had at last "most ample accommodations for recitation rooms."

---

* *Phillips Phonograph*, Oct. 29, 1886: "Forked tongues of flames embraced the Baptist Church, and the sacred edifice crackling and hissing fiercely soon went down in ruins. While this church was burning, about 50 young ladies from the Normal School made an effort to save it. They collected pails and buckets and formed themselves into a fire brigade. All to no avail."

A. T. Stewart carpenters with George C. Purington in the background (far right), 1896. The top floor of the new Merrill Hall is being constructed. The Franklin County courthouse tower can be seen in the distance.

Although the principal expressed satisfaction about the space now available for recitations, he had no intention of giving the impression that other physical needs did not continue. As we have seen, graduations had to be held in Music Hall and many school events of importance had taken place in the old Methodist church before it burned in 1886. For many months, and even years, Purington would dream and plan for the completion of a school building containing, among other things, an adequate assembly hall. His science teacher was aware of this all-consuming interest when he wrote in February 1893: "Mr. Purington has no interest in anything except that new building. He excuses his classes, and locks himself in his office or goes home and draws plans for what he wants. His psychology and civil government classes have recited only twice since the half-term tests. He hasn't yet given his E music test for the first half."

The FSNS principal had heavy responsibilities, both voluntary and mandatory, besides the full teaching load he was forced to carry. These duties included the care and supervision of the physical plant, discipline problems, public relations work without secretarial help, promotion of the normal school idea by means of state-wide speeches, promotion of the school's social life, supervision of its catalogue and circular. He was also adviser to the lovelorn or homesick, and leader of daily chapel exercises. It was little wonder that he occasionally felt the need to get away from it all. Apparently he accomplished this occasionally by giving precedence to non-academic responsibilities. In 1893, for example, he decided that the installation of a ventilating system deserved his supervision. His science teacher noted this priority decision: "They proceed very slowly with the new ventilating apparatus and Mr. P. finds more geniality in the work in the basement than in recitation work, so consequently excuses his classes and stays down there a good part of the time."

George Purington's perseverance was to pay off, for on March 21, 1895, the Maine legislature appropriated $20,000 for alterations of the old brick building, vintage 1865. At first it was thought possible that the building could be repaired and enlarged. A careful examination by architects, however, revealed that the walls were too thin to permit a third story being built upon them. In addition to this, the roof was in bad condition, and the floors and other parts of the building invited serious accidents.

MERRILL HALL, winter of 1897

One result of this building inspection was the decision to tear down the 1864–65 structure and join a new one to the 1888 addition. The architects for the project were Coombs, Gibbs, and Wilkerson of Lewiston; the builder, Theodore L. Stewart; the masons, S. W. Foster and Co.; and plumber, Wilfred McLeary. Although G. M. Coombs was supposedly the chief architect, he was constantly a-ware that his ideas would not necessarily prevail. The principal had been planning too long and had too many dreams wrapped up in the projected building to allow any architect, or combination of architects, to have the last word.* Even the strong-willed Purington, however, could not overcome the obstacle known as "limited funds available." He hoped to have two towers of the same shape on the front corners of the building, but after the smaller tower was constructed, dwindling funds did not permit a larger tower of the same shape. Consequently the present bell tower was built in order to stay within the confines of the legislative appropriation.

The Hon. J. W. Fairbanks, of Farmington, was a trustee of Maine normal schools during this building period (1895–98) and served as chairman of the three-man building committee. (The other two were Henry L. Chapman, of Bowdoin College, and G. A. Robertson, of Augusta.) There was not the same congenial relationship between Fairbanks and Purington as had existed between Merrill and Purington. The FSNS principal thought that Fairbanks was parsimonious and that he did not always have a proper appreciation of school needs. The 1898 report of the State Superintendent included a report of the building chairman, which plainly indicated the pride he felt in the project:

> The new normal school building at Farmington, which the State has so generously furnished for the training of teachers, is a structure ninety feet by seventy feet in size. The foundation walls are of stone laid in cement. The walls of the building are of first quality brick, and are twenty inches thick. The roof is

---

* George C. Purington was not content with his role as adviser to the architects; he participated more directly in the building of Merrill Hall. The teachers' room was of particular interest to him; as a consequence, he painted the ceiling of this room while lying on a staging flat on his back á la Michael Angelo. He was also involved in the carpentry work done by Alexander Stewart and his crew, as revealed by existing photographs. Whether or not he actually swung a hammer or used a saw is not known.

supported by heavy southern pine trusses, and covered with first quality of Monson slate. The basement is well lighted, being twelve feet high in the walls. A portion of this floor is devoted to a large gymnasium, with a hardwood floor, also toilet rooms, with all modern convenient arrangements. One section of this floor is devoted to the storage of coal. The first floor is divided into recitation rooms of convenient size, also a large cloak room, which connects by a flight of stairs with the gymnasium below.

The assembly room in the second story is nearly square, about sixty-eight feet by sixty-eight feet. The seating capacity of this room on public occasions being a thousand people. On one side of the room, above, and in the rear of the teachers' platform is a handsome ornamental balcony for the use of an orchestra, finely finished in quartered oak; on the opposite side are two fireplaces with mantels of quartered oak. Off the main hall is a cozy room, facing the west, fitted with desks, chairs, etc., for the teachers, and is also used as a reception room. This room has a fireplace and the tower on the south also opens into this room, the wood work is of quartered oak and the ceiling of metal handsomely painted.

The halls, corridors and stairways are finished in quartered oak, with metal ceilings, which are used throughout the building, and it is warmed by steam heat and lighted by electricity. Two new boilers were added to the building. The building is well lighted, every room having a cheerful interior. The fitting, furnishings, and apparatus, with few exceptions are the same as in years past, the appropriations not being sufficient to afford new and much needed ones, the trustees not being authorized to expend any monies, except for the erection of the new building. A sewer has been laid from this building to the Sandy River, a distance of 1,383 feet. The appropriations for this building were $40,000 covering four years time in the expenditure. The total cost of the new building is ($39,745.80), thirty-nine thousand seven hundred and forty-five dollars and eighty cents.[34]

The townspeople derived great satisfaction from the new building, and because of a generous and wise policy were allowed to use the new structure. One of the features of August in Farmington at the turn of the century was Old Home Week. From August 6 to 13 in 1900 the town invited everyone who had ever lived in Farmington to come and be received in local homes "with good cheer and hospitality." Wednesday, August 8, was set aside as Public Reception

Day and the new Normal School building was very much involved. The program notes had this to say:

> There will be a public meeting and informal reception at the Normal School Building, in charge of the citizens. Music by Priscilla Alden's Orchestra and the Festival Chorus.
>
> The building will be open for the inspection of the public from 10 o'clock A.M. til the opening of the meeting at 2 o'clock P.M. Attendants will be present to show visitors about the building.
>
> The Normal Building is new, and there are many of our own people who do not know the extent of the facilities furnished by the State for the education of teachers. The building, 165 feet long by 70 in width, is one of the finest in New England. It has been provided with a system of ventilation and heating that is perfect, furnished by two 40-horse power boilers, and one 15-horse power boiler, a Sturtevant heater, and a blower driven by a 10-horse power engine. Each pupil in the building has a minimum of 2,500 cubic feet of fresh air per hour. This system of ventilation is absolutely perfect.

The Farmington Chronicle followed the building of this new schoolhouse with great interest and provided detailed information about it to its readers. One week its subscribers would learn that the Wilfred E. McLeary bill for plumbing was $1,148; another issue of the paper would inform its readers that the birch for the lower floors came from Allens Mills. Later on the town was to learn that the portico cost about $3,500.

Other Activities of the Principal

It would be a distorted picture to visualize the principal during the 1890s as exclusively concerned with improving the school facilities. The Farmington Normal School, or any other normal school of the nineteenth century, took its substitute role as parent very seriously. The father of this school brood was the principal. He was the one who tried all the discipline cases, and he no more would have transferred this responsibility to others than he would have with regard to his own family affairs. But it was not just the rule-breaker who received the personal attention of the principal. On Thanksgiving there were usually ten or a dozen students who could not get home. At least several times such away-from-home students ate their Thanksgiving dinner at the Puringtons'. The principal knew where most of his students lived, not only while they were in Farmington but after they returned home. George C. Purington not only arranged for most of the school sociables, he was usually one of the main entertainers. In the '80s he played at such times a great many flute solos, but as the years went on he was more likely to sing vocal solos.

On July 1, 1896, the principal sent one of his periodic bulletins to the graduates. In it he was careful to stress that the main purpose of his institution was to turn out well-trained teachers. He wanted a greater number of students now that he had the physical facilities, but he insisted that their quality remain high. This was how he expressed himself on the subject:

> The number for whom I have signed diplomas is now just an even five hundred, and it is to their splendid loyalty that I ascribe much of the success of the school. Having secured a building that will be adequate to our needs for many years, all our energies will now be concentrated upon increasing the number of students, enlarging and enriching the course of study and raising still higher the standard of professional work. May I not count on your assistance, more earnest even than in the past, to secure these ends? More students will always be a need, and there is a constantly increasing demand for well-trained teachers. Will you not present to desirable young men and women the importance of professional training, and urge their attendance upon a normal school? In advising students to come here, keep quality always in mind, and though the whole State is our field, do not urge pupils to come here who are not fitted to do our work or who properly belong in other schools. While we would like to see three hundred students here, we do not want them at the cost of a lowered standard or of courtesy to other schools.
>
> Hoping that you may visit us soon in our new home, and wishing you all the blessings of life, I remain, as ever,
>
> Sincerely yours,
> Geo. C. Purington

Two Teachers of the Purington Régime

One of the wisest teaching selections of George Purington was Lillian I. Lincoln. She entered Farmington Normal in 1884, the year that W. G. Mallett entered from the Brunswick-Topsham area. Miss Lincoln was a graduate of Brunswick High School and had further prepared for college by taking a postgraduate course there. Instead of attending college she found it financially advisable to go into teaching. She taught for 54 weeks in grammar school and the Mechanic Falls High School before she entered Farmington Normal. Her ability and experience enabled her to complete the course in one year. Soon after graduation, she was a member of the faculty, which she continued to be until her resignation in 1924.

She became an instructor in geography, geometry, drawing, and Latin. In 1890 she received the advanced-course diploma. Her greatest success was attained in the years between 1896 and 1924 when she was the head of the training school, or Model School as it was then called. The tradition had been for the head of the Model School to stay only a year or two, at least in that position. Fortunately Miss Lincoln was encouraged to break with this tradition. She was to direct the Model School for twenty-eight years.

Miss Lincoln was a person of ideas and alert to the major educational developments of her time. She never allowed herself, however, to become a faddist or a prisoner of any educational theory. She was always determined to find out for herself whether or not the pupils under her charge really liked what some of the non-teaching educators said they were bound to like. When she took over the Model School she accepted the traditional books for a history course, such as had been adopted at Oswego and other top normal schools, but it did not take her long to find out how thoroughly the Model School students disliked what was supposed to give such great satisfaction. She quickly changed to an entirely new set of texts, with gratifying results.[35]

In 1901 the administration started a magazine, *The Farmington Normal*, that seemed to be a revival of George M. Gage's *Maine Normal*. (It lasted through 1904 and was revived again from 1914 to 1921.) Miss Lincoln contributed more articles to this magazine than anyone else, and her ideas on the teaching of history and geography, as well as other subjects, were first printed in this publication. She disclaimed any great amount of originality, but since her time, countless educators have repeated her ideas on the best methods of teaching the social sciences, without realizing, possibly, that such ideas had been presented as far back as 1901.

Miss Lincoln started an article on the subject of history with the truism that success in teaching it depended upon the teacher,

CLASS OF 1897. Back row (left to right): Charles Turner, Carolyn Stone, Nellie Reed. Middle row (l to r): Annie Case, Grace Lilly, Amelia Bisbee. Front row (l to r): Albert Fowler, Leila Barbour, Mr. Mallett, Cassie Brehaut, Moses Corliss.

and no methods or gimmicks could offset a poor instructor. First, and most importantly, the history teacher should have a broad knowledge of the subject and know what to leave out as well as what to include. Although a lesson might be well prepared, its effectiveness might be marginal if the teacher did not have an obvious reserve of information. Many teachers, according to Miss Lincoln, were in deadly fear of being unable to answer the children's questions, consequently they discouraged the asking of them, which was, possibly, the worst thing they could do. Among the evils resulting from such a practice was the encouragement it gave students to accept unquestioningly what they had read.

Teachers should not only have a broad knowledge of history but an enthusiasm for the subject. Without this, Miss Lincoln thought, instructors were generally ineffective, no matter what their other attributes were. She believed that if the teacher had enough enthusiasm for history for the feeling to be contagious, even mediocre students would become interested in history classics. She was fond of using one of her average students as an example: after finally deciding that he liked history, he waded with joy through John Marshall's four-volume *Life of George Washington*.

According to Miss Lincoln, a history teacher with broad knowledge and enthusiasm was well equipped for success, but could not realize fully on these major advantages unless he used certain teaching aids and methods. Children in the Model School were encouraged to bring to class any history book that particularly interested them. Many did this, sometimes because they were really interested in the book and other times to get favorable attention. Miss Lincoln made use of poetry and pictures of historical interest and solicited constantly for as many of them as she could get from the students. In her later years she was to be one of the most enthusiastic supporters of historical movies as aids in generating interest in the subject.

She stressed the value of historical plays whether they were written by professionals or by the teachers or by the students themselves. But she warned the practice teacher not to be carried away by the device. She knew that history in the form of drama was frequently very effective, but she recognized that parents and school authorities were often justified in becoming exasperated by a teacher's over-emphasis on imagination that left no time for an examination of factual material.

She not only encouraged the writing of historical sketches, but wrote some herself, particularly for the annual entertainment, which was the great event of the year at the Model School. The preparation for this extravaganza was memorable. Sometimes costumes had to be made instead of merely being taken out of mothballs. Still others had to be altered just before the eagerly awaited big night. Various plays demanded costumes for elves and fairies, materials for flowers and animals, garments for pilgrims and people of other lands, Greek and Roman draperies, flowing robes for the women, knee breeches for the men, Indian and court costumes, and peasant dresses for folk dances. The sketches were often rehearsed behind locked doors and the secrecy involved in all of this resembled the secret drills before the Harvard-Yale game, or even the military preparations before D-Day.

Miss Lincoln wanted geography and history, whenever feasible, taught as inter-related disciplines. During her early days as a geography teacher, she became critical of the prevailing view of most normal schools that younger children should be confined in their geography to drawing maps of the schoolroom and yard, district and town. This practice was based upon the belief of Rousseau and Pestalozzi that children were more interested in their immediate surroundings than they were in far-away places. Miss Lincoln was unwilling to accept this as always true—even though it meant disputing the findings of two gods in the educational pantheon. She thought there were plenty of little tots who were more interested in exotic and foreign lands than they were in their own backyard and town. Consequently they should be offered an opportunity to learn more about such places despite their tender years.

Above all, Miss Lincoln knew that what the students learned in school about history or geography or any social science subject, was insignificant compared with what they would learn outside the classroom if only they became interested in such subjects. She wanted plenty of time reserved for the youngster who was ready and eager to do outside reading. She provided this by limiting the homework; in fact, there were few who had to study in the evening during their years in the Model School.

Ginn & Company published two books by Miss Lincoln. One was *Everyday Pedagogy,* and the other, *Practical Projects for Elementary Schools.*[36] She had her eye on the rural teacher when she wrote

Everyday Pedagogy. She knew, of course, how limited the horizons were for many such teachers. Many people, including State Superintendent Payson Smith, encouraged her to set forth her findings and conclusions. He wrote the introduction to the book and included in his remarks were these:

> Admitting, then, the very important place of the schoolroom teacher in making the school system effective, and emphasizing the necessity of a sound basis in educational theory for classroom procedure, we find there must be a large place for those who—whether by book, lecture, or sermon—will aid teachers to interpret their theories into sane educational practices. Progress in the making of better schools will be less halting and hesitating, will be less disturbed by unnecessary repetitions of experiments and by much traveling of bypaths with profitless ends, as teachers find ways of coming in contact with the experiences of other teachers and especially those whose business it has been to test daily in the crucible of experience the freshly wrought theory.

Payson Smith was thoroughly aware and fearful of the intellectual isolation of the average rural teacher.

Practical Projects was written in 1924 during the height of the popularity of projects. In answering the inevitable criticism of projects as a fad, Miss Lincoln replied that the project and problem approach to learning would undoubtedly be replaced sometime by something else, but this did not cancel the worth of the project method, a contribution of Kilpatrick, one of the major prophets of the progressive movement. She supported it because of its influence in making teaching less formal. She also thought it a good way to appeal to a child's interests and his desire to do rather than merely hear. There were other methods that were to be avoided because, unlike the projects method, the teacher was likely to limit himself, or herself, to cultivating the students' memory and verbal expression. Almost any method that was provocative and challenging was good; any method that encouraged mental docility was bad. Miss Lincoln's contributions to the classes she visited often cast doubt on conclusions which the class had uncritically accepted. She never ceased in her efforts to make the classroom a place where thinking was consistently expected from all the occupants.

Along with her scholarship, Miss Lincoln was a person of consistent kindness. She was never more provoked than during the occasional displays of student cruelty. She, herself, had a curvature of the spine and undoubtedly had mental scars that dated back to her own childhood. After she accepted two young Russian refugees into the Model School she worried lest the local children taunt the strangers in their midst because of their accent and appearance. So she alerted the Model School teachers to the possibility of trouble. Her precautions may have paid off because, despite the unfamiliar accent and clothes, the refugees received a friendly welcome free of ridicule. Racial or religious insults or slights were never sanctioned at the Model School. Undoubtedly a few practice teachers had some ugly prejudices, but they were not allowed to surface.

In many respects, Miss Lincoln's early career anticipated the progressive period in our educational history. Although teachers were expected to make reports about their students to the head of the Model School, there was no regular report card sent to the homes of the students. The chief difference between the progressive schools and Model School of the early 1920s had to do with their attitudes toward discipline. The Model School was not permissive. The students were not expected to be noisy, unruly, or wandering around the room, even though such activities might have been a reflection of psychic disturbances and not malicious intent.

Lillian I. Lincoln was a strong character and, as such, had her inevitable critics. Occasionally some of her students felt oversupervised, especially when she made strong moral issues of activities that seemed innocuous to her charges. Playing marbles "for keeps" was an example of this. Certainly she was a conscientious supervisor who would have thought she was shirking her responsibilities if she had not become deeply involved in both the moral and mental development of the students. Her total commitment to the many facets of her duties resulted in her acquiring an ability to judge the progress of each child, and critically evaluate the contents of the courses as well as the qualities of the young teacher. In addition to these assets she had a creative ability that was revealed in her writings. When she retired in 1924, the FSNS principal included this evaluation of her services in his annual report to the trustees: "She came to possess a grasp of the elementary school problems seldom equalled by anyone anywhere, man or woman. Her keen discernment as a critic teacher judged with rare completeness the child's progress, the value of the subject matter, and the qualities of the young teacher."

Wilbert G. Mallett

No less wise than George Purington's selection of Lillian Lincoln was the encouragement he gave a distant cousin, Wilbert G. Mallett, to enroll at the Normal School, despite the fact that the young man had not graduated from Topsham High School. Halfway through his high school career Bert, as the young man was called, heard from his sister, Lillian, that Principal Purington had assured her that there were job opportunities in Farmington which would make it possible for him to earn his way through Farmington Normal. In 1884 he arrived in Farmington and two years later graduated from the Normal School, along with his sister and Ella J. Longfellow. (The latter was an FSNS teacher from 1890 to 1892 and then married W. G. Mallett in 1893.) W. G. went to Brunswick High School to finish his preparation for Bowdoin College, which he entered in 1887 and from which he graduated in 1891. This was made possible by borrowing money, receiving a scholarship, and teaching during the winter terms. Like his cousin, George C. Purington, he was a part-time principal of the Topsham High School while a Bowdoin undergraduate. (His college classes were in the first half of the morning so he could devote the rest of the day to his high school duties.)

After W. G. Mallett received his A.B. degree he accepted a position as a substitue teacher at the Normal School. He was not to leave the institution for forty-nine years. During the first eighteen years of his Farmington career, he taught natural science, trigonometry, surveying, moral philosophy, physics, chemistry, zoology, geology, and astronomy. During the years he was principal, he taught school management, school laws, civil government, United States history, psychology, civics, pedagogy, and anthropology. He often contrasted what he called his "dabblings" in subjects to the teacher of Greek grammar who, on his deathbed, regretted that he had spread himself so thin: He thought he should have concentrated on the dative case.

Most normal school courses in later years were here one term and gone the next. No person, or combination of people, could be thoroughly grounded in many of them, certainly not the principal with his busy life. But some of the books and subjects W. G. Mallett knew the best were either unrelated or only indirectly related to the courses he taught. For many years he had an adult Sunday School class and devoted a lifetime of study to the Bible. He was steeped in classical mythology and knew, as only a tutor to his children could know, Caesar's *Commentaries,* Cicero's *Orations,* Virgil's *Aeneid,* and Ovid's *Metamorphosis.* He had a lifelong interest in the Civil War and remembered the details of the more important battles to an astonishing degree. (This enabled him to correct the inaccuracy of a guide at Gettysburg, and he did it tactfully enough for his family to leave the field without injury.)

Certainly there have been those with a wider range of knowledge than had W. G., but I doubt that anyone was able to get more pleasure in using his information. After reading such books as *The Education of Henry Adams* and Sandburg's *The Prairie Years,* he would seek out those who had also read them to discuss them at some length. He had a zest for life that always reached its zenith whenever he was traveling and acquiring new information, or was seizing an opportunity to enjoy the knowledge he had available. An example of the latter was indicated in the first paragraph he wrote to his elder son during a visit to Geneva:

> Here I am in the land of William Tell and John Calvin, John Knox and—who was it who broke the Austrian line of spears by receiving so many in his own body that his compatriots rushed the line at that point? Winkelreid, wasn't it? Here have lived John Milton, Lord Byron, Voltaire, Rousseau. It is a historic old town, you may believe. Do you remember that Caesar found it to be the extreme town of the Allobroges and to keep the Helvetians on the north side of the river burned the bridge across the Rhone? A stone slab by one of the five present bridges identifies the spot of the ancient bridge.

The combination of Purington and Mallett was mutually advantageous. After his year as a substitute teacher, W. G. was promoted to first assistant to the principal. The new teacher thoroughly enjoyed his work, and his chief was delighted that his assistant was so willing and able to share the burdens. Being an assistant to George C. Purington was no sinecure because of the principal's involvement in so many community and state-wide activities. One night he might be organizing a festival chorus in Kingfield; the next week he would conduct the Normal School glee club in Hebron one night and in Norway the following evening.[37]

As had been noted, the principal's science teacher was half a-mused and half amazed that his boss found such geniality in watching the installation of a ventilating system that he had excused his classes in order to witness the event. Listening to recitations, at certain times anyway, was not the best-liked part of Purington's duties. (Despite this he taught in his last years as principal, psychology, didactics, civil government, agriculture, and music.) Traveling he enjoyed. When he was Grand Commander of the Maine Templars he had to do state-wide traveling. He was a very active president of the Maine Civic League, and this involved speaking engagements throughout the State. Like other articulate heads of educational institutions, he gave many speeches on various topics. On his return from his European trip in 1900, he gave talks throughout the State on the Passion Play. His favorite talk on public education was a discourse he delivered on his favorite character, Horace Mann.

Horace Mann and George Purington had things in common. Mann, for example, had the missionary spirit in championing public education and so did Purington. Both of them appreciated the importance of being public relations experts for the successful spreading of the educational gospel. Purington approved of Mann's emphasis on the study of social forces and social organizations. Purington's interest in useful courses was demonstrated when he pushed for the introduction of manual training. Above all he was a Mann enthusiast because he saw in his hero character traits which he thought essential for any teacher: "The ready sympathy, the thoughtful word of encouragement, the helping hand, the sacrificing spirit—all were his," he said.

The many absences of the principal did not interfere with the harmonious relationship he enjoyed with his first assistant. Purington was a man of generous spirit and he was usually quick to give due credit to his assistant. An example of this was contained in a bulletin he sent to the class of 1886 when they were nearing the time for their twentieth reunion. Purington informed the members of the class that one of their number was still his first assistant and he expressed doubt that he could ever get along without him. Neither did he think the community could.

Both Purington and Mallett were what might be called neo-Puritans in the sense of their being moral athletes. They agreed that idleness was a sin and sleeping late was a first cousin to it, because it meant the avoidance of duties that never slumbered even though one had to sleep. Alcoholic beverages were a costly drug that addled the mind, ruined the body, and accounted for the Democratic party. Tobacco was a poison that injured the health, burned up money, and in a foul and stinking way demoralized the youth in his vulnerable years. All such habits were not only physically debilitating, but could be condemned solely on the grounds of their wastefulness and expense. The money, if put to another use, could benefit mankind instead of threatening it with undermined health and profligate habits.

The Purington-Mallett ideology embraced not only a devotion to education. but a zeal for public service. W. G. was grateful all his life for what he regarded as his good luck in obtaining a college education. After graduation, his first responsibility, he believed, was to pay back as quickly as possible his scholarship loan. This would serve a dual purpose: first, it would help with the education of some other poor boy; secondly, on the payment of the debt, the borrower could cease to regard himself as a parasite. The most important duty was for the new graduate to pay back his debt to society by dedicating himself to serve his profession and community.

President Sills of Bowdoin was one of W. G.'s all-time favorites, and part of the reason for this was because the Bowdoin head participated so often in local and state affairs.* W. G. gloried in the fact that he lived in a democratic country, but he always insisted that such a society was doomed if educated citizens failed to participate in their local governments. To be sure, this was not an unusual thought; only his zeal in action was unusual. He liked the idea of belonging to an independent church, such as his Congregational faith provided, but he thought that such an organization, without a hierarchy, made it necessary for its members to work extra hard.

Throughout his lifetime, W. G. gave complete loyalty to any group to which he belonged. This at times seemed to make him intolerant of those who were not Republicans or of his religious

---

* His other educational favorites, based on the amount of praise he bestowed on them, were: Payson Smith, Henry L. Chapman, and William Dewitt Hyde. One of his closest personal friends at Bowdoin was Professor Wilmot B. Mitchell.

persuasion. When it came to a showdown, however, his basic tolerance usually appeared. This was never more apparent than when K. C. M. Sills was selected as president of Bowdoin. Here was an Episcopalian and Democrat, and such a combination for the head of the college was unprecedented. There was reason to fear that such a member of the Board of Overseers as W. G. Mallett would resent and oppose Sills. Instead he sat down, after the new president's inauguration, and wrote this: "Doubtless as time runs on, we old dyed-in-the-wool Republicans who have looked askance at you because you were a Democrat, and were a little shy, too, of one whose ecclesiastical connection was outside the traditional New England fold, will find that one who combines and harmonizes in his own mind democracy in politics and the Apostolic succession in the church is the very one to lead a free college."[38]

Other seemingly inflexible precepts were not always so in practice. W. G. would oftentimes castigate his students for thumbing rides and then, when on the road, pick up a stranger who had signaled him for a lift. He said that any student who smoked or drank should be passed over for financial aid. He frequently interpreted his own ruling liberally. The co-ordination between heart and head was many times faulty, and at such a time, the heart seemed to be the stronger of the two. (He permitted, however, no compromise with dishonesty.) As an ardent admirer of Abraham Lincoln he could appreciate better than most the Sandburg line about the Civil War President: "He could be as hard as rock or soft as the drifting fog."

W. G. was a science teacher during his years as first assistant. Early in his Farmington career, Bates offered him a position in its physics department. This he declined partly because he believed he was not enough of a mathematician to justify a lifetime devoted to physics. Despite this deficiency, he became an effective science teacher. This was partly attributable to the thrill and wonder he felt at the scientific advances of his age. He followed them avidly in the scientific publications of the times, and his deep interest in how the world was changing made an impression on the students. He spoke as a science teacher at many educational meetings and championed more laboratory work in chemistry and physics. He also offered steriopticon lectures at such times as Old Home Week.

True to his normal school heritage, partly derived from Pestalozzi, he used textbooks as sparingly as possible. His classes in geology and nature-study went on walks to learn of things by direct observation. On nature walks W. G. could take full advantage of having been brought up on a farm, for as a youth he had learned to distinguish the various bird calls and songs, the flowers and vegetation in the field, and the trees which he helped his father cut down and then saw.

Roentgen invented the x-ray machine in 1895, and in 1897 W. G. Mallett was giving a series of lectures throughout the State which featured some kind of crude device that illustrated the principle of the Roentgen invention.* (Farmington would not get a commercial x-ray machine until 1915.) *The Chronicle*, always partial to the FSNS science teacher, called the lecture "witty and instructive." Certainly it must have been a formidable challenge to be witty in talking about the operation of an x-ray machine. One of the most popular courses offered by the science department was surveying. W. G. taught it and was in constant demand throughout his adult life as a surveyor. (He was a witness in court one day as a result of some surveying he had done and was interrogated by an unfriendly lawyer. W. G. spoke about the "side of the pole" when he was interrupted by the lawyer who, in his most sarcastic manner, wanted to know how long a pole had had sides. W. G. assured him it had been true for a long time and then went on to say that a pole had an outside and inside, a bottomside and topside. He wanted to know if the lawyer wanted him to mention any more sides—the lawyer did not.) His enthusiasm for and ability to present astronomy were such that Miss Lincoln prevailed upon him to give an annual lecture on the subject to the Model School. This enthusiasm for teaching science even survived an exhausting schedule imposed upon him. There were more than a few days during his years as a science teacher when he taught every hour of the school day. Such a schedule was easily possible for one who, except for infrequent head colds, enjoyed exuberant health. At such times he did not allow himself the sybaritic enjoyment of staying away from school. During his forty-nine

---

* It was often asserted that C. C. Hutchins, professor of physics at Bowdoin College, made the first efficient x-ray tube in America. It is likely that W. G. Mallett's x-ray machine owed its existence to the genius of the Bowdoin inventor. The Mallett diary on March 2, 1898, had these remarks: "Photographed Mrs. Mellen Hayes' arm with x-ray for Dr. Palmer. Picture shows no osseous formation between bones of fore arm."

years with the school his report card showed only a half a day lost because of illness.

W. G. Mallett's philosophy of teaching was similar to that of Lillian I. Lincoln in that it was not doctrinaire or faddish but practical and flexible. First and foremost, he was committed to the idea that a majority of prospective teachers could benefit from having their first teaching efforts observed and commented on by experienced and successful teachers. There were a few, he admitted, who were natural born teachers, but even these fortunate ones had to be reminded about the thin dividing line between the soporific and the stimulating. Although he was on the faculty of a school that emphasized methods of teaching he was not a partisan for any particular one. He thought teachers should be urged to do what they found most effective. Some were able to arouse interest by lectures, others only lulled their classes to sleep by using this method of instruction. He scoffed at those who were inclined to believe that the newest teaching methods were necessarily the best. For himself, he usually preferred the ancient Socratic method of the teacher feigning ignorance—especially with more bumptious students.

In 1900 W. G. seized an opportunity to serve the community, when he ran successfully for the office of superintendent of the Farmington public schools. For three years he would occupy this position along with performing his duties at the Normal School. His success with this school supervision can be judged by an item that appeared in an April 1902 issue of *The Chronicle*: "Congratulations to Prof. Mallett for his re-election as superintendent of schools. Prof. Mallett is very popular among scholars of the various schools, and is ever ready to help pupils if it is within his power to do so. A better man for the position could not have been found." Despite such accolades he eventually found the teaching supervision a little too much. In March 1904, it was announced that he had been forced to quit as the local superintendent. The year 1903 had been an unusually busy one for him. Not the least of his many responsibilities was serving as president of the Maine Teachers Association.

After the death of the editor of the Republican *Farmington Chronicle*, several people of influence in the community convinced W. G. that he should take his place. On August 9, 1905, W. G. Mallett did become its editor, and his eagerness to serve in this new role is reflected in his first editorial:

Along with the Christian church, public school, and public library, the newspaper may be an educative force of the first rank. We desire to fulfill this ideal, and we trust we shall not misjudge the intelligence and moral demands of our patrons in our endeavor to emphasize what is worthy of consideration and imitation and to give but scant notice to those elements in our civil and social life which are best treated when left alone. It may be the proper policy of a newspaper to publish not what the people need but what they want. We shall count ourselves fortunate if our belief is justified as our experience increases, that what the intelligent patrons of this paper need they also want. We desire to publish the news without fear or favor.

For nearly a decade W. G. Mallett was to write the editorials for *The Chronicle*. Needless to say, some of the battles he won, others he lost. One of those he lost was his effort to get the State to support more liberally its existing normal schools rather than increase their number. Here was his editorial upon learning of the possibility that two more Maine towns might be awarded normal schools.

The committee on education is visiting the various institutions in the state for which they are asked to recommend appropriations. Among them are the Normal Schools. These visits seem to be a very important matter, for no action, favorable or otherwise, can be as wisely taken if the institutions are not seen and their needs learned at first hand. But we have an additional suggestion to make and which we respectfully urge. We urge it in view of the fact that at least two other towns in the state are asking for the creation of new Normal Schools. It will be observed by the committee that it is towns, not educators, which are asking for new schools. The Dexter Board of Trade, not the state superintendent of schools, or the board of Normal School trustees, is asking for a new school to be located there. What we urge is that our legislative committee on education, after visiting Maine Normal Schools, go to Massachusetts, or Rhode Island, or Connecticut, and visit at least one Normal School there. We want them to see how those states support and equip a Normal school, and then let them decide whether our Maine equipment and Maine salaries are sufficiently good to warrant the addition to our Normal school system of one or two other schools.[39]

The editorial writer for the local paper was frustrated when he wrote these lines. One reason for this was that he had had to purchase from his own pocket some of the scientific apparatus that he was using for his classes in science; another frustration stemmed from the inability of Farmington to get a much needed dormitory. Castine and Gorham had dormitories but not Farmington. The third source of frustration was the low salary scale for Maine normal school faculties which made it so difficult to compete successfully with the normal schools in other New England States.

Admission and Curriculum Changes (1897–1909)

Throughout the history of the Normal School there was one constant in the midst of changing requirements for admission; that was the regulation that made it necessary for male applicants to be 17 and female candidates 16. Just why these ages were considered sacred and unalterable is not known; other normal schools had decided on these ages too, but the original rationale for them has not been uncovered. There were admission changes which were obviously introduced to sift out the unfit. One of these was accepted by the Normal School board of trustees in Portland, June 29, 1897:

> Candidates for admission to Normal Schools after July 1, 1898, shall not be admitted until they have passed satisfactory examinations in physiology and hygiene, simple equations in algebra, four fundamental rules, common and decimal fractions, denominate numbers and applications of percentage in arithmetic, facts and principles of geography and grammar, and U.S. history, reading and spelling.

The Normal School board of trustees did some further tinkering with the admission requirements on April 15, 1903, when it was voted:

> that Normal candidates be admitted without exams provided they present certificates of graduation from high schools maintaining a four-year course of standard grade. Applicants without these certificates shall be admitted after passing final exams in all common school subjects.

In the FSNS catalogue and circular there was further clarification of who would be permitted to enter the school without examinations:

1. College graduates
2. Graduates of high schools, academies, seminaries, and other secondary schools, having courses of study covering four years and fitting for college.
3. All persons holding State certificates of any grade.

In the first decade of this century, increasing emphasis was placed upon vocational courses in the public schools. W. G. Mallett wrote editorials in *The Chronicle* in which he maintained that it was folly to require so many high-school students to take the academic subjects. He insisted that not all could do well or get any significant benefit from the college preparatory course. The Normal School trustees, in one of their 1905 meetings, reflected this concern with the practical when they went on record as favoring a uniform course of instruction in agriculture for all Maine normal schools.

It was one thing, however, to vote for an agricultural course and quite another to provide a salary for a teacher. A result of the trustees' action was that George Purington,* despite the incredible number of his school and community responsibilities, taught the subject in Farmington. After his death, Arthur M. Thomas, the new science teacher, took over the course. There was one expert, Prof. Wald from UMO, who taught the course in the summer session of 1908. Other than that experience, agriculture in Farmington was in the hands of amateurs. The subject expired locally after World War I. (In the First World War, a so-called victory garden was cultivated under the supervision of Virginia A. Porter. Credit was given at that time for successful growing.)

Another vocational course at the FSNS had more success. This was manual training. At New Meadows Inn** on July 20, 1906, the Normal trustees voted that manual training should be made part of the required work. George Purington, with his Horace Mann enthusiasm for useful knowledge, was a champion of manual training. After the trustees affirmed their support of the subject, the principal set to work to convert an attic room in the new building into a manual training shop. When that was accomplished, he signed Florence

---

* George C. Purington was an active member of the Farmington Grange.

** The Trustees had a gourmet bent in pre-automobile days. They always managed to have their meetings at inns which provided the best food.

L. Walker in 1907 as the first instructor in the subject. She was a fortunate choice. A person of graciousness and intelligence, she was a graduate from Wellesley in the class of 1900. She went on to get her special training at the North Bennett Sloyd School. Before coming to Farmington she had taught four years in the Santa Barbara schools. She stayed at Farmington until 1916 when she was succeeded by Gertrude Knight. In 1919 another fine teacher, Edna M. Havey, was to be the manual training instructor until her retirement in 1947.

The advanced course that was partly designed by C. C. Rounds in 1880 was never as well patronized as hoped for. At a meeting of trustees in June 1898, notice was given that the question of abolishing the third-year course in the three Maine normal schools would soon be brought up. When the trustees met the next year it was voted that it was inexpedient to discontinue the advanced course of study. In the following five years, Farmington Normal offered two advanced courses. One was heavily loaded with professional, or methods courses, and the other was the academic course.

Although only 56 received advanced diplomas from 1880 to 1904, the list of those getting them is a distinguished one. In some respects, the course of study had more in common with present liberal arts programs than it had in common with the heavily loaded classical studies in the liberal arts colleges of the 1880s and '90s. However, those who controlled the purse refused to consider appropriating enough money to the normal schools to finance the advanced course properly. Consequently it died in 1904 and the curriculum became more oriented to professional courses. By 1905 it looked like this:

I. Psychology, pedagogy, school management, school government, school organization, history of education.
II. Reviews and methods of teaching the following subjects:
    a. LANGUAGE—Reading, spelling, grammar, rhetoric, composition, literature, history.
    b. MATHEMATICS—Arithmetic, algebra, geometry, bookkeeping.
    c. SCIENCE—Physiology and hygiene, physics, chemistry, botany, zoology, mineralogy, geology, geography, astronomy, and agriculture.
    d. EXPRESSION—Writing, drawing, vocal music, physical culture.

e. CIVICS—Government of Maine, government of the
   United States, school system, and school laws of Maine.
III.   Observation and practice in the model schools.

The Model School, founded in 1869, had only four grades in the
1880s. An expansion, made possible by an increase in appropriations,
took place in the early 1890s, and by 1894, all nine grades were in
operation. Eventually, under the guidance of Lillian I. Lincoln, the
Model School was divided into three parts; primary, intermediate,
and grammar grades. The primary consisted of the first four grades,
the intermediate of five and six, and the grammar grades were seven,
eight, and nine. For many years, because of this classification, Miss
Lincoln was officially designated as principal of the training schools.
Later her title was Supervisor of Training.[40]

In 1907 the course of instruction in the Model School differed
little from what it was to be for many years. For the benefit of
those interested in pedagogical history, here is what occupied grades
7, 8, and 9 some sixty-five years ago. The primary grades, with their
emphasis on observation and verbalization, still plainly bore the influence of Pestalozzi:

SEVENTH YEAR
Reading—Greek and Roman History Stories and Modern Clas-
   sics
Language—De Garmo, Language Lessons, Book 2, Part 2. Writ-
   ten work daily on topics assigned.
Literature—Study of stories and poems. Work correlated with
   the language and reading.
Spelling—Alexander
Arithmetic—Based on Prince, Book 6.
Geography—Three times a week. Leete's Geography Exercises,
   South America and Europe, with supplementary work from
   Redway, Frye, and many other sources.
United States History—Twice a week. Study by topics, from
   many sources, to the Revolutionary War.
Elementary Science—Lessons in mineralogy, physics, and botany.
Drawing—Based on the Prang course.
Music—Individual sight singing 7. Chorus work.

EIGHTH YEAR
Reading—Modern Classics
Language—Elements of English Grammar, Brown and De
   Garmo. Written work on topics assigned.

Literature—Study of stories and poems. Work correlated with language and reading.
Spelling—Alexander
Arithmetic—Based on Prince, Book 7.
Algebra—Once a week. Boyden, Grammar School Algebra.
Geography—Three times a week during first half year, twice a week during last. Leete's Geography exercises, Asia, Africa, and Australia, with supplementary work from many sources.
U.S. History—Alternating with geography. Study as in seventh year to the Civil War.
Elementary Science—Lessons in botany, chemistry, and zoology.
Drawing
Music—Individual sight singing. Chorus work.

NINTH YEAR
Reading—Stories of English History. Modern Classics.
Language—Elements of English Grammar, Brown and DeGarmo. Written work on topics assigned.
Literature—Study of stories and poems. Work correlated with the language and reading.
Spelling
Arithmetic—Twice a week. Mental arithmetic and practical work.
Algebra—Three times a week. Boyden, Grammar School Algebra.
Geography—Twice a week. United States, with special reference to New England. Study of the world as a whole.
U.S. History—Three times a week. United States history completed. Reviewed by study of development of leading movements.
Elementary Science—Lessons in physiology, botany, and zoology. Astronomy in connection with mathematical geography.
Drawing
Music—Individual sight singing. Chorus work.

SUPPLEMENTARY READERS
Stories of the Greeks.   Guerber
Stories of the Romans.   Guerber
Stories of the Old World.   Church
Stories of the English.   Guerber
American Neighbors.   Coe
Modern Europe.   Coe
Footprints of Travel.   Ballou
North America.   Carpenter

Europe. Carpenter
Asia. Carpenter
Africa. Carpenter
Australia. Carpenter
Beacon Lights of Patriotism. Carrington
Wilderness Ways. Long
Merchant of Venice
Evangeline
Snow-Bound and Other Poems by Whittier
A Christmas Carol
Lady of the Lake
The Tempest. Lamb's Tales

Some Extra-Curricular Activities at FSNS (1895–1909)

Much of the FSNS social life from 1895 to 1909 remained substantially as it had been in the early days of the institution. Some unappreciated and basic developments were already altering society somewhat, but "the big change" that was to transform small-town life after the First World War had not yet begun to operate in Farmington, nor was its impact felt in other main streets throughout the land. During the greater part of the history of Farmington Normal, the two most important social events were the B and D Hops.* A section of the second-year class sponsored the B, and it was held in February or March; a section of the first-year class sponsored the D, and it was usually held in May. Naturally enough, the nature of these two events changed somewhat with the years. It was customary, for example, until well into the twentieth century, for the dancing part of the evening to be preceded by a musical concert or some other form of entertainment. Square dances gradually encroached more and more on the entertainment part of the socials, and then they were supplanted, in turn, by the galop, one-step, two-step, and waltz. Finally in 1916 the fox-trot made its first appearance at a B Hop and soon thereafter crowded out all the other dances except for an occasional waltz. The original plan was for the balcony in the Nordica Auditorium to be used by a choral or instrumental group. It did not work out that way. The balcony proved unable to accommodate a Steinway piano; it attained its greatest use as an

---

* In the Normal School scheme of things a first-year student started with his or her F term, the winter session was E, and the spring term D. The next year the three terms were C, B, and A.

anchor for one end of the decorations at the B and D Hops and when students threw streamers and balloons from it. (Ghosts or angelic figures, in plays or pageants, were sometimes instructed to make for the balcony in order to be above the mundane crowd.)

The railroads played a significant role in determining the nature of the two important socials. In the days before modern roads and mass production of cars, many an event, or series of events, were built around the railroad schedule. Any substantial influx of young men into Farmington could be effected only by train. Furthermore, if young men were to come long distances, a one-night stand was hardly enough to justify what was in many cases an arduous trip. So in recognition of this fact the B and D Hops were extended to two nights, Friday and Saturday. Many of the imported males stayed around until the train left on Sunday afternoon. This long weekend contributed to relieving students of the monotony of monastic living, but it did little for the principal's peace of mind. Inevitably rule-breaking reached its peak during the B and D Hops.

Throughout the history of the Normal School walking to the cascades behind the Fair Grounds and to Powder House Hill had been, for one reason or another, a favorite form of recreation. Once or twice a year, a considerable number of students would climb Mt. Blue. In this period some would reach the mountain by team, or by bicycle, or on foot. During the Purington régime, student mobility was notably increased by the bicycle. The principal was an enthusiastic pedaler and guided many a student bicycler to spots considered too far or too time consuming for hikes. One of the favorite objectives was the cascades on Mosher Hill.

In 1900 the principal used his bicycle skills, developed in the Farmington area, to see many parts of England, Scotland, and the continent. After his return he wrote a series of articles for the Farmington Normal magazine which he called "A-Wheel in Europe." He described with unfeigned satisfaction his disregarding a danger signal to bicyclists that he saw in the Scottish Trossachs. He was proud to write that his bicycling skills were sufficient for him to emerge unscathed after a fast ride down a dangerous terrain. His Mosher Hill trips had proved to be good training for the Trossachs.

In the years before the First World War, sliding was popular among students—and relatively safe. There was no threat whatever from cars, because the few there were could not be used in the win-

THE CLASS OF 1910 making use of the basement gym of Merrill Hall during the winter of 1909. "Hoops again," as the person using the picture at the time captions it.

ter. (The roads were not plowed; a huge roller packed down the snow to produce more comfortable sleighing.) This meant that horses were in constant demand either for hay rides or sleighing of a more exclusive variety. The beginning of many a romance could be traced to a hay ride.

Dennis M. Cole, a Bowdoin graduate and FSNS science teacher from 1890 to 1892, was responsible for the first local classes in gymnastic drill, horizontal bar, vaulting, fencing, and single stick. (The evidence indicates that Cole was a popular teacher. In 1893 he and W. G. Mallett, his successor, went together to the World's Fair in Chicago. Cole went from Farmington to Westfield High, Massachusetts, where he stayed as the science teacher until his death some thirty years later.) He had no space available for a gymnastic exhibition in the Normal building of the early 1890s, so he rented Drummond Hall and organized the Farmington Athletic Association. Ten years later a revival of interest in gymnastics occurred when a basement room in Merrill Hall had equipment installed that led to an emphasis on physical education. The annual letter that Principal Purington sent out in July, 1902, was primarily designed to convince the undergraduates of the importance of exercise and the development of gymnastic skills.

Farmington Normal introduced basketball to the local area in 1902. This was made possible by placing hoops in the new gymnasium. (The ceiling was not high enough for a regulation court. Many learned to shoot baskets here who would have to learn later the extra skill needed to shoot at the higher baskets prescribed in the rule book.) Not only were men encouraged to play this new game, but it was also championed for women by Ella P. Merrill, who had returned to the Normal School as a teacher after graduating from Smith. This took courage in the days when women were ordinarily covered by layer after layer of unmentionables. In addition to this the average woman lived in a prison of whalebones and to emerge from all this for a game of basketball must have been quite an experience. In the magazine, *The Farmington Normal*, Ella Merrill wrote about the new look in physical education:

> When the new building was erected, a large pleasant room in in the basement was fitted up as a gymnasium. It is rather more than 60 by 30 feet, contains a piano, and is supplied with dumbbells, wands, and hoops. Each class is required to devote two

THE FARMINGTON STATE NORMAL BASEBALL TEAM, taken in the spring of 1893. Standing (left to right): George Giddens, short stop and outfielder; Professor Wilbert G. Mallett, outfielder; Harry Small, 2nd base; Allie Tarbox, 3rd base; Will Sturtevant, short stop and outfielder. Kneeling (left to right): Fred Lord, short stop and outfielder; Winfield Buker, 1st base; Harry Mallett, outfielder. Sitting (left to right): Maurice Severy, pitcher; Willis E. Hardy, catcher (age 18).

periods a week to gymnastics. The work consists of various exercises and simple games.

In addition to this class work we are to have, this year, basketball teams which will play outside of school hours.

And it has been demonstrated again and again that a rapid, vigorous, exciting game can be played without roughness, and without loss of dignity, or courtesy, or any of those qualities which the womanly woman desires to possess.

Ella P. Merrill overcame the initial resistance she encountered to the participation of women in basketball and was appointed the first FSNS coach in the sport. Despite her success in temporary whalebone liberation she resigned from the Farmington faculty in February, 1904, to take a position in the Brooklyn Training School for Teachers.

Baseball in the 1890s was a great deal different from what it had been in 1867 when a normal school team introduced it to the community. Wise changes in the rules had helped its popularity, and the game was the unchallenged national pastime. During those years, when there were enough males to field a team, Farmington Normal was represented on the diamond. (Periodically men were hard to find at FSNS. In 1900 the entering class had one lonely male and the 1909 graduating class had 67 women and no males.) In the 90s the scarcity of men made it essential for the science teacher to play on the team, while in 1922, for the same reason, two other members of the faculty, Errol Dearborn and Charles Preble, contributed their services as ballplayers.

A spirited baseball rivalry developed at the turn of the century between Wilton Academy and Farmington Normal. The local reporter went to see, in football weather, October 10, 1901, Wilton Academy defeat Farmington 5-4 in 11 innings. As a consequence, some Academy boys drove over to Farmington in the evening, in a three-seated team drawn by three horses, and serenaded the Normal School principal. They then drove up the street and gave cheers for umpire Wallace Gould and then, to make it even more emphatic, set off several Roman candles.

There were no recognized fraternities or sororities at FSNS until the 1930s, but other extra-curricular organizations were formed or revived in the later years of the Purington administration. In the winter of 1902, another debating society was organized. At one of its meetings, the members agonized over the topic: Was devotion to fashion a greater evil than the tobacco habit?

In April 1902, Principal Purington, who was already in charge of the regional chorus for the Maine Music Festival, took on one more responsibility when he organized the Normal School Glee Club. He had two excellent pianists available, Arthur D. Ingalls and Annie W. McLeary, while Irene Ladd (married Roy Gammon '99) was a featured soloist. Shortly after the formation of the Glee Club, the kind of instrumental group which was attaining nation-wide popularity was organized, the Mandolin Club.

Probably the most durable and successful of all FSNS organizations was the Christian Association, and it first became prominent at about the time of the Glee Club. The founders announced their object in organizing was to grow in the Christian life and graces by means of studying the Bible, prayer, and the cultivation of Christian fellowship. Meetings were held in either Merrill Hall or the favorite picnic spots, weather permitting. FSNS students, with the requirement to attend chapel daily, asserted that such an exercise was quite different from students gathering voluntarily for inspirational and religious services. The Christian Association was in the habit of sending to Camp Maqua, in Poland, Maine, representatives who met with their contemporaries from other schools.

The Farmington Normal was a publication of the school from 1901 to 1904. As we have seen, Principal Gage's 1866 periodical was called *The Maine Normal*, which evolved into the *Maine Journal of Education*, and this had as two of its editors, C. C. Rounds and Roliston Woodbury. Now some twenty-five years later, George C. Purington started another publication. Its life, however, from its inception was blighted by poverty, which was attributable to a scarcity of paying subscribers. Riddled as it was by financial distresses, it staggered on for three years. Lillian I. Lincoln, as the most frequent contributor, used it not only to present her views on the teaching of history and geography, but also to give various bibliographies and lesson plans on the American Indians, Chinese, and Japanese. Hortense Merrill gave an account of some of her travels in the British Isles and the continent, while George Purington described foreign scenes as viewed from a bicycle. W. G. Mallett wrote about the responsibilities of a school superintendent. Student contributions were confined to class parts.

Members of the Model School had their night of extra-curricular glory when they presented their annual entertainment. *The Chronicle* was particularly enthusiastic about the 1905 entertainment. At that time, Miss Lincoln wrote some sketches for the purpose of dramatizing scenes from American history. In the continental drill, Clinton Greenwood was General Washington and Fabyan Turner represented Ben Franklin. Long before Arthur Miller's *Crucible,* the Salem witch craze was said to have been dramatically and vividly portrayed in Merrill Hall.

Farmington Normal usually had an annual course of entertainment consisting of the traditional fare of travel talks, dramatic readings, musicales, and the perennial bell ringers. One of the most popular lecturers to come to Farmington during this period was Henry L. Chapman. Professor of English literature at Bowdoin, he was also a member of the Normal School trustees. Known throughout the State of Maine as a speaker of charm and eloquence, he delivered in his time more talks in Farmington than any other out-of-town person.[41] Edward Thompson[42] was a frequent dramatic reader in the FSNS entertainment circuit, and Donald B. MacMillan told of his Arctic explorations.

The Farmington Lawn Tennis Association was organized in 1890, and a court was built on lower High Street. Many years, however, would have to go by before it became popular among students. Such a day would await the construction of a court next to Purington Hall. In 1905 a golf course was in use near the old slate quarry, and among the players were W. G. Mallett, Judge J. H. Thompson, Richard H. Clapp, and Carl P. Merrill. (The last named was the best.) Neither golf nor tennis, however, was a student sport. Equipment was expensive and not many towns or cities in the State had facilities for golfers or tennis players. Croquet sets were cheap and plentiful, but the recreation in Farmington that seemed to have the greatest patronage at this time was roller skating. A rink was located near the building on Upper Main Street where the Gray Ford Co. was located in the early 1970s, and it did a land-office business.

More sedentary games were checkers, chess, flinch, authors, and whist. Smoking cigarettes for future teachers was inconceivable; even in the cities, a majority thought of the habit as decadent and effete. Chewing tobacco was regarded as a more manly dissipation.

Tobacco in any form, however, was off limits for female teachers, and many communities were almost as intolerant of male indulgence in the weed.

In 1890 George Purington contributed to the better use of leisure time by being the chief organizer of the Farmington Public Library. About ten years later, he made another major contribution by prevailing upon the Cutlers* to give money for the present building. Despite this cultural achievement that did so much for the town, a 1914 dyspeptic reporter for *The Franklin Journal* decried what he considered an alarming decline of reading as a use for leisure time. The writer blamed this on the tango, automobile, bicycle, steamboat, and railroads. Such diversions may have had national effects on reading habits, but local statistics indicate that Farmington citizens were reading more than ever. At a time when the Farmington Normal library hardly deserved the name, it was indeed fortunate that the students had access to a public library far better than the average.

Outside the classroom, graduation week at the FSNS represented the busiest time of the year. Teaching exercises, which had been part of graduation week since the beginning, were very much a part of the program in this period. In 1905, for example, W. G. Mallett taught a model class in physics; Hortense Merrill had one in history; Louise Richards another in arithmetic; Lillian I. Lincoln one in methods; and George Purington demonstrated how to teach school laws and school organization. The senior class had excursions to such places as the Poland Spring House or the Rangeley Lake House in order to hold their class-day exercises. A professional musical concert was featured on one of the evenings during graduation week. The grand finale, with its presentation of diplomas, brought to town many distinguished visitors. The governor nearly always attended, and so did the members of the legislative committtee on education, as well as some member of the governor's council. The principal of Farmington Normal made himself available after the ceremonies to

---

* Nathan Cutler, for whom the building, donated by his sons John and Isaac and completed in 1901, is named, graduated from Dartmouth. For several years before practicing law in Farmington Falls, he was preceptor of the Northampton (Mass.) Academy. Later, he moved to the Center Village where he spent the rest of his life. President of the Maine Senate in 1828–29, he was acting governor for a time after the death of Enoch Lincoln.

introduce in the teachers' room anyone who wanted to meet the governor.

The Completion of the New Building

In 1898, the FSNS principal was pleased and proud when the last touches were put onto the outside of the new building, but he realized better than anyone else that other pressing wants remained. In his July 7, 1898, report to the trustees he listed them:

1. A new chemical laboratory. The present room is utterly inadequate for the purpose.
2. A large addition to our chemical and philosophical apparatus.
3. An addition to our reference library.
4. More textbooks.
5. New Furniture in place of the present antiquated and unhygienic furniture.
6. Another teacher.
7. New toilet rooms for the Model School.

In the ten-year period from 1898 to 1908, many of these needs were to be fulfilled. The most notable failure would relate, as usual, to the library. Both Rounds and Purington made urgent annual requests for more books, but for reasons not too clear, no principal of Farmington Normal was successful in getting anywhere near the number of books he considered essential. It was one of the major frustrations of Rounds and his successors.

The chief internal transformations in the new building consisted of a gymnasium in 1902, a new chemical laboratory in 1904, and a manual training shop in 1907.* The graduation of 1908 was of special importance because it marked the completion of the building outside and in, and it was an anniversary year recognizing twenty-five years of the Purington administration. In honor of this milestone the Farmington alumni presented their FSNS principal with $1,200. (They had given him a trip to Europe in 1900.) Certainly this was a testimony of love and respect, especially considering the lack of affluence among Maine teachers as well as the 1908 scarcity of the dollar.

---

* The manual training shop was on the north side of the top floor and is now being made into offices for the fine arts department. The chem lab was to the east of the manual training shop and was reached by means of a short stairway that led from the manual training room.

Exercises honoring the completed building resulted in a ceremony attended not only by members of the school but by many local citizens and out-of-town guests. The principal gave an account of Farmington Normal from its founding in 1864 to events in 1908 and stated that the entire expense of the building, including furniture and apparatus, was $71,500. He went on to pay tribute to his former resident trustee, I. Warren Merrill, and told of the assistance he had received from him in obtaining appropriations for the first enlargement of the building, of the careful expenditure of this money under Merrill's supervision, and of the remarkable insight of the man into all the needs and requirements of the institution. Mr. Merrill's children presented to the school a picture of their father and then, in recognition of his contributions, the principal announced that the assembly hall, previously known as Normal Hall, was henceforth to be called Merrill Hall. (Another speaker on the program that day was Payson Smith, who had become State Superintendent of Schools in 1907. He served as such until he accepted in 1916 a similar position in Massachusetts. Formerly a superintendent in Rumford-Canton, and then Auburn, he was a tremendous favorite at FSNS, partly because of his personality and partly because of his educational accomplishments. He had a harmonius working relationship with both Purington and Mallett.)

A *Glance Backward in* 1908

Principal Purington was addicted to obtaining data from the alumni concerning their honors and activities, and at the 1908 ceremony he furnished these:

1. Number of FSNS students registered in 25-year period—3,020
2. Number graduated, 1,138
3. Graduates of medical schools, men 55; women 2
4. Graduates of liberal arts colleges, men 55; women 16
5. Teaching in 1907–08, men 41, women 448; college professors 5, high school principals 17, teachers of manual training 8, principals and teachers in academies 13, grammar school principals 30, teachers in Normal and training schools 22, superintendents 26.

Such unadorned statistics cast a limited light on the past; more helpful in this respect was an examination of those who received the two-year diploma and then went on for the three-year course.

There were only some fifty of them, but their influence was all out of proportion to their numbers. Appropriately enough, the first three to graduate from the advanced course were children of the man who pushed for this additional year, C. C. Rounds. Not only were the two Rounds boys to distinguish themselves later on,* but their sister, Agnes, became the chief critic teacher at the Buffalo Normal School before marrying Edwin S. Matthews, an FSNS teacher in 1882–83.

Those who graduated from the three-year course and became FSNS teachers were: Hortense M. Merrill, Lucy Luques, Mary E. Eaton, Julia W. Swift, Lillian I. Lincoln, Ardella M. Tozier, Harriet P. Young, Sara M. Locke, Nellie Skinner, Ella P. Merrill, and Mary Bickford. Of this number Mary E. Eaton and Ella P. Merrill graduated from Smith, and all the others spent varying amounts of time in post-FSNS study.

Frances S. Belcher (1887) received an AB from Vassar and an AM from Columbia; Abner A. Badger (1888) was awarded an AB degree from Bowdoin; Clarence H. Knowlton (1894) was the son of a former Normal School trustee, David H. Knowlton, and received his AB from Harvard; Donald Cragin (1895) graduated from the Harvard Medical School; George C. Purington Jr. (1898) was granted an AB degree from Bowdoin; Harold King, US Commissioner of Lighthouses in the 1930s, graduated from Dartmouth College; and Alma Bradbury (1903) was awarded an LL.B from Boston University. She was one of the last two to receive a diploma at FSNS for the third-year course. The other 1903 diploma for advanced work was granted to Flora Pearson (married Sumner P. Mills) who, instead of going on to study law, became the mother of two lawyers, William and Peter. Her daughter Virginia taught at Farmington Teachers College from 1948 to 1950.

Jane M. Cutts (1887) and Ella Howard (1895) remained for a considerable length of time in Farmington and made important con-

---

* The two Rounds boys attended the Normal School. Arthur C. went on to Amherst College, graduated in 1887, and went to Harvard Law School. While in college he was one of the editors of the *Amherst Literary Monthly,* and at Harvard he was on *The Law Review.* Ralph S. also went to Amherst. He was editor-in-chief of the *Amherst Literary Monthly* and wrote a prize essay for *Lippincott's Magazine* on social life at Amherst. Arthur became a law partner of Charles Evans Hughes. Ralph also became a New York lawyer after receiving his LL.B. from Columbia.

tributions to the life here. The former became a highly regarded English teacher in the Farmington High School before moving on to the Birmingham School for Girls in Pennsylvania. Ella Howard married the Reverend Edwin R. Smith, pastor of the Old South Church from 1895 to 1903. She was the daughter of a former Old South minister, Rowland Howard, and the niece of O. O. Howard, a Civil War hero and founder of Howard University.

The advanced course, initiated and developed by C. C. Rounds, may have had a mere handful of students, but their quality more than made up for their small numbers.

Students in Farmington and other Maine normal schools, who appeared in such 1908 statistics as compiled by Principal Purington, came usually from small towns or farms. They represented various degrees of poverty, and some in their formative years lived on the razor's edge of insolvency. Some were interested in becoming teachers, while others were trying primarily to get away from an unprofitable farm and at the same time avoid the financial dead end of unskilled wages. Many, endowed with the necessary ambition and talent, used the training of the Normal School as a means for becoming doctors or lawyers. They could save enough as a teacher, even though it was not easy, to study law in an office or use their modest savings to go to college or medical school. The hope of upward social mobility kept them going and frequently delayed marriage with its inevitable expenses.

As compared with the present freedom for youth, FSNS rules continued to be incredibly strict. Despite this repression, there were no recorded FSNS blowups. Apparently the students took seriously their parents' admonition to cultivate habits of work, obedience, and self-restraint. Life was real and life was earnest to a degree unknown to the present generation of students. Despite all this, there is evidence that some thought the school rules and regulations unreasonably severe.

Ida S. Colley, 1909, wrote this poem in her scrapbook:

NORMAL RULES

Hurry, hurry in the morning,
Hurry early, hurry late
Such the life of Normal scholars,
Such will ever be their fate.

> All the rules are strict and heartless
> And are very hard to bear;
> First, for health, the Prof. informed us
> Is to run around the square.
> Next important in the black rules
> Is the awful number three
> Oh, for some of us it's easy
> But for some—it cannot be.
> Normals, beware! My tale is ended,
> Look not sad, but rather bright
> For of course these rules are harmless
> If you'll just observe them right.

The last two lines probably meant that a student could get along well enough if she did not take the rules too seriously. There was no dormitory and those who boarded the students often winked at the rules and encouraged their roomers to do likewise. Needless to say, this was not usually difficult to accomplish.

Serious infractions of the rules, at least according to modern standards, rarely occurred. Young ladies were not only protected by layers of clothes, but by layers of innocence and restraint. These were all held together by the protestant ethic which was rarely challenged. An almost complete WASP environment left little room for arguments about the acceptable mores. (Protestant sects did have comparatively minor arguments concerning biblical sanction for such activities as cardplaying and dancing.)

There was very little leakage in the way of alien ideas. This was partly because the faculty of the Purington administration was largely recruited from those who had attended Farmington Normal. Hortense Merrill, Lucy Luques, and Harriet Young graduated in 1881; Mary Eaton and Lillian I. Lincoln in 1885; Julia Swift, Ella J. Longfellow and W. G. Mallett in 1886; Ella Merrill in 1891, Katherine Merrill in 1891, Katherine Abbott in 1892, and Carolyn Stone in 1898. (These were the years they graduated from the regular two-year course; a majority of them went on with the advanced course.) Their lack of degrees should not mislead anyone into believing they all lacked educational qualifications. Harriet Young spent a year of study at Radcliffe; Julia Swift spent a year in Germany studying its school system and then for another year attended a summer session at Clark University; Ella Merrill received the advanced diploma in 1894, and after that, graduated from Smith. Hortense Merrill received the advanced diploma in 1884 and studied languages one summer at the Saveur Institute and another at Oswego Normal. She studied in Paris in 1892–93, in Germany in 1901–02, and at Radcliffe in 1902–03. W. G. Mallett, in addition to his Bowdoin years, studied at Clark, where he went in the summer of 1895 to take courses with G. Stanley Hall.

The science teachers had the greatest amount of formal education, or at least the greatest number of college degrees. Charles F. Warner had M.A. and Sc.D. degrees from Colby; Jefferson Potter (1888) had an M.A. from Brown; Dennis M. Cole (1890-1892) had an AB and M.A. from Bowdoin, and so did his successor, W. G. Mallett. His science successor, Arthur M. Thomas, had an AB and M.A. from Colby.*

Death of George Purington and a Tribute

George Purington left home with his wife on April 29, 1909, to attend the meeting of the Piscataquis County teachers at Dover-Foxcroft. He participated in the convention on the following day and delivered his address on Horace Mann in the evening. The next morning, according to plan, Mr. and Mrs. Purington went to Monson, the old home of Mrs. Purington. They were to be guests in the home of an old friend and Mr. Purington was to deliver his other

---

* One of the ablest graduates in the latter part of the Purington administration was F. Burnham McLeary, great-grandson of Jonas Burnham, a distinguished scholar and preceptor of Farmington Academy from 1849 to 1859. After graduating from the Normal School, Burnham went on, with a scholarship, to Harvard and received there an AB degree. He became an employee of Doubleday, Doran & Co. and a writer and producer of educational and industrial films. In a recent letter, he wrote about the FSNS teachers as he remembered them. (Some of them have failed to make this story because they taught only a year or two in the Model School):

"During the years I attended the Model School and Farmington State Normal School the teachers I was privileged to study under were like Alexander's Ragtime Band— 'The Bestest in the Land.' Miss Longfellow, Miss Cushing, Miss Leland, Miss Clark, Miss Pinkham, Miss Corliss, Miss Stone, Miss Julia Swift, Miss Lincoln—they not only knew how to teach, they knew how to teach teachers how to teach. And as a teacher and counselor for a young man in his formative years your father topped them all."

favorite speech, a description of the Passion Play. This was not to be, for the FSNS principal was stricken with chills that sent him to bed, and on May 6, he suffered from a fatal cerebral hemorrhage.

On Sunday, May 9, 1909, at the Old South Church in Farmington, Richard H. Clapp, quite possibly the most eloquent of all Old South preachers, delivered a tribute to the memory of George C. Purington. After reviewing the honors of the man and outlining his life, he went on to say this:

In St. Paul's Cathedral, London, the tomb of its architect, Sir Christopher Wren, bears this inscription: "Reader, if you seek his monument, look around." Here in our midst, in stately architecture, are the visible monuments of our friend. This church building bears the marks of his wise and devoted planning. He was, through a long period, on the business committee of the church and leader of the choir for many years. The Public Library in its building and equipment owes far more to him than to any other person. For twenty years he had been president of the Library Association. But of all these the Normal School must remain his noblest monument. The building was planned and its construction supervised by him. The efficient method, the noble discipline, the high reputation and influence of the school in all its later years, have their sources largely in his wise and tireless energy. Here was the throne of his power.

He was a masterful personality, born to organize, direct, govern. High responsibility was native to his desire and he bore gracious authority in whatever circle he moved. Wide grasp of facts and principles, quick and firm decision, tenacious purpose, resolute persistence in the course chosen, marked his actions.

This abounding energy of will and intelligence was directed and impassioned by a strong and sensitive conscience. All that he did was vivified by a zeal for righteousness. He felt the seriousness of the moral order of life with its source in the will of a righteous and holy God. He was urgent to make that will effective on earth as it is in heaven. His is the beatitude of those who hunger and thirst after righteousness, for they shall be filled. The great ideals that dignify and exalt life claimed his sane and eager allegiance. In the midst of the day's drudgery he was enamoured of vision and prophecy and hope. For his own profession he claimed the best that ideal and sentiment and method could afford. He held that to the teacher was offered the opportunity for the most fruitful human service. He, in himself, gave proof of his belief.

All sincere purpose and honest effort claimed his earnest sympathy and was felt as a challenge to his power and opportunity to help. The scholar in the school, the young man or woman at the beginning of a career, the needy from whatever worthy cause found in him sage counsel and ready aid. As he was quick in all strong and delicate sympathies, so, also, he had a virile and fiery impatience with all forms of willful stupidity, of meanness, pettiness and iniquity. On occasion he could use the scathing utterance of a noble anger. Let us understand that without this capacity for elemental wrath a virile manhood cannot be. If this high and resolute temper meant sometimes mistakes in judgment and action it needs no apology, for it was inspired by that sensitive honor and fidelity to truth that sought to deal truly and justly with all men.

The range of his interests and his opportunities for travel and intercourse gave him a wide knowledge in many subjects; a knowledge which he took pleasure in imparting in vivid and eloquent speech. He was listened to with delight whenever he lectured on one of his favorite subjects. He was a conversationalist of rare charm. What lucid argument he could employ and what picturesque description. How his language scintillated with humor and bristled with epigram. From what rich fund of reminiscence was he accustomed to draw the stories, grave or gay, that added point and illumination to his address. What treasure of deep and tender sympathy, of cordial good will, of utter devotion to duty, of the joy of great service, was revealed in him as he spoke.

To the charm of eloquent speech was added the glory of song. His gifts as a singer and his enthusiastic leadership in music standards in school, church, and community.

The loss and the sorrow are ours; ours also the solemn and glad assurance of the abiding gain his life has wrought for the world. The man passes; the personality abides. All that he leaves of precious memory and inspiring influence, of thought and sentiment and will incarnate in beneficent institutions, and in lives informed in wisdom and righteousness by his own rich life, abides, potent for good, forevermore. His life goes on in the forces that humanize and glorify our world and in the increasing glory of his noble personality he lives in God.

Great leader, knightly spirit, dear friend, we bid not farewell, but God-speed.

IV. THE MALLETT ADMINISTRATION

The unexpected death of George C. Purington shocked the Farmington community, and the use of every available space at the Old South Church for those who wanted to pay their last respects bore witness to his standing in the town. The flag on the common was at half-mast, and so were the flags at the Abbott School. At an emergency meeting, the library trustees voted to have emblems of mourning hung on the door of the building whose construction George C. Purington had worked for and then supervised. The Pilgrim Commandary, in accordance with its rites, buried the man who had passed through every chair of the Lodge. Coming so soon after the death of the principal, the June graduation exercises were drastically changed. The traditional exercises, extending as they usually did throughout the better part of the week, were eliminated, and in their place was a memorial address by Henry L. Chapman, a personal friend of the deceased. Following this tribute, sixty-seven women were awarded their diplomas.

Unlike the long period of many weeks that separated the Rounds and Purington administrations, the appointment of a principal in 1909 came quickly. The minutes of the trustees' meeting of June 9 indicate there was no discussion about a Purington successor. It was simply voted that the chairman of the board be instructed to cast one ballot for W. G. Mallett as principal of the Farmington State Normal School at a salary of $1,800. As expected, he accepted.

On the Verge of the Modern Era
In the years that followed the Purington administration, the

towns and institutions of Maine and other states were to change more than they had in all their previous history. This was to be observed not only in physical expansion and improvements, but in political, social, scientific, and economic developments. All of this has to be noted and considered in any proper appreciation of the changes in educational institutions that became inevitable, in one way or another, in a radically changing society.

In 1909 Farmington was relatively fortunate in transportation, as it has been ever since 1859 when the first train pulled into the local station of West Farmington. In 1909 passenger trains left Farmington at 8:45 A.M. for Lewiston, Brunswick, Bath, Rockland, Portland, and Boston; at 2:25, for Lewiston, Portland, and Boston. At 9:20 P.M. another train, this one a Pullman sleeper, went to the same three cities. Those who wanted to get to the northern part of the county could use the Sandy River line, with its narrow gauge and toy-like locomotives and cars. In September 1909, the first special train was run to Lewiston for the benefit of those who wanted, for a substantial price, to see the kind of movies that came for a while only to the more urban areas. (The featured movie in Lewiston, at this time, was "The Traveling Salesman." Seats 50 cents to $1.50.)

The railroads, owing to such inventions as the Westinghouse air brake, block signals, Pullman cars, and better-made rails and road-beds, offered the fastest, safest, and most comfortable way to travel on land. Such a means of transportation, however, oftentimes demanded patience from the passengers, because of circuitous routes to nearby towns. Students from Rumford, for example, had to board a train that took them only as far as Canton; they then were obliged to wait for another train that would take them to Livermore Falls; at that point, they would get out to wait for a train that would complete the journey to Farmington, but not until stops were made in Jay, Wilton, East Wilton, and West Farmington. Much of the afternoon would be spent in this kind of waiting and zigzagging. On the day before school began, students from all parts of Maine converged on the town, bringing with them some 150 to 200 trunks. (Moreover, hunting for one's mislaid trunk was frequently no light-hearted sport.)

The owners of three livery stables were doing a thriving business, and the several blacksmith shops were equally occupied. Although the threat of the horseless carriage was considered serious by the

PRINCIPAL WILBERT G. MALLETT (1909–1940) reading a daily motto from his desk in Merrill Hall, later named the Nordica Auditorium.

more prophetic, there were few with enough power of divination to envision broad highways enabling students of the future to leave town every Friday for weekends of various lengths. At that time, automobiles were toys of the rich, priced beyond the reach of the average person. He could console himself, however, with the realization that a car was of limited use. The roads were abominable, and with few exceptions, would remain so for years to come. (The first modern highway here was built to Strong in 1915.) There were local agents for the Stanley Steamer, Buick, and Maxwell, but few in town could afford such cars or had the ability to drive them. (In the years to come, with the mass production of the Model T Ford, otherwise known as "the tin Lizzie," the nation's citizenry would become well versed in the workings of the internal combustion engine.) In 1909, via *The Farmington Chronicle*, the Portland Auto Company advertised a three-week course which was designed to turn a mechanical novice into either a chauffeur or "automobile engineer." One important part of the course was to learn the intricacies of patching tires and inner tubes. The quality of the tires and roads was such as to make probable a blowout on a trip of any length.

In 1909 the town and school were on the verge of a revolution in entertainment. In Drummond Hall, Mabel Austin gave a victrola concert that astounded a good number of people who, according to *The Chronicle*, "had never heard a victrola and had little conception of its capabilities." At Music Hall, the Moulton brothers showed primitive moving pictures and illustrated songs, but this was not enough to satisfy the customers. Professor Hanson, with his "polite vaudeville of comedy, magic, and illusions," had to be called on before the audience considered themselves adequately entertained. In two or three years, the movies would arrive as a satisfactory medium of entertainment, and then it would be unnecessary to call on any Professor Hanson for the customers to feel they had had their money's worth.

On September 28, 29, and 30 in 1909, students had their afternoons off to attend the 70th annual show and fair of Franklin County. The Maine Central gave excursion rates to out-of-towners who wanted to attend this highly regarded event, and the offer was good for those in the State who lived in the most faraway towns. Governor Bert M. Fernald was present on the last day only, but balloon ascensions were one of the features each day. (In ten years time an airplane would thrill the fair crowd with its rolls and loops.) Carlotta, the pacing mare, was also a daily feature. She went around the track twice to complete her act without the guidance of a driver, but despite this handicap, "showed a fast mile."

Bicycling had temporarily lost some of the popularity it had in the 1890s, but there were enough demon cyclers around to get a warning from the local authorities to keep their dangerous vehicles off the sidewalks. Hikers and strollers were given a dividend about this time when the Bonneys gave land between North and Anson streets as a community woods. More ambitious hikers continued to climb Mt. Blue. During the first year of the Mallett administration, a large and distinguished party, which included two of the local ministers, arose early one morning and boarded the Sandy River railroad for Strong. From there they were conveyed by horse and carriages to the foot of the mountain. With one exception, the entire party then proceeded to climb Mt. Blue. (*The Chronicle* delicately withheld the name of the person who went "chicken.")

Events of national importance were being discussed locally. In 1908 the first U.S. airplane fatality had taken place at Fort Myer, Virginia, and Bleriot was about to fly across the English Channel. The National Geographic Society had accepted the claims of Robert E. Peary, and on his return from the North Pole, the Bowdoin graduate had been given an ovation at all the Maine railroad stops between Vanceboro and Portland. Edward Ginn, of the Boston publishing house, had given a salute to futility by announcing his gift of a million dollars to the peace movement. In September 1909, John F. Stevens was elected president of the Oregon trunk line, which was a Hill railroad to be built from the Columbia River to central Oregon and thence to San Francisco. Local readers of *The Chronicle* were talking about the speed of the *Lusitania* which, with Lillian Nordica aboard, crossed the Atlantic in four and a half days.

The Franklin County Medical Society reflected the modest countryside rates in medicine with its announcement that day visits from doctors (6 A.M. to 8 P.M.) were a dollar each. Night visits were from 50 cents to a dollar more. The E. G. Blake Jewelry Store reminded people, via *The Chronicle*, that they need not go without glasses even though they were unable to pay the optician price; just call at Blake's and you were promised satisfactory spectacles for a dollar, the best for a $1.50, and gold-filled ones for $2.50.

The Sandy River narrow gauge and the Maine Central trains pull in at the Farmington railroad station at the same time.

The FSNS Faculty (1909)

The change in command at Farmington Normal meant no significant change in either policies or personnel. On becoming principal, W. G. Mallett decided to take over, with the exceptions of agriculture and music, the subjects his predecessor had taught: school management, school law, moral philosophy, psychology, and civics. (He had taught most of these courses his first year on the faculty of FSNS in 1891–92. He took over the science courses with the resignation of Dennis Cole.)

Arthur M. Thomas accepted the position of sub-principal (a new title) as well as continuing to teach chemistry, physics, zoology, agriculture,* astronomy, and mineralogy. A graduate of Colby, he was for several years principal of the Ricker Classical Institute. Subsequently he was principal of Higgins Institute and then of the high schools in Bar Harbor and Kennebunk.

Although the faculty showed few changes, courses assigned to the various members oftentimes did vary markedly from year to year. Hortense Merrill, who had started in the 1880s as a language teacher, was now involved with English literature and history. (With the dropping of the advanced course in 1904, languages disappeared from the curriculum and would not reappear for over sixty years.) Katherine Abbott** FSNS '92, was employed for twenty-seven years primarily as an art teacher, but she also taught algebra and geometry, and

---

* In 1905, when the trustees had voted for a course in agriculture, Principal Purington apparently felt that as a prominent member of the Grange he should teach it. Coming in the spring of the second year, it was part of the curriculum from 1906 to 1920. It did not seem to be a demanding course and dealt with the physical properties of soil, methods of making seed tests, and conditions for seed germination. It was supposed to awaken an interest in farm life, but there is no evidence that it ever did. In 1921 rural sociology replaced it in the curriculum.

** Katherine Abbott, on her retirement in 1928, received a pension of about $800. The next year Arthur Thomas applied for a pension but was told he was not eligible, and this despite the fact that he had taught twenty years at FSNS and for several years in Maine high schools. Apparently he needed more continuous service in the Maine public school system, since Ricker and Higgins were not public schools. In 1914 Payson Smith had managed to get a pension arrangement of sorts accepted. In a non-contributary plan those who had taught in Maine public schools for thirty-five years were eligible for an annual pension of a sum not to exceed $250; those who had taught thirty years were eligible for a sum not to exceed $200.

initiated a new course in 1910—bird study. In 1909, Carolyn A. Stone, FSNS '98, taught physiology, arithmetic, and physical culture. Virginia A. Porter* taught grammar, English composition, reading, geography, and penmanship. The only specialists were those who taught music and manual training. Florence L. Walker was the manual training teacher and Mary E. Andrews, a fledgling FSNS graduate (1909) taught music in 1909–10. She was succeeded the next year by Franca Camp,** a music teacher of exceptional competence and enthusiasm, who for a total of sixteen years did wonders with choral and orchestral groups at the Normal School.

For many years, George C. Purington had tried unsuccessfully to convince the authorities that he was not the logical person to perform all the clerical tasks at the school. His eloquence was unavailing but his arguments may have been posthumously effective, because in the fall of 1909, the FSNS acquired its first secretary, Mildred Gay. A '99 alumna of FSNS her efficiency relieved the new principal of many clerical chores that had consumed an exorbitant amount of his predecessor's time.

The Coming of the Summer School to FSNS

In the normal school era there was little, if any, pressure exerted upon grade-school teachers to get college or graduate degrees that would involve residence requirements. Although educators were inclined to downgrade the importance of increasing the teachers' competence in subject matter, they did emphasize the desirability of keeping normal school graduates well informed about the latest developments in methods of instruction and discipline. Even more important than this was the urgent need to expand the education of non-graduates whose inadequacies in the rural schools of Maine re-

---

* Unlike other normal school teachers, Virginia Porter was not a graduate of either a normal school or college. Formerly a principal of a grammar school in Pembroke, and then a teacher in Orono High School, she was selected because of her teaching success.

** In 1915 Franca Camp married Arthur D. Ingalls and left teaching for five years. She consented to come back to FSNS in 1920 and remained this time for ten years. After World War II, she taught at the Teachers College for a year. Mrs. Ingalls also taught concurrently with her FSNS duties in the Farmington public schools. Many students who went through the Farmington public school system learned to appreciate her contributions to their musical education.

presented a problem of gargantuan proportions. It was also recognized that nearly all teachers could benefit by meetings that revived their enthusiasm for their professional duties. (It should be stated that some of the meetings fell far short of reaching such an objective.) A general agreement about the need for the exchange of ideas and for stimulating the uninformed and lethargic led to the formation of teachers' associations and summer schools. In Maine the latter were an outgrowth of the county associations. In 1891 the Piscataquis County Association had arranged to hold its 1892 meeting in the summer instead of the fall, and for one week rather than two days. Specialists were hired to give instruction in vocal music, drawing, physical education, pedagogy, arithmetic, history, and geography. More than a hundred teachers responded to the opportunity to take this one-week course. In 1894, two other schools of one week each were held, the first being at the Chautauqua campground in Fryeburg, the other at the Methodist campground in Northport.

These summer sessions met with such a favorable response that the legislature of 1895 passed a resolve giving the State Superintendent authority to establish and maintain annually not less than three summer schools, and made an appropriation for their support for the years 1895 to 1899. From the beginning, the work done in the summer session was designed to bring out of isolation those who were teaching in rural areas. The schools were not permanently located in any particular town, but were held in whatever area seemed to have the largest numbers expressing an interest in this opportunity.

The Maine normal schools believed they had the superior facilities and instruction for summer schools, and eventually the state authorities recognized this and issued orders for the 1908 summer schools to meet in Farmington, Gorham, Castine, Presque Isle, and Fort Kent. The first summer session in FSNS history opened on June 29 and closed July 17. Some 50 students attended and the teachers were: George C. Purington, Katherine Abbott, Virginia A. Porter, Louise Richards (assistant to Lillian Lincoln and teacher of the 7th and 8th grades) and Professor Wald, professor of agriculture at UMO. It was logical that since summer sessions were primarily aimed at rural teachers there should be a course in agriculture taught by an expert. (The bulletin for the 1911 session announced that "summer schools for teachers will be devoted entirely to the object of aiding teachers of rural schools.")

In the first ten or twelve years of Farmington summer schools, the attendance varied from 50 to 75 students. In 1920 attendance reached 100, in 1921 the number was in excess of 200, and in 1925 a record-breaking 414 attended the local summer session. The reasons for the increase in attendance were several: superintendents began to urge teachers in graded and urban schools to attend; young people in the 1920s were showing greater interest in teaching; and the FSNS summer teaching staffs had acquired an excellent reputation. In 1927, for example, Willard O. Chase, superintendent of schools in Old Town, was on the faculty and so was his son, W. Linwood Chase, who was, at that time, a teacher in the Horace Mann School in New York City (later he was dean as well as professor of social sciences at Boston University). Others on the faculty were Margery Gordon, of the New York High School of Commerce, who taught English; Elizabeth Collins, of the Smith faculty, who taught courses in education; while Errol Dearborn, of Farmington, Emma Flinn, from a North Dakota teachers college, and Carrie M. Frost, principal of a junior high school in Boston, completed the staff.

Before the summer schools became as large as they were in the 1920s, and before cars came into common use, summer students, forced as they were to stay in Farmington, became well acquainted with one another, and a camaraderie developed impossible of attainment these days. Bulletins issued to prospective summer students emphasized that afternoons were devoted entirely to outdoor life, rest, and recreation. Socials were frequent, and one day of the summer was reserved for an all-day outing. For several years the narrow-gauge railroad took the entire summer school for a picnic to the Rangeley Lakes area. Enrollment in summer school was encouraged with the announcement that, as in the past, no tuition would be charged and textbooks would be free.

Course of Study and Entrance Requirements

On August 5, 1910, the trustees of the normal schools took another step forward in tightening the entrance requirements. They voted that at the beginning of the 1912 fall term no students would be admitted to a normal school unless they were graduates of a four-year course of a standard secondary school, or could pass an examination in the branches offered in the secondary schools. (The two-year notice was given in order that students contemplating the normal school course might have an opportunity to provide for the required preparation.) The days of attending a normal school without, or before, completing a high-school course were drawing to a close.

In 1910–11 the administration put into operation a new system of practice teaching "whereby every graduate receives three months of training during the second year of her course by assisting in some of the training-school rooms, observing the work as done by an experienced teacher, and giving her own practice lessons."[43] Such tightening of the standards would have warmed the heart of C. C. Rounds, who was so far ahead of his time in urging greater discipline and regularity in teacher training. He would have been happy indeed in 1883 if only he could have written then to the trustees as the FSNS principal did in 1911:

> A gratifying improvement in the standard of preparation for admission to the school is apparent. The general encouragement manifest throughout the state for teachers to prepare themselves more thoroughly for their work has resulted in a larger number than formerly persisting in their normal school work throughout the year rather than pursuing it in a desultory way of teaching one term and attending normal school the next.

An extraordinary number of courses were provided for normal school students. During the first year as part of the curriculum a student took chemistry and physiology the first term, zoology and physiology the second term, and physics the third term. Courses in the other disciplines went by in the same dizzy succession, and it was not unusual for some teachers to have recitations every period of the day. The severe limitations placed upon normal school appropriations made it essential to offer generally only courses that would be of help to future elementary school teachers. It had been a long and hard pull from the days of Rounds to get as many people as there were in 1910 to accept the expense and discipline of two full years in preparing themselves for a profession that still paid barely above subsistence wages.

The Pestalozzian doctrines, which were mentioned in the local press in 1864 as so all-important in the establishing of normal schools, were in 1910 continuing to exert an influence on teacher-training institutions. Manual training and agriculture were for many years pet enthusiasms of Pestalozzi and only a lack of facilities and teaching competence kept them for many years out of the FSNS curriculum. Bird study, with its Pestalozzian emphasis on observation, was introduced as a subject in 1910 (possibly reintroduced), and some of the field lessons the Swiss educator promoted were a regular part of the FSNS geography program. The home geography of Pestalozzi was featured as part of a course taught by Virginia Porter. After learning from field excursions about the physiography of Farmington, the students were asked to draw a map of the town, and on these trips other natural phenomena were studied, such as glacial deposits and landslides.

Home Economics—A New Department

In the July, 1911, meeting of the Normal School trustees it was decided to allocate to Farmington a household arts college, while Gorham was to have a special program in manual training for the purpose of training teachers in that subject. In September, Marion C. Ricker was appointed the first director of the FSNS household arts. She was not only to serve Farmington Normal, but supervise any state-wide work that needed the attention of an expert. A graduate of the Boston School of Domestic Science, Miss Ricker continued her education in domestic science at Columbia, receiving a special diploma in 1911. Her employment was based on an annual twelve-month period and her salary was set at $1,500.

In the beginning the household arts subjects were a part of the regular normal school course, and there was no intention of training anyone as an exclusive teacher of sewing, cooking, and allied subjects. In this period, however, household arts became popular in the public schools, and consequently the demand for teachers increased. To meet this demand it was decided in 1913 to establish a program to train future teachers exclusively in household arts. As a result of this decision, in 1914 the first home economics class, consisting of six students, received diplomas. The next year an advanced course was offered and four won diplomas in the expanded program, while the two-year course had six graduates. In 1917 the Smith-Hughes Act was passed to foster vocational education of youth in the high schools. The bill provided financial aid for preparing teachers in agriculture and home economics by requiring each state to provide a sum of money equal to the amount it received from Washington. By 1921 the graduating class numbered 16.[44]

In 1924, with Helen E. Lockwood as dean, a four-year course

was introduced and all shorter courses withdrawn, although a person could teach home economics in Maine after successfully completing three years. Through an act of the 1928 legislature, Farmington Normal was granted the privilege of conferring the B.S. degree on a class of eight who had completed the four-year course.

The Nordica Concert of 1911

The completion of the main building of Farmington Normal provided an auditorium for many school events that in other days were either considered impossible or needed a rented hall. This did not mean that either George Purington or his successor wanted to keep the new assembly hall exclusively for normal school functions. Both were pleased to be able to offer it for important community events. The Nordica concert of 1911 represented just such a time.

During her lifetime, Lillian Nordica, world famous opera star, was to give three concerts in Farmington. The first was in 1878 in the Methodist Church, the second was in Music Hall, and the third was on August 17, 1911, in what was originally Normal Hall but in 1908 had been re-named Merrill Hall (in 1972 it officially became Nordica Auditorium). The original intention was for Nordica to have her 1911 concert in the Methodist Church. This was primarily because her grandfather, "Campmeeting" John Allen, had been an important member of the church and a lively figure in its revivals. His granddaughter thought it would be appropriate in this way to honor his memory. An offer from the Normal School changed her plans. Merrill Hall had a much larger seating capacity than the church, as well as a Steinway piano which, purchased nine or ten years before this event, was probably the best instrument of its kind in any Farmington auditorium.

The Nordica concert was memorable in FSNS history not only for its location but because many people connected with it were, or had been, affiliated in some way or another with Farmington Normal.*

---

* Years later, when the Nordica Association was formed, most of its original members were either graduates or teachers at Farmington Normal. Arthur D. Ingalls became president; later on Myron E. Starbird was selected as vice-president. Some of those on the board of trustees were: Nina D. Palmer, Zilda Brown, Errol Dearborn, Emma Mahoney, Beatrice H. Mitchell, Florence Fogg, Blanche Applebee, Ermo Scott, Agnes Mantor, and Marguerite Emery.

Miss Carolyn Stone, left, and Miss Louise Richards have come down to the station to see students off on the morning train. In the background, Mr. Mallett has a baggage check, probably for someone who is slow or has forgotten.

David H. Knowlton, onetime trustee of the Maine normal schools, introduced Nordica. At intermission a bouquet of flowers was presented to Nordica by Annie W. McLeary, who had been a pianist in George Purington's first glee club, and in 1911 was a teacher in Nordica's alma mater, the New England Conservatory of Music. In the reception that followed the concert, one of the young men who assisted in guiding people around the Belle Gilman estate was Burnham McLeary of the 1905 class. According to *The Chronicle*, the FSNS principal "was in labors abundant for the comfort of performers and audience."

The Building Program (1909–1940)

It had become increasingly apparent, near the end of the Purington administration, that a dormitory was badly needed. During this period the Farmington Normal, more often than not, had the largest number of students of any normal school in Maine, yet it was the only institution of its kind in the State without a dormitory. (In 1898, the year the main building was completed, FSNS attendance figures had jumped in the winter term to 264. This made Farmington, at least for a while, the largest normal school in New England. The main building, with its widely advertised ventilating system and the promise of scientific and gymnastic equipment, had undoubtedly helped to attract students.) By 1910 many of the local citizens had become unwilling to board students, either because the average citizen was more prosperous or because a rise in prices was not being accompanied by a rise in the going rate for board and room. School authorities knew from the experience of other Maine normal schools that the mass purchasing of food, so important a part of dormitory management, would result in reduced costs.

Several months before the death of George Purington, the Normal trustees had voted to present a request to the legislature for $55,000 to cover the cost of a lot and dormitory. On October 12, 1910, the trustees again voted to recommend to the legislature that the sum of $55,000 be appropriated for a Farmington dormitory. By this time the new principal realized that all available state money was going for a new normal school to be located in Machias. In *The Chronicle,* as we have noted, he complained that only those with political considerations could be responsible for still another normal school when the established ones were denied funds for badly needed facilities. Although the legislature was willing to go on record again in 1911 that Farmington needed a dormitory, the frustration of the principal was not lessened when he learned that no funds were available. In 1913 his efforts were finally rewarded when the legislature provided the funds, and soon thereafter a contract for general construction was awarded the lowest bidder, L. E. Bradstreet & Sons, in Hallowell. Their modest figure was $38,943. (The dormitory was designed by Miller and Mayo, Portland architects. W. G. Mallett rejected their first design and held out for a flat roof. He had his way, even though he was assured that such a shape would make the dormitory look like a penitentiary.)

Students arrived a week late for the fall term of 1914 because construction on Purington Hall had been delayed. When they did come, they found an unfinished dormitory, inadequate furniture, and whenever it rained, a quagmire in front. A possibly unprecedented situation prevailed for several weeks when over a hundred girls were bereft of undelivered mirrors. Fire drills, candy pulls, and victrola records seemed to make life bearable in an unfinished dorm. Later in the year, the furniture did come and the most exciting event of all took place—the installation of a piano. For some ten years the matron of Purington was Mrs. L. Estelle Allen. She was both efficient and well liked by the students. (In 1924, with the building of South Hall, now Mallett Hall, Mrs. Allen transferred to South where she did the purchasing for both dormitories. In 1927 board and room were $5.00 a week. The school year consisted of 38 weeks so the total board and room bill was $190.)

In 1921 the Lodge was acquired and until 1939 was used to house about 20 students. It was located on Academy Street next to the Baptist Church. In the beginning, the Lodge was for women, but in the 1930s male enrollment had increased to the point where it was deemed advisable to convert the house into a male dorm. Mrs. Jane Kendrick, aunt of Mrs. Errol Dearborn, was the matron or house mother. (Later on removal of the Lodge made it possible for the area to be used as a parking space for college commuters.)

Home Economics Buildings

In the earliest year of the home economics program, the sewing classes were conducted in Room 23 at the Normal School building. The cooking classes met at the Annex, a cottage on the present site of Purington Hall. After the first dormitory was opened for business, sewing classes used the reception rooms where cutting tables were set up. (This helped to thaw out some of those who had nearly frozen in the poorly heated rooms of the Annex.) The trustees voted in 1915 to purchase a better house, directly across the street from Purington Hall. It was renovated and the barn remodeled into cooking and sewing laboratories. The so-called Cottage was ready for occupancy in January 1916, and despite its modest name and the outward appearance of house and barn, the refurbished and converted areas were well lighted and had the latest equipment. An elegant touch was applied to the exterior in 1935 with the dedication of the Mary Palmer Garden, located in the rear of the Cottage. The Cottage became a practice house for prospective mothers and home economics teachers when in 1927, Leo Cote, the first Cottage baby, arrived. In succeeding years an annual baby replacement became an important part of the program. In 1930 the Cottage was first used entirely as a practice home with four bedrooms for students and a nursery.

In 1929 a house on South Street, which had been used as a hospital, was sold to the State. It was to serve as the junior-senior home economics dormitory until removed to make way for the college library. It was known as Palmer Hall in memory of Mary Palmer, a member of the home economics faculty from 1924 to 1929.

The Willows

In 1870, Hannibal Belcher, a prominent Farmington citizen, had built The Willows as a private school for girls, with his daughter Lucy in charge. The school was maintained for only some five years, and then The Willows was unused for a considerable length of time. Shortly after the 1886 fire destroyed or damaged the three local hotels, The Willows property was bought by a corporation, refurbished, and opened as a hotel. In the early 1890s several Normal School events, including banquets, were held there. As the years went by, however, it failed to prosper and for many years it was again unoccupied. In 1923, mainly as a result of a big jump in the school enrollment,* it was purchased and put to use as a dormitory.

---

* In 1923 the principal found himself inundated by applications for admission to FSNS. Whereas in 1922 there had been an enrollment of

For nearly fifteen years it was to provide board and room for 65 to 75 students. Mrs. John Mahoney was its popular matron and Mr. John Mahoney was the man in charge. The Willows students became famous for their *esprit de corps,* and many of them felt sorry for those who had to live in other dorms.

South Hall

In 1924 South Hall was built.** It was constructed, except for a few interior modifications, on the same lines as Purington Hall. Moreover, a delay in occupancy, such as had occurred at Purington, was even longer and more inconvenient. The principal's diary for October 7, 1924, reflected his frustration: "Progress on the dormitory is very slow, long waits for the finish and plaster." On December 22, he wrote: "Freeze-ups at South Hall. Mrs. Allen's illness retards the work there." On December 30, there were still more difficulties: "Students return. Electricians behind on contract. Students move into unlighted rooms." A principal's life was not always a merry one—three days later, a fire at The Willows routed him from bed at 5 A.M. Fortunately the damage was slight.

Gymnasium

Normal schools throughout the country have always emphasized the importance of physical education, and Farmington was no ex-

---

about 290, in 1923 the attendance figure was close to 350. A new dormitory, scheduled for completion in 1924, was only in the planning stage. This meant that there was an urgent need for living quarters for an unprecedented number of students. The principal decided to gamble and buy The Willows with his own money, hoping for a later reimbursement from the State. The gamble paid off but not without a price. The Willows was a wooden structure that represented a major fire threat. Of course everything possible was done to prevent serious trouble, but no steps taken could entirely eliminate worrying about the possibilities of a disastrous fire. In the winter of 1925 two fires did break out, but neither one was very destructive and the second one was put out by John Mahoney. No further trouble was experienced, but the threat did nothing for the principal's peace of mind.

** After Mrs. Allen left Purington to relocate at South Hall, Mrs. Lena S. Caldwell became the new matron at Purington. After a short time she resigned and Mrs. Minnie Mantor, mother of Prof. Agnes Mantor, was named to fill the vacancy. At the June, 1940, meeting of the trustees, Carl P. Merrill prevailed upon his colleagues to re-name South Hall and so it became Mallett Hall.

ception. The gymnasium was well equipped and served a worthy cause for many years. As the years went by, however, the need for a separate building for indoor sports and physical education became obvious. Not only was the basement gym used by an increasing number of FSNS students, but by an increasing number of Model School pupils. In 1931, under the efficient and enthusiastic leadership of Errol L. Dearborn, funds were solicited from the alumni for a new gymnasium. Their contributions and supplementary funds appropriated by the legislature made possible the Alumni Gymnasium. Even though it was rather quickly outgrown, it served as a home for some very successful basketball teams.

New Training School Building

From its inception in 1869, the Model School, or training school, increased in size until in 1930 it had about 250 children, who occupied the greatest number of the first-floor rooms in the main building. (As one entered through the front door, the room at the right was reserved for FSNS music classes. On the left, in a room now filled with offices, was a large area for FSNS art classes. The remainder of the first floor was used by the training school.) The number of FSNS students had gone over 450 in 1928 and the combined increase in both grade and Normal School students resulted in a desperate need for more space. The principal of FSNS prevailed upon the Town of Farmington to accept a plan which provided that the town build a new school building on Quebec Street with the State equipping it. The implementation of this arrangement meant the merging of the Town School (located where the community building is now) and the training school. The new school was opened in 1932 and served all the children of the village, who then numbered about 350. In 1942 the Farmington School Board renamed it the Mallett School, and Arthur D. Ingalls from 1932 to 1946 was its first principal. Emma Mahoney and Julia Cox continued to be supervisors of FSNS student teachers.

Semi-Centennial of FSNS Observed

On August 24, 1914, just fifty years to a day from the first meeting of the first class in Beal's Hall, the founding of Farmington State Normal School was observed. The opening event of the program was the Alumni dinner, held in Drummond Hall. It was not large enough to take care of everyone at one sitting, so the after-dinner speaking was delayed until later in the afternoon when people gathered in the old Merrill Hall. (Purington Hall was being built. For many years after its completion the alumni were to be accommodated there.)

George F. Stackpole, the lone male member of the 1866 class (who was awarded his diploma in 1890) was introduced by the principal, and the man who missed his chance to deliver a graduation part in 1866 at last had his chance to address an FSNS audience.* He told the alumni of the gathering in Beal's Hall fifty years before and spoke of himself as a good example of "Kelsey's Menagerie," as some of the irreverent called the student body during the first principal's management. He then went on to pay high tribute to nearly everything and everybody connected with FSNS over a fifty-year period.

The feature of the Semi-Centennial came when Clarence H. Knowlton, FSNS '94 and Harvard A.B., son of David H. Knowlton and Clara Hinckley Knowlton, presented for the alumni a bas relief in bronze commemorating George C. Purington and his twenty-six years of service to the Farmington Normal School. The inscription on it was taken from the tribute to George C. Purington delivered by Richard H. Clapp on May 9, 1909. It read: "George C. Purington, Principal of this School from 1883 to 1909: Knightly Spirit, Inspiring Teacher, Loyal Friend." The bronze gift was another achievement of Cyrus E. Dallin, the noted sculptor from Boston.**

---

* George F. Stackpole was doing splendidly even before George C. Purington in 1890 prevailed upon the trustees to grant him a diploma. He received an A.B. and A.M. from Dartmouth and had a successful career in Riverhead, N.Y., as a lawyer and financier. He wrote a book on his travels in the United States and abroad, and sent in 1912 a complimentary copy to the Farmington Normal library. Unfortunately it has been lost. In a letter to the *Chronicle* in 1890, George Stackpole commented on his delayed diploma: "In your paper received today I see that I was graduated from the Normal School at the last Commencement. I venture to say that in the history of the school I am the only one that it took 26 years to graduate."

** Cyrus Edwin Dallin was born in Springville, Utah, in 1861. He studied at the Ecole des Beaux Arts, Paris, 1889, and the Julian Academy in Paris. He was the recipient of many prizes for his work. These included a gold medal, St. Louis Exposition in 1904; first prize competition for Soldiers' and Sailors' monument, Syracuse, N.Y., 1906; gold

A series of tributes to the character and services of George C. Purington followed the remarks of Clarence H. Knowlton. The first in this series was delivered by Hortense Hersom, '94, principal of the primary department in the Sidwell Friends School, Washington, D.C., and head of Camp Abena at Belgrade Lakes. She spoke about her former principal as a loyal friend; Lillian I. Lincoln commented on him as an inspiring teacher; and Richard H. Clapp* concluded the tributes by describing his knightly spirit.

The Semi-Centennial exercises came to a close with an address by Warren C. Philbrook of Waterville, associate justice of the Maine Supreme Court. What he said that night was not as memorable as his coming back to an institution as honored guest which he had left so abruptly in 1883. In the spring of that year, it may be remembered, he participated in a rebellion against the arbitrary power, as he saw it, of the FSNS principal. Now, in this anniversary finale, he was proving again that time is likely to heal all wounds.

A *Decade of Accelerating Change* (1910–1920)

In this decade a village such as Farmington underwent initially a slow, later an accelerating change in its activities and mores. The 1920s have been credited with producing a postwar social revolution, but the preceding decade prepared the way. In 1910 the movies were too primitive for even the least sophisticated and the automobile was considered a mere plaything. By 1914 the movies were setting the styles throughout the country in manners and fashions. In the same year, a substantial number of people, even with the prospect of higher taxes, were clamoring for the better roads that they eventually enjoyed. By the end of the decade the assembly line and

---

medal, Panama Exposition, 1915. He may be best known to New Englanders for his "Appeal to the Great Spirit" in front of the Museum of Fine Arts. Dallin was a fellow of the American Academy of Arts and Sciences; member of the National Institute of Arts and Letters, Royal Society Arts (London) and National Sculpture Society. He died in 1944. He was at Farmington in 1914 for the installation of his work.

* In 1916 Richard H. Clapp left Farmington for a church in Brattleboro, Vt.; after serving there he was pastor of a Congregational church in Northampton, Mass.; his last twenty years of preaching took place in the United Church of New Haven. Ruth, one of his two daughters, came back to Farmington in the 1920s and was a very active member of the FSNS class of 1929.

mass production of cars would bring the farm and village closer together. Farmington Normal students, in this decade, were beginning to lose the provincialism of former days.

In 1914 they could see in Music Hall any one of these movies for fifteen cents: "A Good Little Devil," starring Mary Pickford, "The Great Python Robbery," "The Tower of Terror," "From Gutter to Footlight," and "The Outlaw's Revenge and Remorse." Those who were partial to historical extravaganza could see "The Last Days of Pompeii," consisting of eight reels, 260 big scenes that included the eruption of Vesuvius. (Admission 25 cents.) On December 1, 1914, all those who liked danger and suspense could go to Music Hall and see the opening scenes of "The Perils of Pauline." James O'Neill, the father of Eugene, was thrilling moviegoers in the "Count of Monte Cristo." The more affluent could go by special train to Lewiston for a D. W. Griffith spectacular, "The Birth of a Nation"; certainly with such a show as that the movies were coming of age.

By 1914 the primitive days of the automobiles were vanishing. All models were less costly than they had been. The average list price, including the most expensive as well as the cheapest, was $2,347 as compared with $2,585 in 1913. The Ford touring car had been reduced from $600 to $550. The runabout that sold in 1913 for $500 sold in 1914 for $450. Henry Ford had just announced that he was to pay a minimum of $5.00 a day to his workers and this kind of wage would make it easier to purchase a Ford. (As the years went on, the Ford would sell for considerably less than these quoted prices.) The number of cars in the United States in 1914 had doubled since 1911 and the number was steadily accelerating. Maine citizens were impressed to get the information that in 1913 over $1,500,000 was spent in the State for ordinary repairs and the maintenance of roads. The Maine legislature, in 1914, voted to build seven miles of road in each county.

Students in the Normal School and other institutions were becoming more aware of the dangers connected with automobile travel. Nearly all had known some one of their contemporaries who had been killed in an accident, and the older generation had its share of victims. But it was not as a threat to life that the automobile was considered a major factor in the changing times. Educational institutions were to learn in this decade the complications arising from a marked increase in human mobility. Many members of the older generation ridiculed the sedan as a mobile bedroom, and much to the eventual distress of anxious parents, that was what the sedan oftentimes turned out to be. Temptation on wheels, plus the long and passionate kisses on the screen, seemed to threaten the accepted morality of centuries.

The twenties have oftentimes been referred to as the "jazz age," but the new music, developing from the old ragtime, was beginning to attract attention in the 1910–1920 decade. Alexander's Ragtime Band was a 1911 favorite and the first recording of the Original Dixieland Jazz Band took place in 1917. In 1915, Vernon and Irene Castle gave a powerful stimulus to ballroom dancing. Their grace and charm helped popularize the new fox-trot, and jazz was enlisted to support the gyrations involved in this ballroom exercise. Dance pavilions, that could be reached by using the new cars, first appeared in this decade.

During these years the theater was attaining greater respectability in the smaller towns, and this was reflected in some FSNS activities. In 1916, in place of the traditional commencement concert performed by professionals, the students performed Shakespearian plays under the guidance of Mrs. Nina D. Palmer. In 1917 another change seemed to be in order, partly because of it being a war year. Consequently, a pageant entitled "Patriotism," was given. Written by Lillian I. Lincoln and staged by Nina D. Palmer, it used over a 100 students in episodes of American history.

The Puritan sabbath was gradually losing its religious vigor. In the early days, many students spent the greater part of Sunday in church. Now, although everyone was encouraged to attend one or more services, there were no mandatory provisions in the rules for church attendance. Near the end of the decade, the sabbatarians were dealt a staggering blow when the students attended a movie benefit on Sunday (Near East Relief). There were even those who went to Togus in order to see baseball games that were legal because they were played on federal property.

With all the changes that occurred in the 1910–20 decade, it should be remembered that some, if not nearly all, features of FSNS stayed about the same. Dormitory rules for women were not substantially changed from 1914 to the 1940s. (The rules were liberalized mildly in the late 1930s for third-year students.) There was no unusual increase in enrollment during this decade, so it was still possible for the principal and a few faculty members to know, usually by the first name, everyone in the student body. The automobile was becoming more popular, but it had not yet joined the ranks of the indispensables. Students, in order to arrive and leave Farmington, were largely dependent on the railroad, which they used sparingly. Consequently, few students departed for home on weekends and this resulted in a continuation of the traditional socials. With the addition of Purington Hall, a greater degree of camaraderie developed because over half the students ate together in its dining room. Thanksgiving dinner was well attended and festive. Chapel exercises were compulsory, daily at 8 A.M. The memorization of mottoes was required for these daily sessions, and if the graduates are to be trusted, most of them look back with nostalgia in recalling their weekly precepts. An example of student days long gone was described in the June 15, 1912, *Franklin Journal*:

> The graduating class of the State Normal enjoyed the annual class day on Wednesday at the Poland Spring House. The trip proved one of much pleasure although the weather conditions were not of the best. The dinner was served at the famous Poland Spring House and the management made extra efforts to add to the entertainment of the guests. The return to Farmington was made on the afternoon train and almost the entire student body was at the railroad station to welcome them back.

FSNS During the War Years

Although the United States, until April 1917, was a noncombatant in the First World War, there was a noticeable FSNS emphasis, before we entered the conflict, on patriotic and martial themes. Agnes Mantor, as the 1915 valedictorian, spoke on "The Spirit of America"; "The Star Spangled Banner" was being sung with increasing frequency; and both the Normal and Model school students were starting off the day with the pledge to the flag. After the United States entered the war, it was immediately reflected in school activities. Recitals and fairs were given at FSNS for the benefit of the Red Cross; Model School children, and Normals too, began to save their money for thrift and war stamps. The State Superintendent got into the act by proclaiming Liberty Day to encourage the sale of bonds.

Normal School alumni played important roles in the patriotic mass meetings in Farmington which were a part of a nation-wide series. The principal speaker at the May, 1918, meeting was Dr. Donald B. Cragin, FSNS '95, graduate of Harvard Medical, and medical director of the Aetna Life Insurance Company. Principal Mallett presided over a June, 1918, rally in which these war aims were advanced: (1) To win the war against autocracy; (2) to make the world safe for democracy and democracy safe for the world; (3) to secure for nations—small and great—safety, justice, and equal economic opportunity; (4) to establish a League of Nations. Local orators were asked to speak four minutes between movie reels or the acts of plays. Their audiences were urged to Hooverize and save their peach stones for use in gas warfare. Each speaker flayed the Kaiser and his Huns and described the horrors of a German victory. Frank W. Butler, FSNS '87, was in charge of this program.

Unfortunately, the war period had its more somber side. In October 1918, Farmington students and citizens were informed of the death of Lieut. Thaddeus Roderick. At the 1917 graduation he had returned from military training to receive his diploma. He was the first local person to be awarded one in uniform and his appearance was greeted with a standing ovation. Over a year later, in the bloody battle of St. Mihiel, Lieut. Roderick was killed while in command of a platoon of machine gunners. In April 1922, his remains were returned to Farmington and a memorial service was held for him in the old Armory.*

General Pershing Comes to Town

In 1918, 1919, and 1920, influenza and its after-effects were widespread and lethal. Although the Normal School was fortunate in having few serious cases, at various times in these three years, the attendance was drastically reduced. In addition to the flu, the Model School, in the spring of 1919 had several cases of scarlet fever. By June of 1920, the flu epidemic was over, the boys had returned from France (a majority had come back the previous year), and the post-

---

* Thaddeus L. Roderick was born in Farmington, April 17, 1893, a son of Joseph and Mary Roderick. He graduated from the Farmington High School and entered UMO but transferred later to Farmington Normal. The day of his graduation he married Dorothy McKeen of Strong. The local legion post was named in his honor.

war mood was to celebrate the deliverance from war and disease. The opportunity soon came.

On June 4, 1920, the citizens of Farmington and FSNS students had an unusual opportunity to pay their respects to a genuine war hero of international stature. This event was made possible after General George McL. Presson, adjutant general of Maine from 1915 to 1921, found out that General John J. Pershing was planning a trip to some of the Maine cities. Anxious for his home town to be honored by a Pershing visit, he talked the former leader of the American army in France into including Farmington in his itinerary. General Pershing accepted the invitation and General Presson was able to acquire the use of FSNS grounds and building.

Among those accompanying General Pershing were: Governor Carl E. Milliken, Adjutant General George McL. Presson, Colonel George C. Marshall, an aide to General Pershing, Colonel Albert Greelaw, department commander of the American Legion, James S. Boyle, adjutant, and the Hon. George W. Norton of the governor's council. (The presence of George C. Marshall that day has remained a little known fact about Farmington history. His appearance here made it possible later on to say that two future five-star generals were on the Normal School stage on June 4, 1920.)

Two of the local Maine legislators extended official greetings to the distinguished group. (They were Wilfred McLeary, father of two FSNS graduates, and Whiting Butler, a brother of three FSNS graduates.) General Pershing proved to be a gracious guest, and there was an exchange of felicitous remarks between him and the FSNS principal. The latter said that instead of imitating the medieval practice of giving General Pershing the key to the town, since everyone knew he had the freedom of it anyway, it was decided to give him a Sawyer print of a local landscape. General Pershing was effusive in his thanks and expressed his special interest in Farmington Normal because he said that he had attended a Missouri normal school before being tapped for West Point. When the chorus, under the direction of Franca C. Ingalls, sang "To Thee, O Country," General Pershing asked for an encore and the request was granted. Barbara Gammon, a daughter of Farmington Normal graduates, presented the General with a bouquet of flowers and then the students lined up to shake hands with him. As the party left the grounds, the girls sang to the tune of "Boola-boola":

> General Pershing, General Pershing, here's to you,
> We are singing, praises ringing,
> We will never find your equal,
> General Pershing, here's to you.*

A few days after the Pershing visit Farmington Normal presented a pageant commemorating the centennial year of the State of Maine. Again it was Lillian I. Lincoln who arranged and wrote the presentations. She and other faculty members selected material from noted Maine authors, including: Longfellow, Laura E. Richards, Sarah Orne Jewett, Kate Douglas Wiggin, and Harriet Beecher Stowe. Nina D. Palmer helped stage the pageant and Franca Ingalls directed the music. Her star soloist was Gertrude Carleton (Turner), a contralto of unusual ability. *The Franklin Journal* recognized her talents: "It is no disparagement to others to say that Miss Carleton is by far the most finished soloist in the Normal School in many years, and that her graduation with the present class will be a distinct loss to the musical forces of the community as well as of the school." General Pershing had told her she sang like an angel and that was praise enough coming from a five-star general.

---

* The kind of adulation bestowed on the General reached a climax in the 1920s after Lindbergh flew the Atlantic. There was a counter-movement to this hero worship, however, and the best examples of this were to be found in the writings of the irreverent and iconoclastic Henry L. Mencken. Three months after the General visited Farmington, Mencken wrote an article for the *New Republic* in which he commented on the General's campaign ribbons.

"Like General Grant, he is without a sword. Like General Grant he wears a sort of soldier's blouse for a coat. Like General Grant, he employs shoulder straps to indicate to the Army who he is. But there is something more. On the left breast of this officer there blazes so brilliant a mass of color that, as the sun strikes it and the flash bangs my eyes, I wink, catch my breath and sneeze. There are two long strips, each starting at the sternum and disappearing into the shadows of the axilla—every hue in the rainbow, the spectroscope, the kaleidoscope— imperial purples, sforzando reds, wild Irish greens, romantic blues, loud yellows and oranges, rich maroons, sentimental pinks, all the halftones from ultra-violet to infrared, all the vibrations from the impalpable to the unendurable. A gallant Soldat indeed! How he would shame a circus ticket-wagon if he wore all the medals and badges, the stars and crosses, the pendants and lavallieres, that go with those ribbons!"

School Organizations and Activities (1910–1920)

At the beginning of the spring term in 1915, a Camp Fire group known as Soangetaha was formed under the direction of Carolyn A. Stone. Such organizations did not have the secret hocus-pocus of Greek-letter fraternities or sororities, but ceremony and symbolism served as satisfactory substitutes. The ceremonial meetings took the form of an Indian Council Fire at which each girl wore her ceremonial gown and headband. Each Camp Fire group, as well as each member, had a symbolic name and emblem. The law of the Camp Fire was: Seek beauty. Give service. Pursue knowledge. Be trustworthy. Hold on to health. Glorify work. Be happy.

Eventually there were four FSNS Camp Fire groups: the Soangetaha, the Pierpole, the Witawentin, and the Aokiya. By the mid-twenties the fires of these organizations, with one exception, were either burning low or had gone out completely. By 1926 there were only two Camp Fire groups and one of these, the Witawentin, acknowledged in the yearbook that it had not been active during the year. Soangetaha, under the guidance of Mrs. Errol Dearborn, was more active and vital than one remaining rival, but the day of the Camp Fire was approaching its end. By 1930 it was time for a different kind of organization to take over some of the social life of the school.

The decade from 1910 to 1920 was not particularly eventful in FSNS athletic events. The girls had basketball teams with the sections in the two classes engaging in intramural rivalry. There were so few males, however, that even in such a game as basketball, FSNS had to borrow a Farmington High athlete in 1914 to enable the small number of FSNS males to engage in informal basketball.

In contrast to the enfeebled state of athletics, musical clubs were thriving and consisted of three groups: the orchestra, mandolin club, and choral society or glee club. By 1920, however, the mandolin club had just about strummed itself out of business, although it had a short revival in 1927. Successors of the mandolin were the ukelele, banjo and guitar. Their popularity with the young has been reminiscent of the mandolin craze, but they were never used by groups of twenty and thirty in the manner of the mandolin clubs.

On March 10, 1916, Home Ec students organized the Home Economics Club, and social and business meetings were held, initially, with regularity. In the mid-twenties this club became increasingly active and held monthly meetings featuring appropriate speakers. Thanksgiving and Christmas were observed by helping out some of the needy families of the area. The club raised money in a multitude of ways—movie benefits, weekly sandwich sales, and the sales of Christmas cards and candy. The money was used for furniture and fixtures for the Cottage, and the residual amount went to charity. One of the most active members of this club in the mid-twenties, and president in 1925–26, was Alfreda Skillin, who was to return later to the department for many years of effective teaching.

During the last forty years of Normal School history, the Christian Association was a thriving organization. In the twenties its Get Acquainted Social helped the homesick and shy. The first great event of the season was the C. A. Fair which, on a Saturday afternoon, made the old Merrill Hall look like a huge emporium with booths for exhibits of manual training, sewing, pictures, candy, and other goodies. Weekly services were held and inspirational talks were given. The Association raised considerable money during the course of a school year and spent it on worthy causes. An annual contribution went to the Seacoast Mission and the Red Cross. The Association helped keep the school medical cabinet supplied and bought many quality magazines for the library. The faculty were encouraged to attend certain conferences with the promise of C. A. financial assistance. The officials of C. A. had their expenses paid to attend an annual conference of C. A. organizations held at Camp Maqua in Poland, Maine.

The 1920s at FSNS

Normal school principals throughout the country were traditionally charged with carrying a full teaching load as well as attending to all administrative details. Before the attendance went up sharply in the 1920s, the FSNS principal did not think of this combination of duties as unduly burdensome; in fact he liked the variety of his job and would have had it no other way. Like others in similar institutions, he assumed responsibility for both the important and the trivial. Part of this was probably his fault because of reluctance to assign duties to others, but wherever the blame lay, the fact was he was engrossed in a myriad of details. When the dormitory pipes overflowed or froze, he was called; when rule-breakers were discovered or suspected of being engaged in their nefarious business, he was called; and so he was when a janitor or chef had been drinking too much, or a light was seen in The Willows during vacation; no problem was likely to be finally solved without his involvement. The principal was not only the monarch of all he surveyed, but the busiest of the hired hands.

Of all his many duties, the most disagreeable, by far, was to deal with rule-breaking. In the 1920s this perennial problem was taking on unprecedented proportions at FSNS, reflecting as it did a sharp increase in attendance, a postwar desire to throw off the Puritan restraints of generations, a reopening of the Abbott School, and the increase in opportunities for misconduct. Some blamed the war for the changes and took comfort in the thought that the nation would recover its sanity and morality in due season. (This would be accomplished after the American soldier had readopted his native mores after temporarily losing his moral bearings in France.) Others, more pessimistic, reasoned that the war had only accelerated inevitable changes in American life.

A social revolution, little suspected by most, was certainly developing in the 1910–1920 decade, but the storm broke in the 1920s, a decade which has had so many inadequate or misleading adjectives applied to it. The FSNS faculty, like other conservative groups, were alarmed when the women began to bob their hair, shorten their skirts, and reduce the remainder of their wearing apparel. (It is hardly necessary to say that this drastic change in youth's appearance was not to be the last occasion for the older generation's becoming censorious and worried.) Coinciding with the changes in our national mores, there had been a very modest liberalizing of FSNS rules, especially as they were concerned with the conduct of young ladies and gentlemen. Along with the more liberal attitude toward the socializing of males and females, however, no corresponding alterations were made in dormitory rules. On weekdays, the women of the school still had to be in their rooms by 7:30; on weekends, there was a 9:30 curfew, with 10:00 possible for unusual occasions, such as an extra long movie.

By 1921, W. G. Mallett had concluded that he needed help in diagnosing and prescribing for an unprecedented rash of rule-breaking. He told the editor of the first yearbook in FSNS history that watching to make sure students were obeying the rules was making him old before his time. So he enlisted their support by creating,

At the George Washington birthday masquerade (February 22, 1915), Principal Mallett and Miss Carolyn Stone represent George and Martha Washington.

with their advice, a student council. This consisted of three from the first-year class and three from the second-year class. With their aid the principal hoped to reduce the number of scofflaws. The experiment in self-government was welcomed by the students, and the principal was to enjoy this opportunity to talk with them and get their points of view about the indiscretions of their colleagues. (Even members of the student council were caught doing such heinous things as holding birthday parties after lights were supposed to be out.) The new student organization did not usher in Utopia, but both the principal and students agreed that it was preferable to one-man rule.

Faculty Changes

In June 1921, it was announced that Hortense M. Merrill was resigning from the faculty after thirty-seven years of service.* Soon after this it was learned that Charles S. Preble** was to join the faculty and offer courses in geography, biological science, and U.S. history. Such important changes in the faculty were rare and served to underline the long service of the teaching staff. Katherine Abbott, appointed by George C. Purington in 1901, was a faculty member for twenty-seven years; Virginia A. Porter, a Purington appointment in 1907, stayed at Farmington for thirty-two years; Carolyn A. Stone was a teacher and then dean, in all for thirty-five years; Franca C. Ingalls, in 1920, was prevailed upon to return for a decade of effective music teaching, and Errol L. Dearborn, the lone male in the

---

* Soon after her resignation from the FSNS faculty, Hortense M. Merrill married Herbert J. Keith. He had graduated from Farmington Normal in 1880, and taught at the Abbott School. (In 1901 he had married Harriet P. Young, FSNS 1881, who was a member of the FSNS faculty for fifteen years. She had died in 1919.) In 1923, while the couple were on a European trip, he died, bringing to a close a very successful business career. He had developed a large industry of preserving and drying eggs and had become an expert on egg production and egg markets throughout the world.

** Charles S. Preble, a graduate of Wesleyan, came to Farmington from Old Town, where for three years, he had been principal of the high school. It was understood that his primary interests were biological sciences, nature study, and geography. The U.S. history assignment was temporary.

class of 1918, after graduating from the University of Maine was asked to return in 1922 to substitute for Arthur M. Thomas who, in 1922–23, taught in the Yale Mission School in Changsha, China. On his retirement in 1953, Errol L. Dearborn was president of the Farmington State Teachers College.

Some School Activities in the 1920s

The first FSNS yearbook made its appearance in 1922 and the person most responsible for it was Arline Coffin. (Her brother, Robert P. T. Coffin, in 1936 won the Pulitzer Prize in poetry.) She was the editor-in-chief, and this first effort was called *Effesseness*, as it continued to be until the end of the Normal School period. The 1922 yearbook, as well as its immediate successors, had a literary section, alumni notes, and detailed descriptions of the year's events and clubs. The first yearbook was dedicated to the principal, and Arline Coffin wrote in the Foreword: "We sincerely hope that the effort we have so gladly put forth in producing this book is not entirely in vain and that the *Effesseness* of 1922 will be the foundation whereon many, many, more successful ones will stand in the years to come." (The first editorial board of the publication consisted of the following: Nellie Flinn, Leora Tomlinson, Vey Merrill, Marion Merrill, Myrtle Beckler, Addie Reed, Sebra Bicknell, Annie Day, Hortense Mackay, Arline Coffin, Julia Cox, Alice Coffin, and Lillian Archibald. Alice Coffin was the twin sister of Arline. Julia Cox was also on the student council. She would play other roles in FSNS history.)

The 1921–22 school calendar, as it was presented in the first *Effesseness*, is called upon here to give a picture of the FSNS which was so remote from the 1970s in both time and life styles.

September 13. Fall term opens with 250 in attendance, 155 of whom are members of the entering classes.

September 16. Reception to entering classes by the Christian Association in Merrill Hall.

September 19. School goes to the slate quarry for a corn roast.

September 20–22. Franklin County Fair. Two half-holidays. Baby dolls a favorite prize with the students.

October 11. Miss Abbott and Mrs. Ingalls attend the Maine Music Festival at Portland.

October 12. Columbus Day but Columbus is not remembered here.

October 17–21. Mid-term exams.

October 26–28. Maine Teachers' Convention at Portland. All the teachers except Mr. Preble and Miss Abbott attend.

October 29. Hallowe'en Masquerade Social in Merrill Hall.

November 4. The Elsie Illingworth Concert Co. of London give a concert.

November 11. Armistice Day Holiday. Very wintry. The Germans should have surrendered earlier in the season.

November 18. Franklin County teachers in convention in Merrill Hall.

November 24–27. Thanksgiving recess, dividing the school into the envied and envying.

November 25. Thanksgiving dancing party in Purington Hall.

December 3. Christian Association Fair. Fine patronage. Glee Club's first appearance for the year. Recitation and dramatic skits add to the evening's entertainment.

December 13. Harold Proctor Concert C.

December 9–15. Final term exams.

December 15. Term closes for Christmas vacation.

January 3. Winter term opens.

January 11. Bird lecture by Charles Crawford Gorst. Remarkable imitation of bird songs.

January 13. Candy pull given by Mother Allen.

January 20. Christian Association gives a straw ride. A delicious supper followed.

January 28. Gymnasium dance.

February 2. Lecture on Russia by Eugene Gruenbaum.

February 6–11. Mid-term exams.

February 11. Valentine social given by the Domestic Science girls.

February 28. Mr. Mallett tells at the C. A. of former members of the Association.

March 6. Chapman concert, W. R. Chapman presenting Julia Floyd, soprano; Gabriel Engel, violinist; Everett Bishop, baritone bass.

March 7. The Chapman concert company the guests of the school.

March 10. *The Little Shepherd of Kingdom Come* dramatization presented by a New York company.

March 15. Concert by the musical clubs of Bowdoin Col-

lege in Merrill Hall under the auspices of the High School seniors.

March 16.   The winter term closes.

March 18.   Massachusetts Alumni Reunion attended by several of the teachers.

March 29.   The spring term opens.

April 17.   The school passes before the bier of Lieut. Thaddeus Roderick of the class of 1917, killed in France.

April 29.   Annual exhibition by the Training School. A little
girl dancing as David danced draws the fire of a local domine.

May 4.   The Salvation Army band from Lewiston gives the
school a short concert on the front lawn.

May 6.   The Home Economics Club gives a successful fair
and food sale at the Cottage.

May 12.   The class of 1922 appropriately observes Arbor
Day by exercises at Merrill Hall and by planting a tree at Purington Hall.

May 12–22.   Miss Abbott and Miss Porter take a trip for
study and recreation under a gift from the Keith Fund, Inc.

May 22.   We are much honored by a visit from Governor
Baxter and Hon. Augustus O. Thomas.

FSNS Mottoes: Nineteenth Century Relic

Daily chapel exercises opened the school day at the Normal
School, and many alumni have remembered those early morning
sessions primarily because of the mottoes. After a short religious program, the principal handed out to the students a quotation of wisdom and guidance which they were expected to memorize. This
custom went so far back in FSNS history that time has concealed
the origin of it.* Records have been preserved of George C. Purington's mottoes, and the practice may have started with C. C. Rounds,
or even Gage or Kelsey.

By the 1920s the motto exercise was as outmoded as the bustle
or hoop skirt. W. G. Mallett, along with others, realized the limited

---

* The memorizing of mottoes was common practice in grade schools
from about 1835 to 1900 when schoolchildren read McGuffey's and
similar readers. These books were full of aphorisms, epigrams, "horse-
sense" philosophy, and particularly emphasized morals and manners.
Judged by the number of people who have claimed they were set on
the right path by McGuffey's quoted precepts, doubt is cast on the
assertion of those who put no store by this kind of approach.

THE FSNS FACULTY AROUND 1916: front left: Louise Richards (Ellis), eighth grade teacher and assistant supervisor of student teaching. Second row (left to right): Franca Camp Ingalls, music teacher; Hortense Merrill (Keith), English literature; Lillian I. Lincoln, supervisor of student teaching; Principal W. G. Mallett; Florence L. Walker, first teacher at Farmington of manual training; Cora Chase, home economics. Back row (l to r): Katherine Abbott, art teacher; Virginia Porter, geography and English; Marion Ricker, first head of the home economics department; Carolyn Stone, first dean of women (at a later date); Inez Rolfe; Arthur M. Thomas, assistant principal and science instructor.

effectiveness of teaching by precept, but he was reluctant to let go of this traditional feature of normal school life. Students were willing to go along with it for several reasons. It was not too onerous a task to learn a short motto and it gave dormitory inmates another excuse to get together to memorize the mottoes.* (Students were allowed to visit in other rooms from 9:30 to 10:00 P.M.) In 1940, as a retirement gift, the Lambda Epsilon sorority indicated an affection for motto memorization by having all the mottoes they had learned collected, typed, and bound in an attractive volume. At the last chapel they presented this appropriate present to the principal, on the verge of his retirement.

By 1940 W. G. had spent over thirty years selecting mottoes, which naturally reflected many of his personal views and much of his philosophy. There were quotations on books, music, manners, health, luck, teaching and teachers, and general philosophical reflections. There were even quotations which warned that it was by imitation and not by precept that we learn anything. In this way the principal was attempting to disarm those who were fearful he did not know that. Emerson contributed the greatest number of quotations, but Goethe, Kant, Confucius, Socrates, and others gave the mottoes a universality in both time and place.

Those on education and teaching reflected Mallett's failure to read many of the books on pedagogy which were being published in the 1920s and 1930s, especially at the Columbia Teachers College. Many of the ideas represented in the motto book were popular among professional educators but some were not. Among those which were, was a quotation from Kant: "To develop in each individual all the perfection of which he is susceptible is the object of education." Margaret Fuller contributed a motto not popular during the progressive era: "Drudgery is as necessary to call out the treasure of the mind as harrowing and planting those of the earth." A quotation that pleased many different schools of thought was from Winterburn, who wrote: "Some old philosopher remarked that in dealing with children he found it well to be a little deaf, a little dumb, and a little blind." It is doubtful that the leaders in educational measurements would have subscribed to the conclusion reached by Dr. Arn-

---

* Many of them found enjoyment in paraphrasing the better known mottoes. An example of this was in the 1925 yearbook: "A wise old owl sat in an oak/The more he saw the more he spoke." W. G. Mallett.

old, of Rugby: "The difference between one boy and another is not so much in talent as in energy."

There were several mottoes on the subject of luck. For many years, children were told by Horatio Alger that pluck beats luck, but more intellectually respectable persons were called upon to promote that idea in FSNS chapels. Emerson wrote: "Small men believe in luck, in circumstances. Strong men believe in cause and effect." Another was by Spurgeon: "Good luck will help a man over the ditch if he jumps hard." It was inevitable that Ben Franklin would be quoted on the subject: "Industry is Fortune's right hand and Frugality is her left." Voltaire was called upon: "Chance is a word void of sense; nothing can exist without a cause." Finally another Emerson quotation: "Good luck is only another name for tenacity of purpose."

Normal schools were promoters of good manners. In a few teacher-training institutions including Farmington, manners was at one time a part of the curriculum. A large majority of the students were from rural areas where their teachers had oftentimes not only been ignorant but rude. Certainly normal schools were justified in administering an antidote for this, and at the same time, emphasizing the importance of good manners on the part of graduates. FSNS students learned from an anonymous philosopher: "Politeness is like an air cushion; there may be nothing in it but it eases our jolts wonderfully." They learned from Lord Chesterfield: "A man's good breeding is his best security against other people's ill manners." An observation that W. G. Mallett was particularly fond of was from Charles Dickens: "A man can never become a gentleman in manner until he has become a gentleman at heart." One quotation was out of joint with the progressive era in education: "One thing I solemnly desire to see our children taught—obedience." This voice from the past was that of Ruskin. Less controversial was a Goethe motto: "Kindness is the golden chain that binds society together." An old proverb admonished: "Grow angry slowly; there's plenty of time."

Horace Mann was a heavy contributor in ideas to the normal school curriculum, and one of the subjects he championed successfully was physiology. Along with this subject, as it was taught in the normal schools, was an emphasis on good health, physical and mental. Emerson made another one of his many contributions to FSNS mottoes in dealing with this subject: "Health is the condition of wisdom and the sign is cheerfulness." At the turn of the century, one of the most famous educators to promote health consciousness was G. Stanley Hall, psychologist and president of Clark University, where FSNS teachers went in the summertime to get the word as passed down by this Olympian figure in American education. G. Stanley Hall posed an easily answered question for the FSNS motto collection: "What shall it profit a man if he gain the whole world of knowledge and lose his own health?"

It was inevitable that the FSNS motto book would glorify books.* C. C. Rounds fought constantly from 1868 to 1883 for a larger FSNS library, and he never was more distressed than during the many times he was unsuccessful in his attempts. George C. Purington, as we have seen, was chiefly responsible for the Farmington Public Library, and both he and his successor served as its president. So in view of all this it was not surprising to find many quotations extolling books. These included Milton's famous, "A good book is the precious life-blood of a master spirit embalmed and treasured up on purpose to a life beyond life." Emerson contributed to every subject, and books were no exception: "A book is a sure friend, always present at your first leisure." Colton contributed: "Next to acquiring good friends the best acquisition is that of good books."

Educators of the 1920s and 1930s who had marked influence on teacher-training institutions were missing from the FSNS book of mottoes. These included John Dewey, William C. Bagley, Edward Lee Thorndike, Lewis Terman, and William Kilpatrick. Many educators of the nineteenth century did make it, however, besides Mann and Hall, including Francis W. Parker and J. F. Herbart. Presidents of liberal arts colleges were well represented, and especially was this true of Charles W. Eliot of Harvard, who made it four times. One of

---

* It was not inevitable that all normal school principals would champion books. The educational philosophy of Rousseau and Pestalozzi produced an anti-intellectual movement, from the very start, in some teacher-training institutions. This was because Rousseau emphasized the superiority of childhood experiences as a way of learning as opposed to the inferiority of book knowledge. He felt sorry for those children who had to depend on books for their information. Pestalozzi, as we have seen, wanted children to have direct knowledge through observation of things themselves rather than through the medium of books. The ideas of Rousseau and Pestalozzi did not necessarily result in an anti-intellectual attitude, but sometimes they did.

his precepts was a particular favorite of the FSNS principal: "The actual problem to be solved is not what to teach but how to teach it."

FSNS Changes in the Early 1920s

By the early 1920s, Farmington Normal students were using the railroads and American Express less and less, although it should be added that a majority of them still depended heavily on the trains.* At this time the Maine Central, in process of being undermined by automobile competition, was showing increasing signs of inefficiency. The B Hop, so important in FSNS social life, suffered in 1921 and 1922 as a result of the increasing confusion of the railroads. In these years freight trains were involved in accidents near Leeds Junction, resulting in the need to re-route passenger trains via Rumford and Canton. The influx of male escorts was consequently delayed over two hours, and this made the arrival hour coincide with the scheduled time for the dance. Because of such things as the Leeds Junction pile-up, the car was in the process of becoming not only a symbol of freedom but the necessary means of getting to places on time.

By 1922 another former plaything, the radio, was about to become a necessity. The first broadcasting station, KDKA in Pittsburgh, was opened in 1920 and broadcast the Harding-Cox returns on November 2, 1920. In the spring of 1922 the Normal School bought a radio, and students took time out to listen to weather reports, dance orchestras, soap operas, and all of this interlarded with the inevitable advertising and static. In a year or two, the broadcasting of professional ball games would help boost the popularity of spectator sports that had also become, as a result of the radio, audio sports. One Farmington Normal student wrote this in her diary on October 17, 1922: "I had the wonderful experience and privilege of listening to the radio over at school tonight. It was the weather report from Newark, New Jersey, and I stood fairly spellbound thinking of the wonder of it. I heard that Mr. Mallett said he felt about it as people used to when bicycles were first invented. They said two-wheeled vehicles couldn't be ridden, and he feels the same about radio, it can't be done."[45]

---

* In 1930, for the first time, the Gorham basketball team came by bus instead of train. Score: Farmington 25, Gorham 24.

In the early 1920s, educational changes included the conversion of normal schools into teachers colleges. The Maine Department of Education and Normal School trustees recognized this development by commissioning Principals William Russell, of Gorham Normal, and W. G. Mallett to investigate the new expansion of education as conducted west of New England. During this trip, from February 20 to March 19, 1923, the two principals also attended the National Council of Normal School Principals and Presidents in Cleveland, and the Superintendents' midwinter meeting of the NEA. In telling of the impressions gained on his trip, Principal Mallett said:

> West of the Atlantic States the normal schools are rapidly becoming teachers colleges of four years but still retaining their two-year courses, and granting degrees for four-year courses.
>
> It is noteworthy that the four-year courses are drawing more men for education than in the East. The western schools are seriously striving to train high school teachers as well as elementary teachers, while the eastern normal schools have left the training of high school teachers to colleges, which have technically given them no training, only education.
>
> The number of buildings, their size and superior equipment, are in strong contrast to the more modest, even meager physical plants in Maine.
>
> The instruction is much more in the nature of lectures, notebook work, and library reading than in some at least of our eastern normal schools.
>
> The actual training of the students seemed somewhat more fragmentary and more incidental than in our own school.
>
> In the normal schools we visited, the same large percentage of native-born Americans was found as in Maine.
>
> Although the financial support of normal schools in large and prosperous states of the West is more generous than in our own State, we failed to get any impression that the final product of the normal school, the trained teacher, was more efficient in the West than in the East, where devoted and enthusiastic teachers on smaller salaries and in smaller buildings and with smaller facilities in general, are educating teachers who are eagerly welcomed into every state in the Union.

These impressions were the result of visiting twelve teachers colleges in ten states extending from New York to Colorado. The observations quoted above were made to a reporter for the first FSNS yearbook. The principal's remarks to the trustees had a somewhat different emphasis in that he pointed, with some degree of envy, to the well-equipped libraries of the West with an adequate number of people to administer them. The FSNS principal, however, had no urge to copy the lectures and note-taking he found in the West. Many times he went on record as agreeing with the anonymous writer who described the lecture system as "a process by which words are mysteriously transferred from lecture notes of the professor to the notebook of the student without passing through the mind of either." He would have agreed with W. H. Auden that too frequently "a professor is one who talks in someone else's sleep." Two years after this trip was taken, Farmington Normal announced that it was instituting a four-year course in home economics that would be rewarded with a B.S. degree.

In the early 1920s school buses began to proliferate in the rural areas, and thus a new set of educational problems was initiated. In some districts men teachers were employed to drive these buses and the salaries for the combination of responsibilities were sufficient to attract more male teachers. This was to explain, to a limited extent, the increase in male FSNS students during the subsequent years.

In the spring of 1921, botany became at the Normal School a course in nature study and included a study of plants, trees, and birds. Much of the work was accomplished by field excursions, and Katherine Abbott and Agnes Mantor were in charge. The following September, this new subject became the responsibility of Charles S. Preble. Thus began the famous nature walks which were often taken at six in the morning.

In 1922, Normal School trustees recognized the need for a modern training school building. However, the only major additions to the FSNS physical plant in the 1920s were to be confined to dormitories, the most notable of these being The Willows and South Hall. In 1921 a minor addition to the grounds brought on a ceremony worthy of the opening of the Temple to Artemis. The commencement exercises of 1921 were begun when a flag-raising took place on the grounds of Purington Hall. Led by a flute and drums, the entire student body of the Normal and Model schools marched from Merrill Hall to Purington and formed around a beautiful new flagpole erected on the north end of the dormitory lot.

The traditional entertainment programs went on apace in the

1920s, and several people involved are worthy of special note. During the spring of each year, William R. Chapman, of New York City and Bethel, Maine, brought some of the leading recording artists of the day to Farmington Normal. Before each concert he paid his emotional respects to two persons, Lillian Nordica and George C. Purington. Year after year, he recounted how much the latter had done for Farmington and Maine music. In a fervid conclusion to his remarks, Professor Chapman would praise the character and magnificent singing voice of Nordica. He would usually end his introduction by urging the town to erect a suitable memorial to her memory. He would have been ecstatically gratified if he had known that Merrill Hall would some day be named for her.*

Among other performers of unusual quality was Tom Skeyhill, an Australian veteran of the Gallipoli campaign of World War I. In a talk of incredible emotional intensity, he described his personal participation in the unsuccessful British effort to wrest Gallipoli from the Turks in order to open the Straits of the Dardanelles for Allied use. Another notable lecture was delivered by Hamilton Holt, the editor of *The Independent* magazine and later president of Rollins College. He was a strong advocate of the League of Nations and talked in Farmington in support of this lost cause.

The spirit of the 1920s was revealed in what the students wrote for publication and how they wrote it. In 1914, *The Farmington Normal*, which had given up in 1904 for lack of subscribers and money, was revived. This time the magazine was under the management of the students, but they were very inhibited and depended on the faculty to carry the burden in writing articles for the publication. The result was that Hortense Merrill had an article on the value of current history in the curriculum, Edna Havey had one on

---

* Chapman was in charge of the Maine Music Festival, which he started in 1897. This famous event was held each year in Bangor and Portland and lasted until 1927, when he decided it had become too much of a burden. Nordica assured the success of the first festival with a promise to sing for it and this she did. George C. Purington trained some of the regional singers who then participated in Professor Chapman's state-wide chorus, but in the 1920s there was no one in Farmington with the necessary time to carry on this program. Professor Chapman in his introductory talk always expressed his regret that Farmington had no festival chorus and warned his audiences that they would be out of practice and out of tune for the heavenly choruses in prospect.

Photo courtesy Natalie Butler

GENERAL PERSHING on the speakers' platform at FSNS on the occasion of his visit to Farmington.

the value of manual training, and nothing in the publication showed any rebellious spirit. There was a joke department, but it was run with propriety and the utmost respect for authority.

Eight years later, with the appearance of *Effesseness*, the mood had changed. This first yearbook included a jazzed-up and revised edition of the mottoes. An example of this was:

> Uneasy lies the head of him who breaks a rule,
> He, most of all, whose abode is Farmington Normal School.

Certainly it had been impossible since the founding of the school in 1864 to have a poem on kissing until the 1920s such as:

> It must have been some mean old maid
> Who never tasted bliss
> Who started that infernal lie
> About the microbes in a kiss.

The movement for women's rights showed up in verse:

> If ever I should get married
> And my husband began to chew,
> I'd fire the rolling pin at him
> And paddle my own canoe.

A poem about bobbed hair indicated it was merely a craze and passing fad, but no moral outrage was involved in the writing of it.

Songs composed by professionals and sung by Normal girls were drastically different in the twenties from previous years. In the 1921 B Hop, "I'm the Sheik of Araby" was a favorite, and the words were a radical departure from those of the past:

> I'm the Sheik of Araby, your love belongs to me.
> At night when you're asleep, into your tent I'll creep.
> The stars that shine above, will light our way to love.
> You'll rule this land with me, the Sheik of Araby.

Kisses that a short time before had been considered a sure sign of an engagement were now treated differently as indicated in Victor Herbert's "A Kiss in the Dark" (1922):

> A kiss in the dark was to him just a lark
> But to me was a thrill supreme.

Other songs that were played at the Normal dances in the twenties were: "I Won't Say I Will But I Won't Say I Won't"; "Whispering"; "Margie"; "I Wanna Be Loved By You"; "That's My Weakness Now"; "Lonesome in the Moonlight"; "Where'd You Get Those Eyes"; "Yes, Sir, That's My Baby"; "Ain't We Got Fun", and "Pagan Love Song."

Many normal school graduates had thrilled to the moral message of Longfellow's "A Psalm of Life." The mood of the twenties was highlighted by a parody of the poem, printed in the 1926 *Effesseness*:

A PSALM OF SCHOOL LIFE

Show me not my poor rank sheet,
That I may not see my grade;
For I hate to show my mother,
Lest her joy in living fade.
Yours are low! But mine are lower,
Yet to pass is still my aim;
Dumb thou art, and dumber gettest
Was e'er spoken to my blame.
To enjoy and not to listen
To what goes on in the class,
To learn before examination
In a solid compact mass.
Hours are long, but youth is fleeting,
And over our heads, both hard and thick,
Will absorb some information
Just as water on a brick.
Lives of scholars all remind us,
We can also be sublime;
And, departing, leave on school desks
Records of our glorious times.

Organizations of the 1920s

Many FSNS organizations had proved their durability by the 1920s. The most notable example of these was the Christian Association, but the Home Ec Club, founded in 1916, also thrived during the 1920s and continued to do so during the entire normal school period. Both organizations were idealistic and took pride in helping the unfortunate. In the 1920s the Home Ec Club announced it had a three-fold purpose: (1) promotion of general interest in forwarding the Home Ec movement; (2) interest in and co-operation with social welfare work; and (3) fostering of good fellowship among members through social activities.

Musical organizations grew steadily in numbers and quality in the 1920s. In 1925, the male glee club was composed of 16 members. (There were 20 men in the 1926 graduating class, whereas in 1923 there were only 3). This outfit usually rehearsed alone, but they combined with the women in public performances. Both glee clubs sang together in an observance of Patriots' Day and again in an oratorio at Easter. Chapel exercises were frequently enlivened by their appearance, and in one year at least, these singers were heard every Friday. In 1926 the orchestra had nearly 30 members and that same year a band was added. The latter organization was formed mainly because FSNS men were competing athletically against New England normal schools and martial music was needed before such battles. At the time of the Gorham game at home, the band usually led a parade through the streets of Farmington. In 1926 anti-freeze for the instruments must have been used because the temperature during the parade was well below zero. (The never-say-die spirit of the musicians may have set an example for the athletes, because Farmington won.)

Throughout the 1920s the student council waged a seesaw battle against sin. The 1925 *Effesseness* noted: "Good weather and good roads seem to be an indication of prolonged and stormy sessions in Room 23, Monday P.M. at 4:30."

Dramatics began to play a more important part in school activities. In 1916, Nina D. Palmer had become the first dramatics coach on the FSNS faculty. (Previous to that year, infrequent plays were directed by members of the faculty who were temporarily drafted for the assignment.) For most of the 1920s, the dramatic coach was Errol L. Dearborn. As the years went on, play rehearsals were to involve a larger and larger part of the student body. The Puritan prejudice against the theater was to become thoroughly exorcised. Farmington Normal, in its last two decades, graduated many enthusiastic thespians who as teachers helped popularize amateur dramatics in countless Maine schools.

For some twenty years, Farmington Normal was not officially represented in athletics. The policy was to prohibit women from competing with other schools, and men were too few for even a basketball team. But by 1922–23 enough of them had registered to justify a basketball schedule, and in the spring of 1923, FSNS organized a baseball team. This was made possible by the previously mentioned heroics of two members of the faculty, Errol L. Dearborn and Charles S. Preble. Although the latter was then in his early forties, an age not generally regarded as young for ballplayers, he proved to be a very acceptable first baseman. Errol L. Dearborn was the right fielder and these two faculty members contributed to a season of surprises, one of them being the defeat of a highly rated Farmington High nine. The basketball players were less successful, but they did have an understanding reporter who was able to explain FSNS defeats without denigrating the players' skills. In the 1923 yearbook, he explained that the game loss to Wilton Academy (41 to 17) was owing to the FSNS right guard being taken from the game in the second quarter. The reporter thought this put the FSNS boys at an impossible disadvantage, but he did assure his readers that they "played a clean and fast game." The game with Livermore Falls was lost 31 to 9, but it was little wonder because "of the low ceiling and waxed floor." The worst breaks were yet to come. In the last game of the season with Mexico High, FSNS lost 43 to 24, but this was because in the third quarter the FSNS center was hurt and rendered *hors de combat*. In the last quarter FSNS lost two more players, and naturally, no team could expect to succeed with so little co-operation from Fortuna. (The suspicion was inevitable that the lost players were lost because of fouls. This, however, was not stated specifically; of course, they may have just been accident-prone.)

The basketball teams from 1926 on needed no apologetic reporter. They defeated their normal school competitors more than half the time, and had several star players who would have done well in any kind of collegiate competition. In 1925, FSNS had a football team with the busy Errol Dearborn coaching the eleven; the next year Lester Starbird took over the main coaching duties with Errol Dearborn assisting.* (Errol Dearborn was not on a forty-hour week. One year he taught every period of the school day while serving as coach of all the male sports and directing the dramatics club. There were probably other duties I have overlooked. In the

---

* Errol Dearborn has denied that he did any coaching of football. I suspect, however, that he was involved by being present at practices and giving encouragement to the players.

twenties, a small faculty failed to expand in accordance with the sharp increase in student enrollment.)

A tennis club was formed in 1927, and by 1930, Farmington racquet wielders had an undefeated season. Track teams, starting in the mid-twenties, have had notable success at various times in FSNS history, and this included in the 1930s two New England Championships.

In the 1920s, FSNS basketball teams always had to rent a hall in order to have any home games or practices. They played in these years in various places. One year they were on the second floor of the brick building across from the post office; other years they rented Music Hall. Finally, in 1931, they had a court of their own with the completion of the Alumni Gymnasium. The track and baseball teams have used Hippach Field in recent years, but the first FSNS baseball nines of modern times had their games near the railroad tracks on the intervale where the high school also played. In the 1920s the Abbott School used their own Hippach Field, although in the summer it was the scene of professional games until the town went deeply into debt as a result of the expenses involved. The tennis team started its career on the court next to Purington Hall, but through the generosity of Ben Butler, they moved to the court at Few Acres.

Although FSNS women were non-liberated in that they were denied interscholastic or collegiate competition, a significant development did take place in their athletic program in the 1920s. In 1927, Marian Allen, the physical ed instructor and daughter of the South Hall matron, introduced FSNS women to field hockey.* This sport became very popular and has remained so throughout the years. In the 1930s, Mrs. Mary Tilton, successor to Marian Allen, enthusiastically supported field hockey, and her efforts did much in further arousing and maintaining interest in it.

In 1926, Virginia A. Porter started a new organization, the Modern Authors Club. Its purpose was twofold: (1) to supplement the regular English courses with extra study of modern poetry, plays and short stories, and (2) to give an opportunity for the development of creative ability. In the first meeting, Miss Porter read parts of *Craig's Wife* by George Kelly, a play which won the 1926 Pulitzer

---

* Marian Allen proved her resourcefulness by putting on a gymnastic exhibition to raise money for the hockey uniforms.

prize. The first discussions about poems and poets involved several New England writers who were then dominating this branch of our national literature, including Edna St. Vincent Millay, Edwin Arlington Robinson, Robert Frost, and Amy Lowell.

Faculty Changes

In the 1920s time began its inevitable breaking up of the old guard of the FSNS faculty. Lillian I. Lincoln, after thirty-seven years of Farmington teaching (twenty-eight as head of the Model or Training School), retired in 1924 to be replaced by Emma Mahoney, who had proved to be a very capable 7th and 8th grade room teacher since the retirement and marriage in 1922 of Louise Richards. As previously stated, Hortense Merrill retired in 1921 and Katherine Abbott in 1928. Agnes Mantor was to teach history and library science, and counting her public service years, was at FSNS for forty-five years. L. Joe Roy, a Bates graduate, was at Farmington from 1928 to 1941 as the replacement in science for Arthur M. Thomas (1909–1929). He also served as the coach of the most successful basketball teams in FSNS history. Stella Dakin joined the faculty in 1929, and for seventeen years was to teach mental hygiene and courses in education and to advise the staffs of the student publications. Ruth Griffiths was the worthy successor of Franca Ingalls and taught music in Farmington for sixteen years. From 1922 to 1953 Julia Cox was a teacher in the training school, then assistant director, and finally, the director. In 1928 Ingeborg Johansen became the school nurse, a new position,* and she served in that role until her retirement in 1945. Ruth Broadbent was the successor of Katherine Abbott, and after she left in 1930, Frances McFaul became the art instructor, remaining as such until her marriage in 1937.

In 1914, FSNS was fortunate to obtain for what is now Merrill Hall the janitorial services of a retired sea captain, William D. Blake. He was a man of character and charm who applied himself conscientiously and effectively to his job. (Besides taking care of Merrill Hall, he joined the Modern Authors Club and was a regular partici-

---

* In November 1928, the Normal School trustees accepted the strongly worded recommendation of W. G. Mallett for a school nurse, the same to be paid from student fees with $300 from a state fund. The school nurse was to become a member of the faculty, and the principal was authorized to increase student fees to $5.00.

pant at its meeting.) In December 1928, he was stricken with what proved to be his terminal illness. Realizing the seriousness of the situation, and wanting his friend to have the best possible care, W. G. Mallett had him moved to his house on 14 High Street, where Captain Blake died on January 8, 1929. A few months after the Captain's death, the FSNS yearbook was dedicated to him with these remarks:

> To the memory of Captain Blake, his faithful service, and loyal, helpful friendship, we the class of 1929, affectionately dedicate our yearbook.
>
> By all the standards which we are accustomed to enumerate as measuring the stature of a real man, here was one who seemed to us to meet the test.

The 1930s at FSNS

The decade of depression that preceded U.S. involvement in World War II was marked at Farmington Normal by several important developments and policy changes. During this period, the trustees limited attendance; the 1933 legislature made tuition of $50 and $100 a requirement in all Maine normal schools; library facilities and services were expanded; a new student publication, *The Mirror*, was introduced; the training school found a separate home; student-faculty government was further developed; athletic and social life for men reflected the substantial increase in male enrollment; sororities and a pan-hellenic council were established; a new gymnasium was completed; academic clubs proliferated; dormitory rules were mildly liberalized; a three-year course was made optional and then mandatory; a state-wide committee revised the curriculum and in 1940, the principal, who had been associated for fifty-one years with Farmington Normal School as a student and teacher and principal, retired.

In postwar 1919, FSNS had some 134 students. In 1922 the enrollment went up sharply to 280, and by 1925, the Normal trustees recognized the difficulty involved in the ever-increasing registration by speculating on the advisability of limiting attendance to 400 students, leaving ten or twenty places open for unusual students. (This meant unusually able students, not unusually slow ones.) In 1925, 180 pupils were in the Model School, and by 1930, the number had risen to 250. Such attendance, when combined with the spiraling of the Normal School registration, turned Merrill Hall into an edu-

Photo Luce's Studio, Farmington, Maine

THE MALLETT SCHOOL, built in 1931, to house the Model School, formerly conducted on the first floor of Merrill Hall.

Left: Emma Mahoney, supervisor of teachers at the Mallett School, 1924–46. Right: Charles Preble, teacher of sociology and geography, occasionally included Model School students on his early-morning nature walks. Photos 1927.

cational ghetto. Moreover, there was not enough money to increase the size of the faculty in ratio to the jump in student enrollment.

In 1927, the school administration issued a bulletin which attempted to discourage some from applying for Farmington Normal: "For the past two years, applications for admission have exceeded the capacity of the school. In selecting members of the entering class preference is given to those whose moral character, health, scholarship, and high school course give most promise of success here. The commercial course is the least satisfactory preparation for Normal School work."

In the 1928 bulletin there was a revival, or at least a re-emphasis, of an admission requirement that went back to the founding of the institution. This was: "Young men must be 17 years old and young women 16." The bulletin then explained the resurrection of this requirement by saying: "Selection must be made because of excess of applications over the capacities of the school." In the fall of 1928, however, another jump occurred in registration and about 450 enrolled. This made it necessary for the principal to control the numbers by more stringent measures. One of these was to limit the registration to those who had been in the upper half of their high school class. Later this was changed to the upper one-third. The administration, however, was reluctant to enforce this requirement because it was well aware of the difficulties involved in comparing performances in the better high schools with those in deprived rural areas. After all the local attempts at controlling the enrollment failed, the trustees, backed by the Commissioner of Education, limited the attendance at Gorham and Farmington to 400 in 1933, and to 375 thereafter. By this method they hoped not only to prevent undue straining of the capacities of these two institutions, but to divert some of the applicants to other teacher-training institutions of the State.

Two of the most persistent problems in FSNS history were student enrollment, whether too many in the 1920s or too few in the 1880s, and the agonizing inadequacy of the library facilities and services. In 1930, when the trustees held their meeting in Farmington, Principal Mallett made another effort to get greater recognition of and resulting action for urgent library needs. Despite the substantial increases in appropriations for Maine normal schools throughout the 1920s, the FSNS library continued to be neglected and diminutive.

(In the 1930s all the books were housed in the rooms in Merrill Hall formerly occupied by the first three grades of the Model School.) In 1930, the chances for a more adequate library seemed improved in the light of encouragement from Augusta. Unfortunately, as the depression deepened, the library lost, temporarily, whatever chance it had to acquire a substantial addition to its book shelves or add to its professional staff. The budget did allow in 1932 for more student helpers in the library and Agnes Mantor added to her hours by agreeing to become their supervisor as well as teaching library science.

In December 1932, the FSNS *Mirror* reflected the new developments that were made possible by transferring Model School pupils to the new building on Quebec Street. "Evidences of a real library are to be seen on the first floor of the school building. A student librarian and volunteer helpers are for the most part directing its use." In 1934, the principal struck an optimistic note concerning library developments when he wrote to the Commissioner of Education: "As intimated in my last report our immediate objective in improving the usefulness of this school is a better library. That objective is being attained. Our library of 10,000 volumes is coming to include the best books of pedagogy as well as other school subjects. The Farmington Public Library contains 25,000 carefully selected books and maintains a liberal policy toward the school of loaning books above fiction levels without fees." The dependence of an institution of higher learning on a town library, in normal times, would not have been encouraging to the principal. He was simply yielding gracefully to the realities of the depression and was finding solace in the working arrangement he was able to negotiate with an excellent town library. (Such arrangements were frequently made in the nineteenth century between indigent normal schools and town libraries.)

In a 1933 meeting of the Normal School trustees, Bertram Packard, Commissioner of Education, reported on the bill passed by the legislature for the charging of $50 tuition for Maine students and $100 for nonresidents. Such tuition was to be charged even if the Maine students promised to teach in the State for a certain length of time after graduation. Consequently, the 1933 legislature changed a policy that had been in effect since the founding of the Farmington State Normal School. The Commissioner, however, also reported that a limited number of scholarships, involving a deferred tuition, would be available.

In 1934 the New Deal came to the rescue of many needy students by creating the Federal Emergency Relief Administration (FERA), and later this was replaced by the National Youth Administration (NYA). These government agencies extended financial assistance to students who were willing to perform such tasks as washing windows, digging weeds, and raking leaves. For all such menial tasks the FSNS worker received 30 cents an hour. For a skilled employee such as Harland C. Abbott, known as the fastest typesetter in Errol L. Dearborn's printing establishment, the pay was 40 cents an hour. (Two others, Will Havey and Alton Hyer, became top professionals in the printing business.) No NYA helper could make more than $15 a month, but this amount in the depression years sometimes represented the difference between solvency and insolvency.

Student laborers had their critics, not the least of whom was Reggie Berry, the redoubtable and outspoken janitor of Merrill Hall. Errol L. Dearborn, in charge of the student workers, defended his crew when he announced that as a result of a special study, he found the NYA helpers to be above the average in their scholastic attainments. Moreover, photographic proof has been uncovered revealing that at least some of them were involved in reasonably useful and constructive assignments.

Federal assistance to needy FSNS students did not mean that out of gratitude a considerable number of them would become converts to the New Deal. Maine students, as in other areas, reflected usually the political ideology of their parents and teachers. Although a Democrat had been elected governor in 1933, the State in national elections was to remain overwhelmingly Republican for some time to come. (Agnes P. Mantor was one of the few Democrats at the Normal School. In 1935 she was granted a leave of absence to serve for two years as an administrator in the Maine WPA program.) In the 1930s the Farmington faculty contained no one who was trained as a teacher of economics. There were no funds available for any such specialization, but this was of concern to few. It was generally believed that in training elementary and junior high teachers, there was no need to include a course that called for a critical examination of the malfunctioning U.S. economy.

However, radical and milder leftist ideas were in the air at this time and were no respecters of state boundaries. Some of them were listened to and discussed at teachers' conventions. George S. Counts might appear as a speaker and deliver a scathing critique of class bias in American school board membership; Charles A. Beard was to shock some by his economic interpretation of the Constitution; Harold Rugg was sometimes invited to explain his social science texts in which he had attempted to combine such subjects as history, geography, sociology, economics, and political science for the purpose of explaining, and occasionally deploring, modern industrial civilization; and John Dewey, the most frequently mentioned educational philosopher, was often attacked or defended by some who had never read his writings, or by others who had never understood what they had read.

Some school boards, after hearing that heresy was stalking the classrooms, would examine the texts born out of the depression and would then demand that they be proscribed. Such action would usually be caused by the emphasis placed on an economic interpretation of history. Some school board members were aware that Karl Marx was the father of Communism and, as such, was the best-known promoter of the economic interpretation of history. It was to no avail that the harassed teacher of social science could quote from the Founding Fathers, especially from James Madison, to prove that the Communists had no monopoly on economic interpretations.

The disputes of depression days were set aside when people began to concentrate on "the gathering storm" which developed into World War II. The war and postwar years avoided the depression and unemployment of the 1930s, and the kind of challenge to U.S. institutions that had marked the depression period was not repeated. The cold war, however, was to produce its own brand of grief to many teachers.

Two FSNS principals, Gage and Purington, edited during their widely-spaced administrations publications that were, for the most part, vehicles for faculty articles on education and travel. In 1914, FSNS students started *The Farmington Normal* (the same title as the Purington publication). Both faculty and students contributed to this periodical but it had an unsteady and irregular life and finally went out of business in 1922 with the appearance of Arline Coffin's yearbook. Nine years later, a new FSNS publication was issued. In

+++
"Each for the Good of All"
+++

| Boost Your School | # The F. S. N. S. Mirror | Hurrah The Mirror |

Vol. I, No. 1   FARMINGTON, ME., MARCH 1931   Price 10 cents

The New Gymnasium

The project of a new auditorium - gymnasium for Farmington Normal School seems now to have taken definite shape. Requirements of such a building have been furnished Bunker & Savage, architects, Augusta, and they have prepared preliminary plans and a sketch of external appearance, the latter being reproduced upon this page.

The former Methodist parsonage buildings and lot on High Street, next south on the Public Library and Training School playground, have been bought recently by the state for the school. It is proposed to locate the new building across the western end of the lot and continue it northerly thirty feet on the school playground with the main entrance in the north end upon the playground toward Academy Street.

The building will be of red brick with trimmings of white cast stone. It will rise about 30 feet above the cement underpinning and the ground dimensions will be 90 x 60 feet. The roof will be a tar and gravel specification with interior drainage. The interior arrangement provides for an ante-room and ticket office in the front end and a thirty foot stage in the south end. Balconies will extend around three sides of the hall which will be sixty by sixty. The basement, one-half its height above ground level, will contain lockers, showers, gymnasium director's office and heating arrangements.

This building has been conceived as a school project. With no prospect for several years that the state can build it, the school, encouraged by the support of recent classes, has resolved to carry its construction forward to a point which will make it available for some of the most urgent needs. This school of four hundred students which includes fifty young men has very inadequate quarters for its physical culture and athletics program. The basement room in the school building served very well for the past thirty-five years till the greatly enlarged school and the greatly increased program of physical training has now come to demand better facilities. Furthermore, the new building will serve important auditorium purposes.

To erect such a building and make it suitable for use will cost from fifteen to eighteen thousand dollars. We expect the state will assist in completing the building when funds become available in a few years. In the meantime the building will possess few embellisments but will be substantial and adequate for use.

The school is organized for support of the project under the leadership of E. L. Dearborn, Chairman, and already $1500 are in hand. The school will raise $1500 a year. Last year the school paid $800 for a hired hall for its athletics and dramatics activities and saved several hundred dollars for the gymnasium fund.

The school now earnestly solicits aid from the Alumni. Perhaps we can make it an alumni building. Some alumni of more than average means may wish to assume a large share in that work. We hope so, but to make it an alumni building givers of small amounts also must be large in number.

(Continued on Page 3 — Col. 5)

E. L. DEARBORN

THE GYM

"A gym you say?"
"Why, yes indeed!"
So fall in line
And all take heed.

The plans are made;
Now all we need
Is help from all
And we'll succeed!

"This is the forest primeval," remarked Joe Pillsbury as he stroked his lip.

Mr. Mallett's Trip to Detroit

Mr. Mallett left Farmington Wednesday, February eighteen, for Detroit to attend the mid-winter meeting of the National Educational Association and Conference of Normal School Principals and Teachers' College Presidents. Mr. Mallett traveled in company with Principal Russell of Gorham Normal and other New England delegates.

Some two hundred fifty normal school principals and teachers were in conference February twenty and twenty-one to discuss standards and rating of teacher training institutions.

The theme of the N. E. A. sessions was, "Working Together for the Children of America". One of the outstanding speeches was by E. W. Butterfield, State Commissioner of Education in Connecticut, on the subject, "The School and Community". Rear-Admiral Richard E. Byrd was the guest of the Department of Superintendence and addressed the general sessions Monday evening, February twenty-three. He gave an illustrated lecture of his recent expedition. On Tuesday evening, February twenty-four, the National High-School Chorus gave a grand concert in the Masonic Temple which contains the largest public auditorium in Detroit. The chorus, under the direction of Hollis Dann of the Department of Music Education, New York University, numbered over five hundred voices, representing practically every state in the union. The National High-School Chorus gives a glimpse of what is possible in school singing.

At the request of the committee on Assembly Programs, Mr. Mallett gave a very interesting report of his trip and the meetings at the assemblies of March five and six.

F. S. N. S. Teachers State B. B. Champs

Basketball season opened in the fall with favorable prospects of a winning year for F. S. N. S. All but one of the previous season's club were back to share their part of the task, and some valuable material had entered with the first year class. These two separate groups soon became one body, of which each was working for the team as a whole.

No player was regarded as superior to the others, but each one was considered a necessary asset for a smooth-working, winning quintet.

Pillsbury, a gift of the first year class, was an invaluable pivot man, because of his ability to surpass all comers in getting the tip-off, besides the many rebound shots his unusual height allowed him to make.

A more steady, dependable guard than Perkins, is hard to find. The position he plays is often lacking in due praise because many spectators judge a player by the work he does under his own basket. That is not the criterion by which every player should be judged, because each position requires different qualities. Many times, Perkins was alone to guard two, and sometimes three players, who were passing the ball down the floor to attempt a shot at the basket, but his clever work and quick thinking often prevented the opponents from scoring. What would be the advantage of the Farmington Normal Five scoring points, if there was no sturdy obstacle to prohibit the opposing team from caging baskets?

But there would be no use in merely preventing the opponents from scoring, if our favored quintet could not ring a few also. We find that quality in Webber who certainly has an art for pulling up the score. When in action he shows a continuous fighting spirit that does much to encourage the team. We see a hubbub, the spectators gasp, they think the play is lost, but no, — for among that muddle the ball shoots upward for a true basket. That is the way Webber works, and he certainly did much toward making the team successful.

The shortest person on the team was Fenwick, but size was no handicap. His quick dashes, in and out, here and there, wrested the ball from rival players so unexpectedly that at times they were at sea for a moment, during which excitement Farmington had an opportunity to score.

Last year's Captain, Ingalls, played a more stellar game than ever, as a running back. He seemed to have something in common with the baskets, for he counted many points from difficult angles in the corners of basketball halls. This also was a great help in running up a score; and he aided in holding the opponents' score down by recovering the rebound from their backboard, thus robbing them of a chance for a second shot at the basket.

A capable sub was found in Marble, who could be put into a game without changing the calibre of the team for the worst. He, too, was a fast player and could get baskets with comparative ease at quite a distance.

The team's record of 18 wins and 3 losses, includes the Normal School Championship of Maine — two wins over Gorham giving F. S. N. S. the Chrisskoss cup for the year 1931. An early season win over Houlton, one of the leading high-school teams of the state, did much towards encouraging the boys to greater effort for a successful team.

The defeats were at the hands of a New Brunswick team, the House of David, professionals, who were undefeated in 25 games in this state, and the Bucksport Seminary team which was crowned the State of Maine champions.

The record is as follows:

F. S. N. S.	32	Jay High School	21
F. S. N. S.	46	Livermore H. S.	14
F. S. N. S.	47	W. S. N. S.	26
F. S. N. S.	72	Ricker C. I.	12
F. S. N. S.	17	Woodstock V. S.	30
F. S. N. S.	30	Houlton H. S.	15
F. S. N. S.	35	Kent's Hill	25
F. S. N. S.	27	Castine Normal	10
F. S. N. S.	34	Jay High School	21
F. S. N. S.	39	Castine Normal	25
F. S. N. S.	71	Alumni	20
F. S. N. S.	23	Gorham Normal	17
F. S. N. S.	36	Gorham Normal	27
F. S. N. S.	31	House of David	57
F. S. N. S.	36	W. S. N. S.	28
F. S. N. S.	36	Bucksport Sem.	47
Our Scores	564	Oppon. Scores	402

"B" Hop

The annual "B" Hop, given by the second year class, was held at South Hall, Saturday evening, March 14.

The dining-room was transformed into a ball-room effectively decorated with Japanese lanterns and beautiful panels of Japanese scenes, designed and painted by students in the art classes. The side and overhead lights were made into Japanese lanterns, which gave a subdued and colorful effect. Jennie Starrett, who was at the head of the committee on decorations, was highly complimented on the beautiful appearance of the hall.

The orchestra played in an improvised Japanese garden, enclosed by a white fence over which flowers of various shades were climbing. Foster Sanborn, chairman of the music committee, was indeed fortunate in securing the Mainonians to provide the music for the evening.

The patrons and patronesses were Mrs. Tilton, Miss Mantor, Miss Lockwood, Miss Manser, Mr. Roy and the class president, Reginald Ingalls.

The living-room with its cheery fireplace and collegiate atmosphere, appealed to many. Helena Purvis and Dorothea Towne had charge of the arrangement of this room.

(Continued on Page 3 — Col. 4)

March 1931, the FSNS *Mirror* appeared and was unique for the institution in that each month students were to give their opinions and present school news. It came to be issued ten times annually and was partially financed by a student activities allotment. In subsequent years, under the enthusiastic supervision of Stella Dakin, it gained stature and was eventually rated a first-class school newspaper by the Columbia Scholastic Press Association. This FSNS paper had some able editors and columnists who tried to capitalize on their wit and ability to extract juicy tidbits from the local scene. Helen Kane, with her "Oh, Mr. Poster," was a popular presenter of the local low-down, and her worthy successor was Edna Hollywood. Philip Quinn and Robert White ran a column called "Vanity Fairgrounds," and after the graduation of White, Quinn carried on alone. In later years, Robert White became one of the editors of the Portland *Sunday Telegram*. Phil Quinn, a wit of many *bon mots*, was a victim of a fire a few years after his graduation from Farmington. Mickey Maguire developed his itch to write when he served as a sports writer, and a future member of the FSNS Hall of Fame, Gwilym R. Roberts, was the author of a column he dubbed "Upsen Downs." Clifford N. Oliver was in charge of a somewhat more intellectual column than the others, devoted as it was to the literary world.

The first big story handled by the *Mirror* was an account of the organizing of a new student-faculty cooperative government. This was a result of Errol L. Dearborn's study in New York University with Professor Ambrose Suhrie. As had been noted, the first student group to participate in governing the school was the student council formed in 1921. The Suhrie-Dearborn plan did not supplant the student senate, which the council had become, but represented a means of including the entire student body in the affairs of the Normal School.

The student and faculty cooperative government had three main branches—the faculty, the students, and faculty-students. The president of the faculty group was the principal, and the student assembly consisted of all members of the school. The student senate had twenty-four students, four of whom were officers of both the student assembly and the student senate. The faculty-student branch of the government consisted of eight committees. Every student in the school belonged to one of these, and since there were twenty-four faculty members, three of them were appointed to each committee.

They met on Thursday during the last period of the day. The business each committee transacted and its effectiveness in attaining objectives depended, of course, on the quality of the leader as well as the enthusiasm of the entire group. A brief summary of the work done by the early committees may help the reader to understand how the students were involved in school affairs.

Admissions, Scholastic Standing, Self-Help Committee

The first meetings were spent in reviewing policies and working out credits for extra-curricular activities. One of the more important projects was to find out what preparation high school students needed to enter the Normal School. This committee, as well as the others, made a study of parliamentary law as a result of trying to conduct business in the most expeditious way.

Assembly Programs Committee:

Two members were chosen periodically from this committee to have charge of chapel duties and the lost-and-found box. Also, one member was chosen each month to keep accurate and up to date the social calendar.

Attendance and Permissions Committee:

Went beyond its charter to give parties, the proceeds of which were used to buy books for the library. One quarter they devoted to the study of parliamentary law. They clarified men's rules and the policy governing them.

Dormitory Life Committee:

Formed to make the FSNS strict rules as palatable as possible. It handled such matters as laundry privileges, seating arrangements in dining rooms, light cuts, and the extension of the right of the house president to give black marks for the infraction of house rules.

Field Service, High School and Community Relationship Committee:

Took charge of the school during the State Teachers Convention in October when nearly all the faculty were attending the Convention. It sponsored and operated the superintendents' conference in March. At this time, superintendents from all over the State would meet in Merrill Hall to talk over problems of the young teacher.

This committee also sent speakers to Maine high schools to talk about the opportunities available to those with normal school diplomas.

Recreation Committee:

Took care of the tennis courts, game room, and other recreational facilities; sponsored the Winter Carnival and Better Health Week.

Social Training Committee:

This committee's function included arrangements for the Holiday Dance, dinners, and teas, and social training in the form of presenting programs in chapel designed to illustrate correct etiquette; it also presented dancing school and bridge parties.

Publications and Publicity Committee:

Published the *Mirror*, address book, and handbook; spent some time discussing the problems of journalism.

In 1933, another organization was added to the student government—this was the Judiciary Committee. Its function was to deal with cases of misdemeanor reported to it from house courts, matrons, deans, committees, and the principal of FSNS. The Judiciary was not intended to be a detective agency or Gestapo; consequently, no judiciary members could report directly to their own group. Principal Mallett appointed three faculty members to the judiciary, and the president of the student senate appointed seven students.

In 1929, the Normal School sent, for the first time, a faculty member, Emma Mahoney, and two students, Lulu Owen and Helen Murray, to the New York conference sponsored by the Eastern States Association of Professional Schools for Teachers. This was an annual event, and faculty and student delegates met to discuss questions common to teacher-training institutions. The 1929 appearance of a delegation from FSNS set the pattern for the future; for each subsequent year Farmington Normal was to be represented.

Dorothea Hodgkins Small, in 1932, made one of the more important contributions from the local institution when she gave a six-minute talk during which she described the newly installed FSNS student government and told the delegates how Farmington Normal's program is interpreted to the supporting public. The reporter for *The Franklin Journal* was impressed by the fact that the speaker would be asked to stand before a microphone to enable all in the Pennsylvania Hotel auditorium to hear her.

The student senate in 1933–34 was under the strong and enthusiastic guidance of Charles Gillis. He may have been the first student in FSNS history to make a strongly worded protest against what he regarded as a benighted and illegal policy of the school establishment. This had to do with the administration's toleration of the recently formed sororities and fraternity. Gillis wanted them put out of business because such organizations were banned in the high schools of Maine and he thought that what applied to them should also apply to all public institutions. This may have been a landmark in the history of FSNS protests, but it failed to receive any support from state authorities. (Years later, Colonel Charles Gillis would defend estimates of Army intelligence in Washington, D.C. as they were considered by the Board of National Estimates.)

In 1935 the delegates to the New York conference were concerned with a topic many of them probably thought was a distinctly modern development, namely "Beyond the Textbook." A professor from the State Normal School in Geneseo, New York, explained the use of current literature as a supplement to textbooks in the education of teachers and students. A panel then discussed the use of the magazine in education. In 1870, C. C. Rounds was writing about this subject for *The Maine Journal of Education*. The only difference was that Rounds did not limit the teacher to newspapers and magazines in getting help beyond the textbook; he thought a teacher should go to the original sources in order to check properly on textbooks. In 1916, Hortense Merrill had written an article on this 1935 topic. She had delivered her paper to a Franklin County Teachers' Convention and it was later printed in *The Farmington Normal*. The same educational problems seem to appear and reappear with regularity, even though the majority of each generation may believe they are the first to grapple with them.

In June 1931, the FSNS *Mirror* reported an important decision of the Normal School trustees. It ordered normal schools to stay out of secondary teacher-training, except in those subjects which were already included in the curriculum. The trustees, however, added that they were convinced that Maine normal schools would have to be put on the same level in training elementary teachers as that of normal schools of neighboring states. Consequently, an optional third-year course was introduced in Farmington the following year, and in 1934 it was made mandatory. The FSNS principal accepted the trustees' order reluctantly because his initial thought was that the Maine pay scale for elementary schoolteachers did not justify the expenses that were involved in the mandatory third year of study. Later he concluded that not only a third year was advisable, but also a fourth.

The 1930s witnessed a marked increase in FSNS organizations, especially those involving men. Principal Mallett, in his 1938 report to the Commissioner of Education, expressed his pleasure and satisfaction with the number of males who had been entering the school: "The increase in the number of men entering work in education through the Normal School and following it up by securing the bachelor's degree at the State University augurs well for trained material in the future for both teaching and superintending of schools." These were to prove prophetic words, for in the 1930s and the first two years of the 1940s, FSNS graduated many males who were to distinguish themselves as teachers and superintendents. Farmington Normal was to be greatly strengthened by the capable graduates who returned to teach at the institution, and the State of Maine has a large number of highly regarded superintendents who graduated from FSNS during this period. Some of the male graduates have attained their greatest recognition in other states, one of the more illustrious being Harvey Scribner, chancellor of the New York City schools from 1970 to 1973.

The increase in male enrollment after 1925 made possible a greater activity in men's athletics. The basketball teams of the late twenties were first-rate, and by the mid-thirties, the Normal School had enough men to be represented in basketball, tennis, track, and baseball. (The two years of football in the mid-twenties had proved this sport to be too expensive.) In the 1930s, Farmington joined the New England Teachers College Athletic Conference, which consisted of Gorham, New Britain, Rhode Island College of Education, Hyannis, Salem, Danbury, Keene, and Fitchburg. In the 1930s, Farmington was to enjoy a better-than-average athletic record in competition with these New England teacher institutions. The tennis team was undefeated in 1929–30, with twenty-four consecutive victories, and it claimed a somewhat nebulous New England championship. Under Dr. James Reed, the cross-country team won twenty-five consecutive victories and the state normal title three years in succession. Dr. Reed also coached Farmington in 1936 and 1937 to two New England track titles.* The baseball team had a .500 record even though the uniforms looked like hand-me-downs from a Salvation Army collection.

No sport at FSNS could rival basketball as a generator of interest and emotion. Being a winter activity, it was able to take advantage of the snowbound weekends that found most of the students unable to get home. Moreover, Farmington, throughout the first half of the 1930s, had a varsity five which could more than hold its own with its rivals. During the 1930s, such players as Bill Webber, Joe Wagnis, Joe Pillsbury, Vince Barrows Davis, Mickey Maguire, Jack Harriman, Tom Connor, Gutty Talbot, Frank Barrett, Dick Hall, Laurel Gardner, Charley Wright, Jim Conway, Phil Soderquist, Joe Wenckus, Bill Russell, Bo Witham and coach L. Joe Roy were local household words because of their basketball reputations. The interest and excitement produced in the Alumni Gym during the 1930 weekends would have had to be experienced to be believed. (Farmington Normal sponsored an annual tournament for the high schools of Franklin County. This laid bare an intertown rivalry that exploded with a deafening roar in the new gym, a pandemonium that was not always free of acrimony.)

Even though all the conference games were considered to be of crucial importance, there was one game during the season that was advertised as "The Game of Games." From the mid-twenties through 1933, this contest was with Gorham. Not only did this climactic contest produce a persistent and ear-shattering din within the modest confines of the Alumni Gym, it was preceded by a march that might have heralded the opening of the Olympics. An hour before this athletic Armageddon was scheduled to begin, the students gathered in front of South Hall (now Mallett Hall) ready to march in a grand parade. The double line of students was formidable, and the cheers and yells not only indicated the excitement of the hour, but a life-preserving effort to keep from freezing in the sub-zero tempera-

---

* Some of the track stars were: Melvin Preble, Wilson Smith, Charles Bottiggi, Bob Chassie, Norman MacWilliams, Chuck Card, Earle Trask, Reggie Watson, Paddy Vose, Doc Robinson, Phil Soderquist, Jim Conway, Wendy Eaton, Sonny McLeary, and Don Graham.

tures. The bitter cold, moreover, did nothing for the efficiency and musicianship of the supporting band or legion drum and bugle corps. Many of the students had torches made of brooms that were well soaked in kerosene. (For the statistical-minded, the 1933 torches used 15 gallons of kerosene, 130 burlap sacks, and 12 spools of copper.) After the brooms were handed out and lighted, a trek began that would take the students around the main streets of the town. In addition to the torches, some of the more enthusiastic citizens contributed firecrackers to the festivities. These may have added to the success of the parade, but when some of them exploded in the narrow confines of the gym, their popularity plummeted.

The Gorham-Farmington game represented a natural rivalry, but Louis Chrissikos, a Gorham restaurant owner, added an extra ingredient to the competition when he contributed a cup that was to be held for a year by the winning team. Perpetual ownership awaited the time when Gorham or Farmington would win for three successive years. In 1933 a strong Farmington aggregation retired the cup by defeating Gorham 67 to 24. This game was to mark the beginning of a five-year hiatus in the basketball competition between Gorham and Farmington.

The attempts to find a substitute for Gorham in this Game of Games were not altogether successful. In 1934, Machias replaced Gorham as Farmington's major rival, but this was to last for only that one year. Once again the torchlight parade swung into action and again the severe cold added to the excitement and stimulation. (The winter of 1933–34 was the coldest in the history of the local weather bureau.) As the parade passed Merrill Hall, a noise from the past was heard when the bell in the tower was rung vigorously but without spectacular sound effects.*

After Farmington defeated Machias 46 to 34 in this short-lived Game of Games there was a dance, followed by a banquet at Purington Hall. Such events were in honor of the teams, cheer leaders, and the appropriate in-charge committee members. At midnight everyone went home in order to get enough rest to reassemble the next morning at the Broadway Theater (now the State Theater) to see the Marx Brothers in "Duck Soup." Extra acts consisted of slides cover-

---

* In 1935, 1936, and 1937, the Game of Games matched Salem and Farmington, but this rivalry also proved to be too artificial and forced.

ing a variety of school topics which were the work of school writers. Some of the killjoys on the faculty exercised their traditional right in considering some of these messages to be of questionable taste and humor.

In the afternoon a winter carnival was held in a large field near Bonney Woods. *The Franklin Journal* described these events as "culminating in the breath-taking thrills and spills of the ski jump." Knowing the terrain of the jump, it is rather difficult to believe that the event could be accurately described as "breath-taking." A large number of enthusiastic students, however, were entered in the modest-sized jump so that what the meet lacked in later-day professional standards and derring-do, it made up for in spirited competition.

In the evening the Mainonians, playing in the Alumni Gymnasium, furnished dance music for the grand carnival ball. The King and Queen won their crowns by being the highest point winners in the stirring events of the afternoon. Mrs. Mary Tilton, the very competent FSNS gym teacher, recognized with appropriate symbols Richard Morton as king and Flora Worthley as queen of the carnival ball.

Music by the Mainonians was a common and welcome advertisement for local 1930 dances. This highly-regarded dance outfit had its beginnings at Farmington Normal. The increase in male enrollment at FSNS had not only strengthened men's athletics, but added another dimension to the FSNS music program. Although the sound of jazz in the late 1920s was one of cacophony to many of the older generation, the FSNS music teacher, Franca Ingalls, did not join in this rejection of the new syncopation. With her encouragement, seven young FSNS musicians formed a dance orchestra in 1928. They originally called themselves the FSNS Dance Entertainers, but as the years went on, and the FSNS musicians graduated, they took the name of the Mainonians.

The town of Madison made a major contribution to this FSNS jazz outfit. In the twenties, the Madison Boys Band was an excellent organization and it had developed many fine musicians. To the FSNS dance orchestra it contributed Red Golding on the trumpet, Roger Snell on the drums, and Wannie Russell on the bass horn. Other musicians were: Don Nichols and then Puss Ingalls on the banjo, Stud Studley on the piano, and probably the best performer of them all, Myron Starbird on the alto sax.

Lester Starbird, the best trombonist in the area, gave important outside assistance to the FSNS group. After the FSNS Entertainers became the Mainonians, the most important outside addition was Jimmy Sutcliffe. In 1932 he took over the direction of the band, and his Nash car was indispensable in fulfilling engagements. The Mainonians were certainly the best dance band in the area and one of the best in the State.

The building and completion of the Alumni Gymnasium constitutes a much more interesting story than what is usually encountered in similar constructions. This was partly attributable to the amount of work and planning that was provided by Errol L. Dearborn. Not only did he give hours of his time, but he managed to whip up the enthusiasm of others who wanted so badly to have a place of their own to play basketball. By December 1931, the Alumni Gymnasium was near enough completion to make it usable for athletics, and to a considerable extent, for social and dramatic activities. The following summer and fall saw the completion of the interior of the building, and during the school year of 1933-34, furnishings were installed. The April 30, 1935, issue of *The Franklin Journal* announced that FSNS had accomplished its purpose in its drive to sell enough tickets to a Dramatics Club play to clear the debt on the Alumni Gymnasium. Almost every conceivable method had been employed to raise money for erasing the Gym debt. In celebration of this achievement, the student body, on April 26, 1935, participated in the hanging and burning in effigy of "Old Gym Debt." It was delayed justice that the second and present college gymnasium should be named for Errol L. Dearborn.

The Training School, as the new Model School was often called until it was renamed the Mallett School shortly after Mallett's retirement, presented more than the usual problems that are involved with new structures. In April 1932, *The Franklin Journal* revealed that a score of workers had been employed undoing the plastering that had been improperly done by the contractors. The sand was found to be unfit, with the result that the plaster was too brittle. An expensive job of replastering took over two months to complete, and the total cost to the bonding company was about $40,000. This was a considerable amount of money in those days, especially when it is realized that the original cost of the entire building was estimated at about $100,000.

Farmington, as has been stated, was selected in 1863 as the town for the first normal school in the State partly because the railroad came to West Farmington at that time. By 1932, it was obvious that Maine railroads were in trouble and might be headed for disaster. Buses and private automobiles were offering increasing competition and the railroads were desperately trying to compete with them by offering special excursion rates to almost anywhere. Finally the announcement came that after August 1, 1932, no through train would run between Farmington and Portland. The narrow gauge, after serving northern Franklin County for over fifty years, discontinued service in 1932 but resumed its work in April 1933. In May 1935, after this brief resuscitation, the narrow gauge expired. It was sold at public auction for less than $25,000. In a few years Farmington was to lose its passenger service, and the days of the baggagemaster checking some 200 FSNS trunks would be only a memory to record in such a history as this.

By 1930, there were three sororities. The first one, Phi Nu Omega, was formed in 1925, the second was Phi Mu Sigma, and the third, Lambda Epsilon. In time, a pan-hellenic council was established with representatives from all three. An organization embracing all the sororities was to reduce as much as possible the bickering and tensions that are sometimes a part of secret society rivalries.

Naturally the men got into the act of forming secret clubs, and in the late twenties, two local groups were formed: the Absoloms and Sigma Omicron Sigma. The Absoloms were the smaller of the two and were heavily loaded with musicians. In 1931 these two outfits merged to become Kappa Delta Phi, a national educational fraternity.

Although the women of FSNS did not have intercollegiate athletics, they were not lacking in intramural competition. At the close of the season, there were many well-attended basketball tournaments played between classes, dormitories, and departments. Other sports for women included badminton, volley ball, horseback riding, and field hockey. In 1937, an outing club known as Fast-Teco (the acronym was in anticipation of Farmington State Teachers College) was organized by L. Joe Roy and featured picnics, skating, hikes, camping trips, and other outdoor activities.

There were organizational developments in the arts and sciences. The Dramatics Club in this decade was renamed Plays and Players

Photo Luce's Studio, Farmington, Maine
A semi-formal dance in the Alumni Gym. "The Holiday," 1938.

and was fortunate to have two enthusiastic directors, Ernestine Merrill Whitten and Charlotte D. Meinecke, who served in that order from 1935 to 1942. The Natural Science Society, established in 1934 under the leadership of Clyde C. Taylor, was devoted to furthering the study of natural sciences beyond the requirements of the school curriculum. Charles S. Preble and L. Joe Roy lent faculty support to it and encouraged camera enthusiasts, star gazers, and nature lovers to pursue their hobbies and expand their scientific horizons. The Modern Authors Club, guided by Virginia A. Porter, was holding meetings twice a month and continued to have a large membership. (In the 1930s, Mrs. W. G. Mallett gave an annual review of the latest books.) The forty-year-old Christian Association was showing its age at times, but it had several spurts of energy in the 1930s. The Home Economics Club had two meetings each month and frequently listened to out-of-town speakers. The musical clubs were flourishing under the capable leadership of Ruth Griffiths. In 1931, Charles Towle reorganized a debating club,* and in 1936, James Whitten, now a history professor at U.M.P.G., breathed new life into it.

During the 1930–1940 decade, unusual honors were bestowed upon three FSNS alumni. One of these was H. Arthur Sanders of Livermore and the FSNS class of 1885. In 1940, Colby College, in the person of President Franklin W. Johnson, awarded Sanders an honorary degree but without alluding to his FSNS diploma. The citation read:

> A native son of Maine; graduate of the University of Michigan and Doctor of Philosophy of the University of Munich. For many years Director of the School of Classical Studies of the American Academy of Rome; recently retired as Chairman of the Department of Speech and General Linguistics at the University of Michigan.
>
> Author of many scholarly papers and works, among them the publication of the Old and New Testament manuscripts in the Freer Collection; educator of scholars; a teacher both witty

---

* The December (1931) *Mirror* was inaccurate by a wide margin when it asserted that for the first time in the history of the school a debating society had been formed. Actually, the first subject for debate in 1931 was the same as one of those debated by the 1885 club: "Resolved, that the present ranking system should be abolished in secondary schools and colleges."

MERRILL HALL (now Nordica Auditorium) before the removal of the Greek statuary.

GWILYM ROBERTS as a senior in
1937. Ten years later, he became the
national president of Kappa Delta Phi.

and wise; an acknowledged authority on the interpretation and dating of manuscripts in the classical tongues.*

Another FSNS alumnus who attained national attention in the 1930s was Harold D. King. Born and brought up in West Farmington, he married Edith Thompson, daughter of Judge and Mrs. J. H. Thompson, of Farmington. He graduated from the FSNS two-year course in 1898 and from the three-year course in 1899. He then went on to graduate from Dartmouth in 1903. After college, he took a position with the Coast and Geodetic Survey. During his eight years there, he qualified as a master mariner. In 1911, he transferred to the Lighthouse Service, and after serving in the early 1930s as deputy commissioner of lighthouses, became commissioner in 1936.

A Washington staff correspondent for the *Christian Science Monitor* applauded the appointment of Harold D. King, and among other things, wrote: "Daniel C. Roper, Secretary of Commerce, is basking today in the glow of general approval over having made an appointment in his department based exclusively on merit."

From 1894 to 1900 the FSNS geography teacher was Melvin J. West. His son Roscoe attended the Model School, and after his family moved to Massachusetts, became a fifteen-year-old graduate of Needham High School. He then came back to Farmington and graduated in 1910 from the Normal School. After earning an A.B. degree from Harvard, he became the Farmington superintendent of schools. (He was succeeded within three years by William Woodbury whose father, Roliston, was C. C. Rounds's assistant from 1867 to 1879.) Roscoe West was to become superintendent of schools in Rockland, Maine, and then in Needham, Massachusetts. In the 1920s he was appointed the director of elementary education in New Jersey, and in 1931, he was elected as the president of the prestigious Trenton Teachers College, which he made in the ensuing years more prestigious. Rutgers recognized his important contributions to New Jersey education by awarding him an honorary Litt. D. Dr. West's last public appearance in Farmington was in 1939, when he gave the FSNS commencement address.

---

* Lillian I. Lincoln tutored both H. Arthur Sanders and W. G. Mallett in Latin in helping them prepare for college. Principal Mallett tried to get Professor Sanders as the speaker for the 50th anniversary of Farmington Normal, but this distinguished graduate was out of the country on a sabbatical.

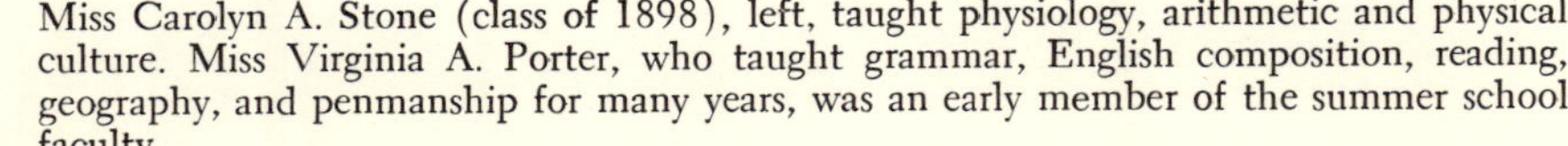

Miss Carolyn A. Stone (class of 1898), left, taught physiology, arithmetic and physical culture. Miss Virginia A. Porter, who taught grammar, English composition, reading, geography, and penmanship for many years, was an early member of the summer school faculty.

On June 17, 1939, about 400 graduates of the FSNS returned to celebrate seventy-five years of the school's history. An alumni orchestra, consisting of twenty-two members under the direction of Ruth Griffiths, furnished the music. (This was an excellent orchestra. It included Anna Austin Small on the cello, Iola Perkins on the viola, and two violinists of the present Bangor Symphony, Arthur and Euleta Webb.) Mrs. Luna Hodgkins, FSNS '99, presided, and the occasion was honored by the presence of Bertram Packard, Commissioner of Education of Maine, who gave an interesting account of the early normal school movement.

Principal Mallett then pointed to the fact that 1939 marked the 100th anniversary of the first normal school in United States history as well as the 75th anniversary of Farmington Normal. He told of the meaning of the word *normal* as used in teacher-training institutions. It was taken from the French and referred to the establishment of norms, or standards, in teaching. Principal Mallett went on to speak of C. C. Rounds and in appreciation of the latter's difficulties during the pioneering days of Farmington Normal. "He was a pedagogue of a very high type, though somewhat autocratic; an able scholar, a man of training who inspired others to follow, a leader of men, thoroughly versed in the new principles of normal schools."[*]

Harland C. Abbott spoke for the student body on this 75th anniversary and expressed his appreciation of the school as he found it as an undergraduate. Years later he would make other speeches at the institution after it had become a college, but then he would be on the administrative side of the fence.

One of Principal Mallett's favorite students, Doris Bridges, completed the program by delivering an encomium with an account of the accomplishments of the principal throughout his FSNS years. She stressed in particular his New England work ethic that was reflected in the many tasks he had willingly assumed in the school and in the community.

---

[*] The 1883 revolt of the greater part of the faculty attests to his autocratic ways, but on the positive side, Rounds was not only well versed in the new principles of the normal schools, but as has been noted, helped to formulate many of them. Nicholas Murray Butler, in his autobiography, *Across the Busy Years*, specifically mentioned Rounds and wrote this about him and his colleagues: "They were the real leaders of a profession and they represented that profession not only before their several constituencies but before the nation."

Another tribute to the principal came at commencement when Roscoe West stated in his address that no one had had more influence on his life than W. G. Mallett.

In the principal's 1939 and 1940 diaries, there was no mention of these praises. Characteristically, he merely wrote: "This is the end of my teaching career. It began the first Monday in December, 1884, in the home school. Dec., 1887, I began my second term in the same school. At Christmas time in 1888 began at Five Islands. In September, 1889, began my duties as principal at the Topsham High School. From 8 to 10:30 every day I was in my college classes."

In June 1939, Virginia A. Porter and Carolyn A. Stone, with a combined total of sixty-eight years of FSNS teaching, retired. They did so without any fanfare, because the announcement of their decision was delayed publication until September. Appointed by George C. Purington to the Farmington staff in 1907, Virginia A. Porter for thirty-two years taught geography and handwriting and English literature. In 1926 she founded the Modern Authors Club and was its enthusiastic adviser for thirteen years. Possessor of no college degree she did possess knowledge of both her students and the books she urged them to read.

Carolyn A. Stone graduated from Farmington Normal in 1898 and became one of its instructors in 1901. With the exception of two years at New Britain Normal, from 1903 to 1905, she would spend her teaching years at Farmington. She was to become the dean during the swift changes in manners and morals that took place in the 1920s and 1930s. At times she undoubtedly felt like a female counterpart of King Canute trying to keep back the tide or Horatius at the bridge. Throughout her trials, however, it was obvious that she was a woman of unusual kindness and warmth. Whenever a student became seriously ill, Dean Stone would invariably volunteer to accompany the student to home or hospital. The last graduate catalogue (1957) was dedicated to her and was a testament to her continuing interest in and knowledge of Farmington Normal graduates.

Agnes P. Mantor succeeded Dean Stone and was quite a different type in that many of her interests went well beyond the schoolroom. From 1935 to 1937 she was state director of women's activities in the WPA. From 1937 to 1939 she was president of the state Federation of Business and Professional Women's clubs. In the 1940s she served on the state Personnel Board to administer state employment on a merit basis. She ran unsuccessfully for the Maine legislature on the Democratic slate in the days of unbroken Republican successes in this area. After the entrance of the United States into the war, she became vice chairman of the Women's Division of Civil Defense and assistant state director for women's activities. All these nonacademic tasks did not prevent her from occupying important educational offices. For several years she served on the Executive Committee of the Maine Teachers Association and in 1942 was president of the organization. (Local papers asserted that she was the first classroom teacher to occupy this high position.) The naming of the library in her honor was a recognition of her contributions to this vital part of the college program.

Lorey C. Day

Succeeding W. G. Mallett was Lorey C. Day. A graduate of Clark University, with a master's degree from the same institution, he was for five years superintendent of schools in Livermore Falls and then had that position for nine years in South Portland. Retiring and somewhat uncommunicative, Principal Day served at FSNS during a distressing time for educators. A little over a year after he became the head of Farmington Normal, the United States entered World War II, and some developments that had been anticipated for the early 1940s were postponed. Before Pearl Harbor it was thought likely that by 1942 or 1943 a fourth year with a B.S. degree would be established at Farmington. The April (1942) *Mirror* announced the elimination of such a possibility. Lorey C. Day had reported to the school newspaper that because of the scarcity of teachers, Commissioner of Education Harry V. Gilson had concluded it would be unwise to introduce during the war the fourth year and B.S. degree. This meant, among other things, that the teacher institution at Farmington would continue as Farmington Normal until the end of the war.

After the bombing of Pearl Harbor, nearly all activities of the faculty and students reflected United States participation in the war. A local campaign was waged as part of a national drive to collect books for soldiers, sailors and marines. This was a signal for the FSNS Entertainment Committee to swing into action with a house-to-house hunt for expendable books as their part of the Victory

                                          University of Maine

LOREY C. DAY, principal of FSNS from 1941 through the end of the school year 1944–45, with Shirley Curtis. Photo 1941.

Book Campaign. Proceeds of FSNS plays were sent on to the American Red Cross. The first play which served this noble purpose was "The Kink in the Male Animal." In September 1942, a normal school calendar was set up with a 5½ day week and a consequent reduction to 34 of the school weeks. This was "to release labor earlier in the spring and to keep the cost of education down by the shortened year." FSNS Home Ec students were active in British Relief, and the entire FSNS was reported as throwing its full support to the Russian War Relief. The Integration Committee of the FSNS student government organized a community drive for recreational equipment to be sent to servicemen. There was a scrap roundup, and all the FSNS teachers were involved in defense programs of one kind or another. Gwilym R. Roberts, basketball coach in 1942–43, had barely enough men to carry out the FSNS schedule. In fact, one night the coach found it necessary to insert himself into the line-up in order to carry on with five players. In 1943–44 Charles S. Preble was granted a year's leave of absence to teach geography at the University of Maine in Orono. The same year Gwilym R. Roberts devoted three days of the week to FSNS and three to Colby, where he was a physics instructor for aviation cadets. Those who felt the need of relaxation in the evening could see at the local theater "Private Buckeroo," starring Harry James and the Andrews Sisters, or "Bugle Sounds" with Wallace Beery, or "Burma Convoy" (Death Rides Every Terror-Strewn Mile).

Shortly after Pearl Harbor, on January 12, 1942, W. G. Mallett died. The papers said the event was unexpected and sudden, but those closest to him knew better than that. Almost a lifetime of absorption in educational problems had ended abruptly with his retirement in June 1940. Nothing could adequately fill the resulting void in his life.

Like George C. Purington, W. G. Mallett had been a community leader as well as school principal. For forty-five years he was a church deacon, and during some of that time, served as president of the State Congregational Conference. For ten years he wrote the editorials for *The Farmington Chronicle*. In 1907 he became a trustee of the Franklin County Savings Bank and its president in 1931. In 1910 he became a trustee of the Farmington Library Association and its president in 1938. For nearly twenty-five years, he was county chairman of the American Red Cross, and almost the last thing he did was to build a fire in the vestry of the North Church in preparation for a Red Cross meeting. He served the town for three years as its superintendent of schools and was elected several times to the local school board. For thirty years he was an overseer of Bowdoin College. Certainly such contributions overfulfilled his debt to society.

In the January, 1942, issue of the *Bowdoin Alumnus*, Wilmot B. Mitchell wrote a memorable and appropriate tribute to his Farmington friend. Included in his remarks were these:

> Mr. Mallett's lifework has been teaching. For eighteen years he was instructor of Science in the Farmington Normal School, for thirty-one years its Principal, and since 1940 its Principal Emeritus. Few men, if any, have had more influence than he in advancing the cause of education in Maine. All these years he has been not only a teacher but a teacher of teachers. Like most successful teachers, he has liked not only books and experiments and abstract problems but also people. Human beings have always been interesting to him,—their peculiarities, their limitations, their innate powers and latent possibilities. As a result he has followed the careers of his students with understanding and affectionate interest long after they have left the school. It has been my good fortune to meet at teachers' conventions and summer schools and elsewhere many graduates of Farmington Normal. I have never met one who did not speak enthusiastically of Mr. Mallett. I like to think that today he lives in many minds made better by his presence.

The Fire

In 1945, the last year of Farmington State Normal School, as well as the year of Allied victory in Europe and Asia, a fire swept through parts of the home economics Cottage and adjoining clothing laboratory. It not only caused damage estimated at between $15,000 and $20,000, but the explosive flash-fire threatened the lives of a class of freshmen girls who were sewing under the instruction of Margaret Mades. The next-door neighbor and Baptist minister, Albert Henderson, saw the flames and rushed over to warn all those concerned of the need for quick action. The classroom was emptied with all due haste. Teacher and students were forced to exit by the rear door, for the main door of the clothing laboratory was in flames. Marian Stover Leighton (FSNS '38) and her baby Terry and the Cottage girls left by the front door of the Cottage and sought temporary refuge at the Hendersons.

The interior of the clothing laboratory was converted to ashes. All books were destroyed and ten sewing machines burned. The refrigerator room, attic, Cottage kitchen, laundry, and dining room were either burned or blistered. In addition, the upstairs Cottage rooms were badly smoked, and long after the fire, crews of student helpers devoted their energies to cleaning up the mess.

Gorham Normal delivered six of their sewing machines as a loan, and local friends supplied others. Temporarily classes met in the Mallett Hall dining room and the inevitable fire sale was held. Eventually plans were carried out for refinishing and improving the Cottage facilities. Some hoped that a brand-new structure would be possible immediately, but that would not be realized until the 1960s.

FSNS, from 1942 to 1945, was in the doldrums, with sparse attendance and reduced programs, but many of its graduates were distinguishing themselves with their contributions to the war effort. The proper telling of the exploits of those who joined the military would result in another book of similar size to this one. Those who gave their lives for their country were:

James E. Bernadini	1931
Donald E. Curtis	1935
R. Donald Fish	1939
William Russell, Jr.	1939
Robert F. Violet	1940
Richard A. Yorke	1940
Mason Prescott	1941
C. Robert Mercier	1942

Farmington Normal: A Summing Up

The major objective of the early normal schools was to improve the quality of elementary school teaching. The leaders of the normal school movement rejected the contention that good teachers are born not made. They said repeatedly that special training was as important for teachers as it was for those in other professions. Champions of normal schools recognized the inadequacy of building character by learning moral precepts, and pointed to the lack of mental challenge in merely memorizing textbook information. Part of the normal school idea was that by spending time in preparing interesting classes and by appealing to the affection of the child, teachers could maintain discipline more satisfactorily than by the use of force or the threat of force. Mark Dunnell, E. P. Weston, and A. P. Kelsey

EXAM TIME in Study Hall (class of 1942).

were three pioneers in the Maine normal school movement. Graduates of liberal arts colleges, they concentrated on what they regarded as the most serious shortcoming of the educational system, namely, the State's elementary schools. Rousseau and Pestalozzi had convinced them of the importance of learning by doing rather than passive memorizing, and this was to be part of the normal school credo from Horace Mann through John Dewey.

FSNS principals, in speeches and articles, never ceased to emphasize the need to elevate the prestige of the teacher of young children. Principals Kelsey and Gage were keenly aware of the need to improve the teacher's standing in the community as a prerequisite for attracting better teachers. C. C. Rounds, throughout his Farmington administration, was frustrated and even embittered by his inability to get legislation passed that would prevent the untrained and ignorant person from entering the teaching profession. Several times W. G. Mallett decried the dominant stereotype of the schoolmaster such as portrayed and popularized in Washington Irving's *Ichabod Crane*. Payson Smith, attuned to and sympathetic with normal school objectives, frequently pointed with dismay at the teacher's low pay and lack of social status, and at the minimal mental stimulation available to the average rural schoolteacher.

The normal school movement oftentimes had a moral earnestness that was of a religious intensity. George C. Purington spoke throughout the State on the life and principles of Horace Mann, and the two had much in common. Both thought the schools could promote temperance so effectively as to remove alcohol as the chief cause of poverty and degradation. Both men believed in the schools as the means of instilling and reinforcing the virtues of honesty, thrift, and uprightness. Both thought that public education could eliminate the greater part of social and economic injustice as well as vanquish crime. The millenarian dream of such men as Mann and Purington went far in explaining the ardor with which they attempted to solve educational problems.

In the nineteenth century, strong support for and interest in Maine normal schools came consistently from the governors of the State. In 1866, the first year of FSNS graduation, Joshua L. Chamberlain expressed his admiration for the new normal schools. In 1872 Governor Sidney Perham said: "The Normal Schools at Farmington and Castine are doing excellent work. Two hundred and sixty-four graduates of these schools have taught in our public schools the past year, besides a larger number of those who have not graduated." Nelson Dingley, Jr., when governor of Maine in 1874, stated that "probably no money expended in educational directions yields larger returns. No one who has watched the progress of our common schools for the past decade can have failed to discover a striking improvement in methods of instruction, coming largely from the influence of our normal schools." In the 1880s, Governor Frederick Robie, of Gorham, was an effective champion of teacher-training institutions.

Despite these words of praise, normal schools were always in dire need of material support such as would have made possible adequate libraries and at least a minimum of scientific equipment. Many members of the legislature were not convinced that normal schools had proven their worth. Some legislators were probably inclined to doubt the value of libraries, especially for prospective elementary schoolteachers. Normal schools were considerably less successful than the State University at Orono in getting desired appropriations.

The poverty-stricken rural districts supported their own schools and were jealous of their independence. This explained why they opposed so successfully Rounds's proposal to recognize the normal school diploma as a teaching certificate. Consequently, for many years, despite the formation of the Maine normal schools, the school agent could continue to fill a teaching vacancy with his local candidate, who might have no teacher-training or ability to derive benefit from such an education. The normal schools waged a long and valiant struggle against the low teaching standards of rural areas before they made substantial progress in improving the situation.

Farmington Normal always had an impressive number of able graduates, but throughout the nineteenth century, many FSNS-trained males were likely to leave teaching after fulfilling their tuition commitment. Many concluded, after considering comparative financial rewards, that teaching was only a way station for those who had the courage and drive to escape from the profession. There were others who found the teaching offers from neighboring states irresistible; fortunately there were those who stayed in Maine and made valuable contributions to its educational progress.

Critics of the normal schools have contended that teacher-training institutions downgraded intellectual achievements. It has been alleged that schoolteachers, more often than not, have been unable to claim any intellectual life of their own, so have naturally been unable to generate any interest in their pupils for attaining intellectual goals. The presence of so many mediocrities, the argument goes, discouraged the ablest students from entering teaching. A 1950 article in *Life* magazine included the observation and opinion that "a great many of the teachers colleges bring an inferior faculty and an inferior student body together in an inferior physical plant."

There is no inclination here to deny the partial validity of such criticism. In the latter stages of FSNS, there were faculty members who belittled academic excellence and exalted in its place such nebulous objectives as adjustment to life situations. Furthermore, there were occasional students whose intention to teach posed a potential threat to some child's education. Normal school principals can be pointed to who have not only denied the desirability of intellectual training, but have insisted that such a thing was impossible. FSNS principals, however, had no such anti-intellectual bias; moreover, they usually refused to recommend an inferior person or weak student for a teaching position. All of them were scholars who had been brought up in the liberal arts tradition. (This did not prevent W. G. Mallett from criticizing his alma mater for what he regarded as its indifference to the art of teaching.) The excessive paternalism of the normal schools reflected the times. In Farmington the paternalism of the principals and teachers not only took the form of enforcing puritanical rules and regulations, it also reflected a genuine affection for and interest in the students. This covered not only their undergraduate days at Farmington but the later teaching and marriage years. FSNS graduates reciprocated and have always been noted for their loyalty to the school.

For good reasons the normal schools of Maine have been superseded, but they served in their day the noble and useful purpose of substantially improving the quality of elementary school teaching.

PART TWO

ERROL L. DEARBORN, first president Farmington State Teachers College, 1945–53.

I. THE DEARBORN ADMINISTRATION

During World War II, any attempts to work out a new and satisfactory curriculum and to make other changes or adjustments in anticipation of the conversion of Farmington Normal to a teachers college, had to be held in abeyance. There was at this time a serious shortage of teachers; to have added another year for teacher preparation would have only aggravated the situation. (The FSNS *Bulletin*, from at least 1934 on, proclaimed that Farmington Normal was also a bona fide teachers college because of the B.S. degree granted by the home economics department. Such a proclamation, however, was insufficient to obtain for FSNS official and legal recognition as a college. A legislative act would be required for that.) The war had delayed the making of educational decisions throughout the land. Hence, the coming of peace found an accumulation of problems that had to be faced. Many of those who had been supporters of teacher institutions throughout the years not only had their sharp disagreements with the liberal arts proponents, but also held divergent educational theories among themselves. Their never-ending disputes covered the pages of educational journals. In postwar years, such disagreements were to be very much in evidence as teacher institutions again began their intensive soul-searching.

Farmington was no exception to this introspection. The problem of how to make teaching more effective and the profession more appealing to the young was highlighted during the war by the withdrawal of many successful teachers from the profession in favor of more lucrative means of earning a living. Many were serving in the armed forces, and whether or not they were to be permanently lost to teaching had yet to be determined.*

On July 19, 1945, the long-awaited legislative action took effect which converted the Farmington State Normal School into the Farmington State Teachers College. Whatever other changes were in the offing, the new institution had become by statutory order a four-year college of higher learning, granting bachelor of science degrees in elementary and junior high school education as well as in home economics. Also on that day, State Commissioner of Education Harry V. Gilson announced the appointment of Dr. Errol L. Dearborn as the first president of the new teachers college. (Mr. Day had resigned at the end of the 1944–45 school year, to become superintendent of schools at Kittery.) Dr. Dearborn was a logical choice. He had been on the faculty of Farmington Normal since his graduation in 1922 from the University of Maine. At various times he had continued his education at Harvard and at New York University, eventually receiving a doctor of education degree from NYU in 1942. Since 1929 he had been vice-principal of Farmington Normal.

As indicated previously, few males attended Maine normal schools during the first quarter of the century. Hence, nearly all classroom teachers in the elementary and junior high schools were women.

---

* One of the first encouraging signs concerning the future of teaching in postwar Maine was contained in a letter written to the Kappa Delta Phi alumni. The date for this was May 1, 1947; the letter was signed by Jerome Audet, president, and Gwilym R. Roberts, trustee of the fraternity: "Past letters have given news of the 162 former members of the Zeta Chapter who were in the service. Of these 162, 160 decided that they preferred civilian life; only two are reported to be still in the service. The much advertised weaknesses of education as a career do not seem to have made too much of an impression upon Kappa members; 53 Kappa alumni are now engaged in it, while another 46 have gone back to school, generally to prepare themselves for that same profession.

"Among those now engaged in educational work, 24 are teaching in junior high or elementary work, 21 in high school teaching, 6 are teaching in colleges from Maine to Georgia, and two are superintendents of schools. 32 have returned to FSTC or other schools to pursue undergraduate work, while 14 others are in graduate schools. In all, then, of the 200 alumni traced by this letter 99 are known to be engaged in teaching or in going to school."

Men, when any could be found, were usually either principals or superintendents. In the latter half of the 1920s there was an increase in male enrollment, partly because the teacher shortage brought higher salaries, especially in the wealthier states. With the onset and deepening of the depression, men increased in numbers at FSNS. In many instances this was because the institution offered an opportunity to obtain a low-cost education prior to earning the remaining degree credits at Orono. After the United States entered World War II there was a return to the previous ratio of men and women at Farmington, the demands of war being what they were. The greatest imbalance was reached in the spring of 1945 when only one male, Dean Murch, a discharged navy veteran, was attending FSNS, but this lonely figure was to get considerable male support in 1945–46. The 1946 *Effesteco* presented an all-veteran basketball team and there were pictures to prove it. One was of the veterans in their military uniforms, the other showed them in their basketball attire.

Although the war was over in August 1945, many of those who had participated in it did not have time to get back from foreign lands, or get their release from wartime occupations before the college year began. The result of all this was that there were only 173 students at the opening session of Farmington State Teachers College. In 1946–47, the enrollment was to go up to about 250, seventy of them men, and by the early fifties the students numbered over 300. (This was still substantially less than the 350-400 of the 1930s.) Although the men who had attended the Normal School were likely to reappear in 1946–47, other war veterans from Maine were more likely to use their G.I. Bill to attend the more prestigious liberal arts colleges or universities.

The men and women who did re-enroll at the newly-converted Farmington Teachers College found many of the former FSNS organizations and practices basically unchanged, but some of them were to become quite different from their antecedents. At FSNS chapels, until the 1940s, the faculty had sat on the stage in the Nordica auditorium (Merrill Hall from 1908 to 1972), and their early morning appearance had had various effects on those who faced them from their student seats. (Perhaps it would be an understatement to say that none of these effects was inspirational.) Now, in 1945, the faculty were no longer on 8 A.M. display, and furthermore, chapel itself as an involuntary exercise was under fire. In the December (1947) *Mirror,* the question was asked: Are chapel exercises three times a week really necessary? The person who asked this question expressed doubts about it and found all such occasions "excessively boring." Only a few years before this iconoclastic editorial appeared, students had attended daily chapel with hardly a discouraging word.

The response to this postwar unrest was to make chapel voluntary, but it was soon evident after the rule went into effect that unforeseen numbers of students felt no inner compulsion to attend chapel. Hence, FSTC assemblies were again made mandatory, and as the years went by, many hours were devoted in FSTC faculty meetings to discussing the most effective and appropriate penalties for those who were incorrigibly indifferent about college assemblies. One or two of the faculty wanted to reduce the grade point average of the absent miscreants, but this draconian suggestion was not regarded by the majority as fit punishment for the crime. Chapel attendance continued to vex an uncertain faculty until the unprecedented increase in students during the mid-sixties made it impossible to seat everyone in the assembly hall. So a lack of space settled one of the most time-consuming problems in FSTC history. This meant that printed bulletins, initiated in 1955, were to be the sole device for keeping undergraduates informed about college activities. Some felt greatly aggrieved that other advantages attendant upon having the entire college get together were to be sacrificed. There is no question that by 1966 the days of the old-time FSNS and FSTC camaraderie and cohesion had been drastically reduced as the State College, established in 1965, began its rapid expansion.

During the almost eighty years of Farmington Normal history, 10 P.M. was considered the inviolable hour for retiring, unless an infrequent event of monumental importance prevented the student from getting to bed at the usual time. The first major break in such a schedule occurred during the first year of Farmington Teachers College. The rules were liberalized to permit students to stay out until 10 on weekdays and 11 on Friday and Saturdays evenings. In a year or two, the hour was advanced to 12 for one evening a week. In early years, students had not only been compelled to retire by 10, but to return to the dormitories by 7:25 on weekdays. The 1946 changes in the rules marked a turning point by determining new hours of propriety. Students seen on the streets after 7:30 were no longer regarded as refugees from justice.

Social historians have oftentimes commented on the speed with which certain sartorial taboos have come and gone; the rules governing the attire of FSTC women represented no exception to this general observation. In the 1950s at Farmington, kerchiefs were permitted on the heads of future teachers if they were worn at breakfast, Saturday noon, and at meals preceding formal dances. Slacks were apparently held in lower esteem, for they were allowed only at breakfast on Saturday morning. (It is assumed they could be worn in the dormitory rooms if the shades were drawn.) The records would indicate that the sometimes spectacular miniskirt and pants ensembles were greeted in the sixties with comparative indifference. By this time the arbiters of local fashion had undoubtedly concluded that resistance to national and international trends was useless.

A majority of FSNS organizations were continued into at least the early FSTC years, and some are still thriving. Only the names of some have been changed in order to observe the acronym necessities. The yearbook *Effesseness* became *Effesteco*, and after the Farmington State Teachers College became Farmington State College, was forced to change its name once more. This time it was to adopt the State of Maine motto, *Dirigo*. The FSNS *Mirror* became the FSTC *Mirror* and then the FSC *Mirror*. In 1970 it was transformed into *The Baked Apple*. (Research has not produced any explanation for the most recent renaming of the publication. Certainly it was not because of the role played by the apple in the story of original sin. Perhaps it is because *The Baked Apple* does not try to mirror events, like its predecessor, but merely indicates the taste of the one doing the baking.)

In 1943 the Agnes P. Mantor chapter of the Future Teachers of America (FTA) was established in Farmington. This was an organization designed, among other things, to assist in the recruiting of high school students for teachers colleges and teaching careers. (With enrollment plunging during the war years, many faculty members had their classes scheduled in such a way as to leave free afternoons or free days in which teams of one faculty member and several students could visit high schools in an effort to entice students to prepare for teaching careers at Farmington.) In the days of the assemblies, the

FTA would sponsor programs that observed National Education Week, Horace Mann Day, or paid homage to other educational heroes and activities. In 1957 this teacher-oriented group became known as the Student Educational Association of Maine (SEAM). It established what was known as Career Day, at which time prospective teachers in their senior years at high school would be invited to visit the Farmington campus. In this way those who were undecided about teaching as a career would be given the opportunity to learn more about the profession. SEAM has also run beano and dance parties, playdays for Mallett School children, and exchange programs with other teacher institutions. In the early sixties SEAM became moribund, but it recovered and was active again in 1965. The revival has continued to the present.

The Normal School faculty-government was altered somewhat with the coming of the Teachers College but remained fundamentally the same. (The committee structure of the 1930s was still standing but was being altered constantly to meet changing conditions.) In 1948 two new organizations were formed: a coordinating council and a dormitory council, which was to last for twenty years. Headed by four students elected by the student body, the former also had four faculty members appointed by the president. The Dormitory Council was composed of an ex-officio member and some student members who made it because of their campus positions. These included the presidents of the four classes and the presidents of all recognized college organizations. The council was expected not only to push for desirable changes in rules and regulations, but had specific duties such as printing the handbook and running the senior dance.

The Dormitory Council was to take the place of the Dormitory Committee, which had proved to be somewhat unwieldy in law enforcement. The continued usefulness of this group is attested to by its present activity. Those who have served on the Dormitory Council have responded to more emergencies, some of them late at night, than those in any other campus organization. Dormitory leaders know the significance of the biblical observation: "Those who watcheth over Israel neither slumber nor sleep."

Some schools officials retained their titles and responsibilities in the conversion process, while other positions were either altered or added in accordance with the changing functions of the new college.

Nettie Rounds, first employed as the secretary of W. G. Mallett, became the first bursar in FSNS history and retained that title until her retirement from FSTC in 1953. During the Dearborn administration, Marie Pecorelli Kearney became the first registrar, although Mrs. Rounds had performed the duties customarily assigned to this position. In 1946 Clinton Nichols became the first vice president of the FSTC, but this position was dropped temporarily with his resignation in 1948. In 1949 two new positions for deans were created when Harvey Kelley became dean of instruction and Clayton Reed dean of men. In 1950 Ruth E. Williams was appointed dean of women, a position she would hold for twenty-two years, the longest such tenure in the institution's history. In 1953 Clayton Reed would become the first male director of student teaching and John Mudge would assume the duties of dean of men, a position which he would hold for twelve years.

The faculty, excluding those at the Mallett School, numbered 26 in 1946. Before the war there were 22, but the drop in wartime enrollment brought about a corresponding reduction of the faculty; by the end of the war, there were only 18 FSNS instructors. Four years after the war, in 1949, the number had jumped to 26, of whom only three had been at the college as long as five years. During this same period the Campus School was also hard hit by resignations.*

Immediately after World War II, it was apparent that the old order was ready to give way to the new. In 1946 Arthur D. Ingalls retired. He had been principal of the Farmington Town School from 1907 to 1931 and the Mallett School from 1931 to 1946. Emma Mahoney, after twenty-three years of service as director of student teaching, gave way in 1947 to Julia Cox. Stella Dakin, after serving in the American Junior Red Cross from 1945 to 1949, came back in the latter year as the dean of women. Apparently as vital as ever on her return, she was taken ill in the spring of 1950 and died a few months later. In 1948 Helen E. Lockwood retired after serving for twenty-

---

* In post-FSNS days, the training school was sometimes called the Campus or the Laboratory School. An extensive, if not excessive, time was spent in periodically discussing the most appropriate designation. This search for the perfect name was not confined to the local scene; the National Education Association, for reasons imperfectly understood, constantly worried about what to call training schools connected with teachers colleges.

Left: Agnes Mantor at the stacks in the old library in Merrill Hall. Right: Helen Elizabeth Lockwood, dean of the Department of Home Economics, 1923–48.

five years as dean of home economics. It was during her administration that the department attained a state-wide reputation for excellence. The following year Margaret Mades, a member of the Home Ec faculty since 1934, resigned to accept a position at Penn State, and then moved from there to Skidmore College. In 1948, Mary E. Tilton, for twenty years the head of physical education at FSNS and FSTC, resigned to pursue her career on Long Island, New York. The English department lost Ruth Somers when she accepted a position at the Worcester Teachers College. In 1946 Ruth Griffiths, the highly successful FSNS music instructor, went to the Plymouth Teachers College and was succeeded by Ruby Blaine, who continued and expanded the musical organizations of the college.

Of all the resignations, the most noteworthy for the greatest number of alumni occurred in 1949 when Professor Charles S. Preble retired. His career went back further than that of any other faculty member. He had completed nearly forty-four years of teaching, with twenty-eight of them spent in Farmington. The first professional geographer in Farmington history, he was well known to both sluggards and early risers for his 6 A.M. nature walks. At forty-odd years of age he was the FSNS first baseman; at seventy he was to make one of his many climbs of Mt. Katahdin; at seventy-six he substituted for Myron Starbird while the latter was studying at Clark University; and at ninety-one he explored by airplane the coast of Maine. Author of the New England section in the geography textbook, *Our Home State and Continent*, he also wrote a forty-page pamphlet, *The Teaching of Maine Geography*, as well as articles in the *Journal of Geography and School Science and Mathematics.* [1]

Those who joined the FSTC faculty in the 1947–54 period tended to stay on for many years. In fact, some were to spend all, and others nearly all, of their teaching careers in Farmington. Among those who became addicted to Farmington life were: Mabel Hastie (successor to Helen E. Lockwood), Clayton Reed, Ruth E. Williams, Julia Ksionzyk, Gladys Taylor, Myron Starbird, Martha Wasgatt, Lawrence Stofan, Robert Bigelow, Elsie Grote, Julia Eaton Van Zanten, John Mudge, Eleanor Wood, Shasta Boynton, Madeleine Parker, and Harland Abbott; Helen W. Gordon and Dorothy J. Sweatt were to be longtime stalwarts at the Mallett School before they joined the UMF Department of Education. The 1959 faculty was almost

Top left: Ruth E. Williams, dean of women, 1950–73. Right: Lawrence Stofan, professor of psychology and baseball coach. Bottom left: Dr. John E. Mudge, dean of men and science professor, 1953–65. Right: Chef Bonney in Purington Hall.

identical with the 1954–55 membership, and 23 of the 26 would be at the college five years after that.

Social activities were much the same in the 1945–53 period as they had been in the years of the Normal School. Until the college began its spectacular expansion in the mid-sixties, there were only three sororities, which were formed from 1925 to 1930. During this period Kappa Delta Phi (now Kappa Delta Chi) continued to be the sole fraternity on the campus. (Its national president in 1947 was Gwilym R. Roberts.) These social organizations continued to sponsor dances and entertainments of various quality, much as they did in pre-1945 days. The Winter Carnival and Coronation Ball continued to hold the spotlight during one weekend in February, and even though the college was not divided into alphabetical sections, there were dances that were the descendants of the B and D Hops. In postwar years the hoopla that had characterized rallies before the Gorham game was again on display, usually in the coldest part of the winter. Several rallies threw in an extra feature—a snake dance through the main streets of the town. Even the sorority and fraternity hazing of normal school days, which was being abandoned in most parts of the country, was continued at Farmington in its merry, and sometimes sadistic way.

The conversion to teachers college did not bring with it any new building activity. But despite the failure of the State to finance any new construction from 1924 to 1954, there were during this period purchases of property that seemed significant to the more prescient. In the 1930s the Methodist parsonage, situated south of the public library, was sold to the Normal School, and the Baptist residence, which was next to it, was acquired in 1945. In 1937 the Kappa Delta Phi fraternity took over the Abbott School dormitory; the fraternal organization was able to house about fifty men. In 1950 the present Franklin Hall was bought and converted into a women's dormitory. Accommodating about fifty students, it was exclusively a senior house and known by the temporary name of Dearborn Hall.

In addition to the acquisition of property in this thirty-year period, postwar agitation mounted for badly needed construction. The long-felt yearning for a respectable library was reasserted in an October, 1946, editorial in the *Mirror*. The following year the Campus Planning Committee was carrying on discussions concerning the pos-

sibility of adding a wing to the Alumni Gymnasium. The lack of
legislative response to such suggestions reinforced the belief of many
that the physical plant could be improved only by the joint efforts
of FSNS students, faculty, and alumni.

Merrill Hall, known so long as the Administration Building, had
been much too crowded in the late twenties, and this was recognized
by the State when it gave financial assistance for the furnishing of
the training school building that combined the Model and Town
schools in 1931. In the early fifties, Merrill Hall was to go through
another space crisis, for it housed at this time the offices of the president, deans, bursar, college nurse, faculty; the college bookstore; the
Edith Clifford library; a student lounge; a snack bar; the college
print shop, and thirteen classrooms. (In the 1940s and later, nearly
all the faculty were assigned to one large room, the very one whose
ceiling had been painted years before by George C. Purington. There
was only one telephone for some thirteen faculty members, and the
students had their conferences with the faculty in this office. To compound the confusion and add to the noise, this one telephone was
only an extension line from the office phone below, to which faculty
receiving their extension calls were summoned by a buzzer.)

Acting upon the assumption that the Lord helps those who help
themselves, a decision was made in December, 1949, that planning
should be immediately undertaken to raise money for a new college
building which would be known as the Mallett Memorial Building.
Students, faculty, and alumni were to cooperate in this project. C.
Everett Page, captain of the only football team in FSNS history,
was to head the drive for the alumni, while the faculty and students
organized a Memorial Building Committee and pledged to raise
$15,000.

Members of the college met initially to draw up revenue producing schemes that, hopefully, would result in a major financial contribution for the construction of this student union and bookstore.
The most successful method for raising money proved to be the Bea-
ver's Den. This was a booth at the Franklin County Fair which, under the dietary control of Gladys Taylor, was to sell vast quantities
of food. For the next several years the Building Committee saw to
it that sustenance was provided all those on the fair grounds who
were either hungry or willing to eat more than they wanted in the
interest of a worthy cause. At the Den, students and faculty worked

together in a democratic and harmonious relationship. The sharing of duties in serving food, washing and drying dishes, cleaning up the booth, and staying awake as night watchmen added another dimension to faculty and student camaraderie. Part of the denouement of the Memorial Building story was to unfold during the Scott administration, the remainder in the Olsen regime.

During the Dearborn administration, the athletic program was almost exclusively confined to basketball. (The women had field hockey as well as basketball, but they continued to be limited to their traditional intramural competition.) With the return of discharged war veterans, Professor Roberts became the first FSTC basketball coach and served during the first part of the year 1945–46. Mickey Maguire filled in during the latter part of that year, and Charles Nelson succeeded him in 1946–47. In the fall of 1947, Joe Wenckus, an alumnus and co-captain of the 1938–39 basketball team at FSNS, was signed up as coach. In 1949 his coaching paid off, for the FSTC Beavers won the New England State Teachers Athletic Conference championship. The sharpshooter of this quintet was Fred Rogers; he was to score over 1,000 points during his career and was elected team captain during his last three years at the college. In 1951 Joe Wenckus resigned and Albert Doran replaced him to direct the basketball teams from 1951 to 1953. During this period two present Farmington educators, Kenneth Marks and Verne Byers, were basketball standouts at FSTC.

After serving in 1955 as president of the New England State Teachers Athletic Conference, Professor Doran became more involved in teaching history and less in the athletic program. Hence a greater part of the burden of coaching was assumed by Professor Lawrence Stofan. The last year of the Dearborn regime witnessed the re-introduction of baseball, which had to be accomplished at minimal expense. This meant, among other things, much searching for lost baseballs and a meager choice of bats unless the individual player was wealthy enough to buy his own. Professor Stofan was prominent in the return of baseball to Farmington. He was to serve for eight years as the coach of this low-budget sport as well as mentor of basketball. And all of this was added to what appeared to be a rather formidable teaching schedule.

In 1953–54, a turnabout occurred in the legislative attitude toward appropriations for college construction. In 1953, Dr. Dearborn,

Moving books into the new Mantor Library, May 1956.

Interior of the Mantor Library. (Photo spring, 1965.)

WINTER CARNIVAL in the 50s. Snow sculpture being judged by faculty members
(l to r): Rose Lambertson, Martha Wasgatt, and Else Grote.

after three appearances before the legislature, was able to reach an understanding which assured Farmington of a building for the library. Unfortunately, the first-mentioned amount for this purpose was reduced to an inadequate $300,000. This was made even more inadequate by the stipulation that it must be a library-classroom building. A large amount of the space was to be used for four classrooms. This all proved costly; in fifteen years, at inflation prices, a substantial addition to the original building would be necessary.

Soon after a new library was assured, Dr. Dearborn announced his retirement after thirty-one years on the Farmington faculty, the last eight of which he had served as president. During these years he was noted for the number of services he was able to render. Some semesters, in his early years of FSNS teaching, he had taught every hour of the school day; in the evening, he was likely to be found either coaching dramatics or basketball. He was the supervisor of NYA workers, operator of the FSNS and FSTC print shop, as well as performer of many other extra-curricular activities. After taking over the direction of FSTC, he was confronted, as has been noted, with the need to find faculty replacements. In 1946 the average salary was about $2,700; this presented an obvious problem to one who was faced with the necessity of rebuilding a faculty. A question of paramount importance was: What were to be the major differences between the nineteenth century normal school and the twentieth century teachers college? Some of the answers to this will involve us with the accreditation story as it unfolded during the Scott administration.

Dr. Dearborn belonged to the Purington-Mallett tradition of participation in community affairs. Deacon at the Baptist church, he was a member of Rotary and past commander of the Roderick-Crosby Post of the American Legion. During World War II he served as chairman of the Franklin County Red Cross drive for three consecutive years. Both Dr. and Mrs. Dearborn have given generously and consistently of their time to alumni activities, including the editing in 1957 of the *Alumni Catalogue.* The highlight of the annual alumni luncheon on May 19, 1973, was the presentation of the first Distinguished Alumni Award to the first president of the Farmington State Teachers College.

DR. ERMO H. SCOTT, President of Farmington State Teachers College, 1953–66.

II. THE SCOTT ADMINISTRATION

The Accreditation Story

The major purpose of the Farmington State Teachers College as envisioned in the 1940s was to be reaffirmed many times, and it served as the introduction to the 1954 accreditation report:

> It is the purpose of Farmington State Teachers College to educate teachers who will guide children toward effective living in a democratic society, a type of living satisfying to them as individuals and, at the same time, characterized by active group participation for the social good. To meet this challenge, teachers must be people with broad knowledge and skills, which continually increase as they work. They must be possessed with characteristics and attitudes which will make them helpful and effective guides in the growth of children. They must be persons who, because of their professional interest, knowledge and skill, will maintain high standards in their teaching and dignify it as a profession.

Such a statement of purpose was not highly controversial, but work on curriculum revision in the postwar years brought on a clash of opinion. The faculties of the two teachers colleges and the three normal schools in Maine were expected to work together in this effort. (From 1945 to 1952 Gorham and Farmington were the only teachers colleges in Maine.) At a meeting of the administrators, Dr. Dearborn expressed the opinion that it would be desirable to work toward getting a more functional curriculum in teacher education, and that in order to obtain this result an entirely functional approach should be tried. He recommended that departmental lines and subjects, as they were then established, be put aside for the time being

227

and that the curriculum be based on the following categories: (1) The art of communication; (2) The art of appreciation; (3) Living in a social world; (4) Quantitative aspects of living; (5) Scientific aspects of living; and (6) Preparing for a profession. The Commissioner, Harland A. Ladd, approved of this approach and recommended its adoption. The other administrators agreed to give it a try.

As a result of this action, chairmen and members of six committees (one for each category) were selected from the teachers colleges and normal schools. But little was to be accomplished, and after a few years, efforts in curriculum planning seemed to swing back to the individual college. The failure of collective action can be probably attributed to several facts: too great a distance separated the members of the committees; no one who accepted the functional approach was available to coordinate and encourage the effort; faculty changes were so numerous that it was difficult to maintain committee leadership; and the untimely death of Harland A. Ladd removed the key supporter of the functional plan.

Dr. Ermo H. Scott succeeded Dr. Dearborn, and the new president had his own ideas on curriculum planning. He needed little, if any, time to adjust to the problems confronting him at Farmington. As deputy commisioner of education from 1948 to 1953 he had occupied a position which called upon him to be deeply involved in shaping policies for Maine teachers colleges. His adult life had been spent in teacher education. A graduate of Castine Normal* and the University of Maine, he had served as vice principal of Castine Normal before becoming president of Castleton Teachers College in Vermont. In 1948 he returned to the State of Maine to accept responsibilities which gave him an excellent view of state-wide conditions in the teacher institutions.

Upon entering his new duties as president in 1953, Ermo Scott made it clear that he was bringing with him a personal commitment to try for FSTC accreditation. As deputy commissioner of education he had seen and participated in the comparatively new proceedings involved in the accreditation of teachers colleges. He was not at all sure that Farmington would qualify in the initial test,

---

* Although Dr. Scott was not a graduate of Farmington Normal he was related to it by marriage. In 1931, Molly Blaisdell, a graduate of Farmington Normal, became Mrs. Ermo Scott.

being acutely aware of the inadequacy of the physical plant as well as of the fact that this was the first such attempt by any Maine teachers college. Furthermore, the other presidents in Maine were giving him no encouragement, for they drew back from what they considered a premature effort. He decided, however, to take the bold course of action, for the initial test would be helpful in the identification of problems, the acceptance and articulation of common purposes, the determination of institutional strengths and weaknesses, and the means of providing a lever to move the legislature.

In order to prepare for the inspection, President Scott appointed soon after his arrival in Farmington a central planning committee consisting of seven members under the chairmanship of the dean of men, John Mudge. This committee provided direction for seven sub-committees. The structure was designed to collect, analyze, and coordinate data for the use of the accrediting associations. In the 1954 report that FSTC sent to the inspection teams, certain changes which were considered significant were listed as having taken place between 1948 and 1952. These were: (1) the introduction of the course on Child and Curriculum; (2) the strengthening of the academic program in English, science, and social studies; (3) the introduction of the course, Personal Problems, for freshmen; (4) the broadening of the physical sciences; (5) the development of a more functional English program; and (6) a better provision made for a broader elective program.

Some of these so-called significant changes are too broadly expressed for us to evaluate them from this distance—perhaps it would have been difficult enough from any distance. Even with more specific information, it was probably painfully challenging to make meaningful judgments about such terms as "strengthen," "broaden," and "more functional." According to today's standards, the curriculum would appear to have had an excessive number of professional courses; of the 128 hours required to graduate, 124 were required courses, and the offerings in science were broad without depth. There was a general course in the physical sciences and one in biology, but there were no specific courses in physics, chemistry, geology, or anthropology. Neither did the budget allow for specialists in political science, sociology, or economics. (The geographer and historian who taught these social science courses may have made them rewarding experiences for the students, but the faculty involved were frequently unhappy to be attempting to teach in areas in which they had limited formal preparation.)

Farmington was denied accreditation in its first try, but the decision came as the result of a split vote. There was reason to be hopeful. Hayden L. V. Anderson, years later the first person to be awarded an honorary degree at UMF, become in 1954 the dean of instruction. Before taking up his duties in Farmington, Dr. Anderson had been the superintendent in the Caribou-Limestone area. Past president of the Maine Teachers Association, he had graduated from Gorham Normal and later was to receive an M.A. from Bates. As the dean of instruction he soon became aware that the entire program at Farmington was lagging badly. He also became intent on determining other deficiencies in the curriculum by sending out questionnaires to seniors and alumni to assist him in identifying the weak spots in the teachers' preparations.

After two and a half years at Farmington, Hayden Anderson resigned as dean of instruction to become director of professional services in the State Department of Education. Professor Gwilym R. Roberts temporarily took over Dr. Anderson's former duties, and soon after assuming office, announced that a student-faculty committee had been formed to revise the curriculum. It was destined to work on this assignment for a year and a half. One of its major achievements was to revise the elementary-junior high schedules in such a way that both seniors and juniors could take electives together as long as the second semester of the junior year and the first semester of the senior year each contained a quarter year of student teaching for all students. Clayton Reed, as director of student teaching, was reluctant to exchange two separate quarters of student teaching for a semester of teacher-training in the last year. When he became convinced, however, that this revision was necessary to provide reasonably large classes for electives, he abandoned his adamant stand against it and thus cleared the way for previously unavailable electives. This change was undoubtedly of great help in getting accreditation for FSTC later on.

Another glaring deficiency in 1954 was the library. Some 20,000 volumes were on the shelves, but a disproportionate number of them consisted of books on pedagogy. Many of these were never too stimulating even in the years when they were supposedly marking out new educational trails. Fortunately work began on a new library building the same year the accreditation team cast jaundiced eyes on the old one. The important relationship between library growth and accreditating standards was emphasized by Agnes P. Mantor in the March (1960) *Mirror*:

> Our college library by its growth in size, number of volumes, and student use may be said to be indicative of the growth of FSTC toward the true maturity of a college. Substantial additions in the field of philosophy, literature, world geography, and history mark library growth in fields that need rich resources.
>
> In the years previous to Farmington's accreditation, the library budget for books consisted of the income of the Edith Clifford fund, $1,350, with state money supplying magazines, newspapers, and supplies. To meet accreditation standards the book budget was increased and now a greater number of acquisitions will be made each year.

Today Farmington's well-run library is about twice as large as it was in 1954, but even so, meager spending for books has been the order of the day until the last few years. The records would indicate that a usable and respectable library has been established mainly through the pressures exerted by accreditation standards. As far back as 1943 the FSNS library was criticized for falling short of such criteria. In that year the *Mirror* tied the modest local library goals to national standards: "As part of a plan to attain the standards set up by the American Association of Teachers Colleges, the school facilities are being enlarged by room extension and new books are being added in an attempt to reach the 15,000 mark."

The failure to gain accreditation in 1954 was followed four years later by the appearance in Farmington of another New England inspection committee; this time Farmington was to receive regional approval. Headed by Dr. Ralph Burns of Dartmouth,, the inspection team also included the president of the Plymouth State Teachers College. (This was of interest to the historian because in 1883 Rounds had left Farmington to become the head of the Plymouth Normal. Now in 1958 a successor of his was to vote for Farmington accreditation.) Along with the approval went many suggestions for rounding out a better balanced program. First on the list was a strong recommendation for a foreign language department. French and German had been offered at Farmington in the nineteenth century,

CANDY • GUM
POTATO CHIPS
CIGARETTES

but were taken from the curriculum after the loss in 1904 of the three-year course. The restoration of modern languages was to prove difficult; it was not until 1969 that this recommendation would be acted upon. For sixty-five years English was the only language taught at Farmington.

In 1961 the National Council for Accreditation of Teacher Education (NCATE) awarded the FSTC provisional accreditation. This was good for three years. Three inadequacies needed correction before full accreditation could be granted: (1) policies which related to the programs for the elementary group and home economics department appeared to be too divergent; (2) standards for admission to the college needed to be raised and more clearly defined; and (3) it was questioned whether or not 45 or 50 hours of professional education left sufficient time for a general education.

The provisional accreditation status of FSTC was prolonged for one year in 1964 because of extenuating circumstances. By December 21, 1965, the delayed report to the NCATE was submitted not by FSTC but by the renamed Farmington State College. (This change in name did not reflect actual changes in functions but only the anticipation of making the institution multi-purpose.) The report included a description of major developments at Farmington:

> Instructionally and with the aid of a Federal Grant, expanded course offerings in both Special Education and Elementary Education have been realized. It would appear that, shortly, the College will be in a position to expand its major in Mental Retardation to include a program for preparing teacher-therapists in the fields of Speech and Hearing. In Home Economics Education, all professional and supervisory functions, hitherto shared with the State Department of Education, have been consolidated within the campus authority and personnel.
>
> Since the 1960 report, the official accession of the college library list has increased about 28%, from 25.5 to 32.6 thousand volumes, with an additional 200 volumes in process of listing. In addition, a Special Education Curriculum collection of over 2,500 volumes is being maintained. The current periodical list has been extended from 97 in 1960 to over 230 in number. Student usage has been disproportionate to the actual numerical increase in enrollment.

The establishment of Fulbright scholarships was an international feature of postwar developments in the educational world. Farming-

Top: Eleanor Wood as faculty adviser of the *Mirror*. Middle: Amanda Winter, now Mrs. Charles Murray, at bat (1959). Above: Snack Bar in the cellar of the Administrative Building in the 50s.

ton was involved in the program both by having one of its faculty study in a foreign land and in receiving a visitor from abroad. At the 1953 commencement, with his mother in the audience as a member of the 50th reunion class, Professor Gwilym R. Roberts heard the surprise announcement that he had been granted a Fulbright for a year's study at the University College of North Wales at Bangor. The next year traffic came the other way when Mohamed Gamal El Din Mokhtar of Cairo, Egypt, with the assistance of a Fulbright, devoted several weeks at FSTC in studying educational problems.

A decade later, President Scott spent several weeks in Nepal studying the educational system of that nation in preparation for the visit to Farmington of one of Nepal's leading educators, Ahmed Pradhan. The purpose of Ahmed Pradhan's visit was to study an American teacher-education institution as a possible pattern for the development of a similar program in his country. The crash in Switzerland of the commercial plane upon which Ahmed Pradhan was coming to the United States resulted in the tragic death of the Nepal educator and the end of this promising experiment in international education.

Janitorial Services

It is doubtful that any public building in Maine has had more effective janitorial attention, over a sixty-year period, than what Captain Blake, Reg Berry, and Bill Harrison provided Merrill Hall. Reg Berry was a native of Bear River, Nova Scotia, who joined in 1915 the 85th battalion of the famous Scottish Highland Kilties of the Canadian Army. In 1931 he was employed at FSNS as a part-time janitor of both the Alumni Gym and Merrill Hall. Students not only noticed that his broom swept cleanly, but were amused that he did not hesitate to speak with the utmost frankness about everyone and everything. When the venerable Greek statues in the Nordica auditorium finally showed the weakness and mortality of work done in plaster of Paris, it was Reg Berry who led the charge that divested the room of such tragic figures as Laocoon and his sons about to be done in by avenging and remorseless sea serpents. It was a historic day in the fall of 1949 that saw Reg prove what an eager iconoclast can do to over-age statues of the Olympian gods. (George C. Purington encouraged the graduating classes to buy something for Merrill Hall as their legacy to the Normal School. Oftentimes these gifts were historical or literary pictures; at other times they were Greek statues. Although hidden from view, these Greek heroes, during the passage of the years, had begun to disintegrate. A 1949 refurbishing of the Nordica auditorium required their temporary removal; it was during this period of renovation that the alarming condition of these plaster of Paris objects was first fully appreciated.)

Bill Harrison was a custodian who belonged to that vanishing breed who have taken seriously being the inheritors and exponents of the New England work ethic. "An honest day's work" was something more than expression to him. Unflagging in his effective physical activity, he was a marvel to those of us who compared the amount of work he could get done with that accomplished by ·persons in similar jobs at other institutions. Even though he was not as likely as Reg to make gratuitous remarks, he was no person to hedge on issues. Students and faculty alike enjoyed their conversations with him in the corridors as he continued to sweep clean everything in sight. The Christmas decorations prepared annually by Bill and his wife Frances, onetime manager of the college bookstore, contributed greatly to the genial atmosphere of the college's basement snack bar.

Expansion of the Physical Plant

One of the major accomplishments of the Scott administration was the expansion of the physical plant, but this was sometimes a frustrating project. Although by the mid-fifties, the days of minuscule budgets and consistent denials for new buildings were over, this was not immediately apparent after the installation of the new president. In 1955 a Farmington request for a dormitory was turned down ($325,000 was the amount asked for) and the pessimists were saying that the days of austerity had returned. However, better and even unprecedented developments were in the offing. On March 8, 1956, President Scott announced that the State Board of Education had approved $1,484,000 for capital improvements at Farmington. In September 1958, the college was granted permission to purchase the Sweet, Gray, and Lovejoy properties on Main Street, and then the three houses were razed. After that the Willard house was moved to Knowlton Avenue, creating the necessary space to build the first Farmington dormitory erected since 1924. (In a 1967 dedication service, the dormitory was named for President Emeritus Ermo H.

Scott.) In 1958 the White and Newman properties on High Street were purchased and their houses razed to make way a few years later for a home economics science building. The science wing was named for Professor Emeritus Charles S. Preble and the auditorium for Arthur M. Thomas, assistant principal and science teacher at FSNS for twenty years. The home economics wing honored the first head of the department, Marion C. Ricker; the lounge was named for the head of the department (1948 to 1965) who planned the wing, Mabel Hastie. Even while this building was being completed in 1962, construction was already being started on the Dearborn Gymnasium, located on adjacent land, part of which had been bought in the 1930s and 1940s.* Long-range planning was thus able to combine with the highly successful efforts of the Scott administration in its sustained drive for a first-rate physical plant.

But even the completion of four buildings from 1960 to 1964 failed to convince President Scott of the immediate desirability of increasing student enrollment. His guiding philosophy, which he shared with a majority of the teachers college presidents in the State, was to insist that enrollments should be strictly controlled in order to preserve a reasonable faculty-student ratio. Faculty growth, student enrollment, and capital development were regarded as interrelated and interdependent. A disproportionate growth of any one of these

---

* A note from Dean Gwilym R. Roberts has provided interesting information concerning the acquirement of the property now occupied by the Dearborn Gymnasium: "The Dearborn Gymnasium was located on three parcels of property. The southernmost was the site of the Home Economics cottage or Home Management house; when this building was razed in 1962 the Look residence on Main Street, purchased in 1958 and briefly used as a college dormitory, filled this function. The northernmost lot was the site of the Methodist parsonage, used as the Home Economics Annex in the 1930s and razed during World War II. The middle lot was the site of the former Baptist parsonage, gained in 1945 by an exchange in which the Lodge on Academy Street, used as a dormitory in the 1930s, was transferred to the Baptists for use as a parsonage.

"From its acquisition in 1945, the former Baptist parsonage on High Street had been rented to various faculty members for a residence for their families, with students sometimes also rooming in the building. Among faculty families occupying the building were those of Mrs. Gladys Taylor, Dean Robert Bigelow, Dean Harvey Kelley, Dean John Mudge, Nurse Gladys Fowler, and Mrs. Cassie Ames, who operated the snack bar in the basement of Merrill Hall."

three elements would represent an undesirable imbalance. However, one urgently-needed dormitory for women was built in the early sixties; this was named for the first dean in FSNS history, Carolyn A. Stone. (Since her 1939 retirement, two other honors had come to her. In 1955 she received a citation for meritorious service to FSTC and in 1961 she was given the title of Professor Emeritus of FSTC.) Only the doubling of the faculty from 1965 to 1968, and the building program, made it seem justifiable to Dr. Scott's successors to allow the number of students to go from 515 in June, 1965, to 1,022 in September, 1968, to 1,338 in 1971, and to 1,538 in 1973.

Institutional food has a well-known reputation and no college history would be complete without some story that involved a student protest having to do with the quantity and quality of dormitory fare—at least as evaluated by highly critical undergraduates. One night in October 1953, Farmington students were to attract national attention when they rebelled at what they considered too much hash and too little food. (NBC carried the story of this student rebellion.) In the Mallett Hall dining room discontent broke out when some 75 of 100 students staged a walkout less than five minutes after they had been seated for the evening repast. Obviously this rebellion had been planned, for hungry students (but well enough nourished to carry placards) gathered on the dormitory steps with posters carrying such demands as: "Down with Hash and Bananas," "Serve Us Don't Starve Us," and the most pathetic cry of all, "We Want Food." This last demand was shouted repeatedly from the dormitory steps.

The college managed to emerge from this crisis without any identifiable epidemic of malnutrition, or even breakdown of administrative authority. But as the years went by and the college increased in enrollment, it became increasingly difficult for it to run its own food program. Finally in September 1964, Slater's, the largest contract food service in the world, was charged with the responsibility of feeding FSTC students. (FSTC, in hiring Slater's, set a precedent; it was the first of the Maine state colleges to sign a contract with a professional food service. Richard Lowe, a long-time employee of the company, received the appointment as manager.) A lack of dining space, however, made it difficult for even a professional outfit to perform its mission well. By 1965 some 500 persons were served in rotating shifts in the Purington Hall cafeteria, which seated only 156 at a time. This intolerable situation was corrected, at least temporarily, in August 1966, with the completion of the Dining Center on South Street. Built and equipped at a cost of approximately half a million dollars, it also had a snack bar and was designed for possible expansion. Such foresight was fortunate, for the doubling of the number of faculty and students from 1965 to 1968 made the building inadequate shortly after it was opened for business. The 1973–74 doubling of the size of the dining facilities, in connection with the new Student Services and Study Center, remedied a problem of several years' duration.

Despite the building boom of the early 1960s, the budget regulations were sometimes embarrassing to those who wanted the campus to look as attractive as possible. The library, for example, was open for business in May 1956, but even as late as May 1963, the building had no proper landscaping. This was because a lack of flexibility in budgeting prevented the use of state funds for such a purpose. The Coordinating Council of faculty and student representatives allocated $500 from its treasury for the overdue landscaping, and it was hoped that this amount would be matched by alumni donations. The faculty were not neglected, for they were also encouraged to make personal contributions to the project.

In the 1960s, increases in the number of grade-school students and those enrolling in special education, were reflected in additions to existing buildings. By 1965 it was imperative to build an addition to the Mallett School. Consequently, 11,000 square feet of classroom space was provided at a cost of $210,000. Here was another reminder of the spectacular rise in construction costs. In 1931 the original training building had been erected for $100,000. In the 1960s, special education experienced a steady growth in numbers of students and faculty as well as expansion of its work area. In 1966 a speech and hearing clinic, directed by Richard Holmes, was added to the special education program, and in 1968 essential facilities for it were installed in Merrill Hall.

The building program of the 1960s provided space for more students, and at the same time, the successful campaign for higher faculty salaries helped to strengthen the quality of instruction as well as facilitate an increase in numbers. The shape of things to come was apparent in the early 1960s as the *Mirror* carried several headlines to the effect that the FSTC would have some 1,200 students by

1970. The 1965 budget was evidence that the State had committed itself to enlarging the functions of the former teachers colleges. Whereas the annual appropriation for normal schools in 1900 was $31,000, in 1965 the state colleges received $3,800,000. Moreover, in this same year, $5,000,000 was made available for capital outlay.[2] In anticipation of enlarged functions Maine teachers colleges became in 1965 Maine state colleges. Having shed the word *teachers* from the title, it was expected that the new state colleges would not only train teachers, but provide programs for non-teachers and perform important regional and state services. An institution that had been one-purpose for over a hundred years was on the verge of becoming multi-purpose.

Near the end of Dr. Scott's administration (1964–65), 11 of the 36 members of the faculty were graduates of FSNS or FSTC. (Four years later the ratio was 13 out of 70.) Among these graduates were three key figures in the Department of Education: Arlene Low, Clayton Reed, and Burleigh Shibles. Coming back as a student right after his war services, Clayton Reed joined the faculty in 1947. (During his career he was awarded an M.A. and had completed course requirements for a doctorate.) First a teacher, then a dean, he became director of student teaching in 1953, a position he held until his death in 1969. A person of character, he also had the good judgment to compromise in deadlocked situations. As has been observed previously, this willingness was particularly valuable in the 1950s when there was so much argument as to what should be contained in the curriculum.

After a few years of successful teaching at the Mallett School, Burleigh Shibles was assigned to the FSTC faculty. An unusually able teacher of reading, he also contributed to the extra-curricular life of the college. This he did with effectiveness, diligence, and enthusiasm. (Gwilym R. Roberts, Clayton Reed, and Burleigh Shibles put in many years of service as advisors to Kappa Delta Chi.) In 1969 Professor Shibles earned his doctorate from Boston University and a full professorship at UMF. The following year he joined the faculty at Boston University.

Arlene Low has been on the Farmington faculty for over twenty years, and during that time, earned an Ed. D. at Columbia. She has served as director of student teaching and as chairman of the elementary education department.

The three members of a highly-regarded geography department, Myron Starbird, Eldred Rolfe, and Albert Mitchell are all graduates of either the FSNS or FSTC. From 1949 to 1963 Professor Starbird carried on alone as the FSTC geographer. In 1963 Albert Mitchell was added to the department, and Dr. Rolfe in 1966. These three graduates have not only been effective classroom instructors but writers of articles for geography and other journals, as well as officers in organizations for professional geographers.* Accreditation teams have singled them out for distinguished work in their field and their professional credentials have been earned in the top graduate schools for geographers. Myron Starbird, developer of the department, retired in 1974 after releasing the chairmanship to Dr. Rolfe in the previous year.

Dr. Anna A. Small, while serving as director of the Franklin County Counseling Service, accepted in 1965 an FSC appointment as professor of education and psychology. Later she was to become the head of the section in special education concerned with problems associated with disturbed children. In the early thirties at FSNS she was a superior musician and popular undergraduate leader. In 1972, after serving with distinction for some seven years on the UMF faculty, she was taken ill, and died soon afterward.

Other graduates or former undergraduates of Farmington who have proved their competence on the UMF faculty are: Verne Byers (a mathematician who was captain of the FSTC basketball team of 1950–51); Clifford Oliver (another mathematician who proved his versatility in 1934 by conducting a literary column in the FSNS *Mirror*); Robert Martin (biologist of the mammalogist variety who has recently been studying the location and behavior of bats in Paraguay); Elizabeth Marks (a 1953 cover girl in a home economics magazine); Alfreda Skillin (dynamic undergraduate leader who served

---

* Prof. Albert Mitchell is, at present writing, president of the New England-St. Lawrence Valley Geographical Society. He has been state coordinator for the National Council for Geographic Education. He has had articles published in the *Journal of Geography, The Maine Townsman,* and *Field and Stream.* Dr. Rolfe has also been coordinator for the National Council for Geographic Education and is the representative and adviser for Gamma Theta Upsilon (international honorary geographical society). He is also the editor of *The Maine Geographer.* Earlier, Professor Starbird was active in these societies as well as being the author of the article on Maine in the *Book of Knowledge.*

two non-consecutive terms on the Farmington faculty); Harland Abbott, Carlene Hillman, and Gwilym R. Roberts. Because these last three have held important administrative posts at UMF, a further word about them would seem to be in order.

In 1949, when Myron Starbird became the FSTC geographer, his former position as principal of the Mallett School was assumed by his eighth-grade teacher, Harland Abbott, the same person who spoke for the FSNS students in 1939 on the 75th anniversary of the institution. After receiving an Ed.D. from Harvard in 1960, Dr. Abbott was appointed the FSTC dean of instruction, in which position he played an important role in the hiring of faculty and in the supervision of undergraduate instruction. Before his retirement in 1974 he was assistant to the president. One of his many contributions to the successful operation of the college has been the collection and preparation of material requested by the accreditation teams in their visits to the campus since 1961. Probably an even heavier burden has been his supervision of the graduate studies, with all their attendant uncertainties, and the program for adult education.

Carlene R. Hillman was appointed director of the home economics department in August 1965, on the retirement of Mabel A. Hastie. Dr. Hillman graduated from FSNS in 1942 with a B.S. degree in home economics. Later she was to receive an M.A. from Cornell and a doctorate from Penn State. In 1954 she went to Douglass College (part of Rutgers University) as an assistant professor. In 1960 she returned to Maine as a supervisor of state home economics programs; in 1962 she joined the Farmington faculty. The home economics program at Farmington has been singled out consistently for its excellence; the number of accolades have not diminished during the administration of Dr. Hillman.

The doyen of UMF, in years of service, is Gwilym R. Roberts. As a matter of fact, Professor Roberts was the precocious doyen of classroom instructors at FSTC long ago, having earned the title as far back as 1949. The heavy faculty losses from 1939 to 1949 gave him, in his eighth year at Farmington, a senior rating which usually comes only to the more venerable. In addition to being a Fulbright scholar, he has devoted two academic years to graduate study at Columbia. In 1957–59 he was interim dean of instruction and played an important role in the badly-needed revision of the curriculum. Returning to full-time teaching, he became in 1965 the official head of the history

CURRICULUM COMMITTEE (1962–63): Left to right: Ronald Brann, Robert Bigelow, Martha Wasgatt, Mabel Hastie, Eleanor Wood, Lawrence Stofan, Harland Abbott, Ross Fearon (?).

JUDICIARY COMMITTEE (1962–63). Front row: Louise Higgins, student member, and Julia Ksionzyk, teacher of clothing design in home economics. Back row: Clayton Reed, supervisor of the student teachers Training School (1953–68), and student member Leighton S. Smith.

department. Professor Roberts has written articles for local and historical journals, has been in state-wide demand as a speaker, and has wielded an impartial gavel as the moderator of Farmington town meetings. In 1970 he went over again to the administrative side of the academic street to head the Division of Arts and Humanities, while continuing to teach history on a part-time basis.

The 1950s were not years of notable athletic success at FSTC, yet bright spots occasionally appeared. In 1954–55 the basketball team broke even with eight victories and the same number of defeats. In 1956–57 a winning season of eight to five was enjoyed. The stimulus of winning seasons was experienced by the baseball team in 1959 and again in 1961. In 1962, Roger Wing, former star outfielder at the University of Illinois, became the baseball coach. In his second year as the FSTC baseball mentor, Coach Wing led the Beavers to a second-place finish in the northern division of the New England State College Athletic Conference. The climax in baseball success was reached in 1965 when the FSTC nine emerged with an impressive eleven to two record. In 1966, the last year of the Scott administration, Roger Wing, as athletic director, decided to transfer his coaching to golf and soccer. As his baseball replacement he appointed Len McPhee, former star athlete at South Portland High and UMO. The new coach led the Beavers nine to an eleven to four season. Behind the pitching of Paul Wheeler, Truman Libby, and Bob Miller, and the hitting of Charles Reed, Roger Reed, and Glenn Burleigh these two 1965 and 1966 teams were the most successful of any baseball club in the history of the institution.

In the early 1930s, tennis at FSNS, starring such racket wielders as Roger Snell, Wannie Russell, and Neale Howard, was not only popular but highly successful. For reasons obscured by time this sport vanished from the local scene during the 1930s without making any reappearance at a later date. In the spring of 1962 golf rather than tennis found enough support to be added to the FSTC intercollegiate program. Furthermore, none other than the present head of the Department of Education, Professor Ross Fearon, became the first coach of the sport at FSTC. He was to remain in this position until Roger Wing took over the duties in 1966. The won and lost record from 1962 to 1966 indicated an exorbitant number of FSTC slices and hooks. To use a cliché of sports writers, Professor Fearon was "building for the future." Three outstanding UMF golfers were to arrive at the college after Professor Fearon had laid down the burden of his coaching duties in 1965.

However, an educational event in 1961 involving the first FSTC golf coach was of more importance to the institution than the introduction of any sport. FSTC in that year initiated a program quite different from the traditional normal school offerings, designed as they had been to prepare students for conventional teaching in the elementary and junior high schools. New demands of society were recognized when Professor Fearon joined the faculty as the head of a small but promising special education department, a unique area for teacher training in the State of Maine. Twelve students were originally enrolled for this kind of training; over the ensuing years this department was to have continuous growth until by 1973–74 the enrollment had gone up to nearly 400.

Developments in 1964–65 had indicated other changes in the future make-up of the college. One of these was a degree program for graduate students. Opened in the summer of 1964, it could claim, by September 1965, an enrollment of over 100 students. The new designation of "State College" was significant. It meant, among other things, the elimination of the time-honored need to sign upon entrance a certification of intention to become a teacher. Moreover, the availability of more courses in general education appealed to those who had no intention to teach. Another FSTC innovation was the adult education program.

In retrospect the year 1965 seemed to mark the most pronounced turning point in Farmington's history. These twelve months witnessed many events of unusual importance, and after 1965, institutional changes were to accelerate to an unprecedented degree. The one-celled teaching institution was acquiring and preparing for responsibilities previously unforeseen in its hundred years of training teachers. It was a year of building dedications and bulldozing for the future. In May the gymnasium was dedicated to Dr. Errol L. Dearborn with Emery L. Mallett, a son of Principal Mallett, delivering the tribute. In June the Mantor Library was dedicated, with the person for whom it was named modestly wondering about her worthiness for the honor. In the summer, the future growth of the college was brought to local attention as three large houses were demolished and a fourth removed to create a building site. As previously noted, the 1965 baseball team had the finest season of any in modern times.

The 1965 September enrollment showed the greatest upswing in recent Farmington history. Some 240 freshmen registered, a 38 per cent increase over the 1964 class. The year also marked the beginning of a sharp increase in faculty positions to preserve the student-faculty ratio. The centennial celebration, one year late, was observed in the spring of 1965 when Dr. Dearborn, Professor Starbird, and Professor Roberts joined forces to present a hundred-year history. (This chronicle of FSNS and its successors would have been greatly improved if only their manuscripts could have been retrieved.) Finally, this *annus mirabilis* proved to be a vintage year for beauty, for Shirley Hawes was Blueberry Queen; Gail Wildes, Carnival Ball Queen; Barbara Calogero, Kappa Delta Phi Sweetheart; Marilyn Yeaton, New England Maple Princess; Sandra Howatt Taylor, Maine Dairy Princess; Diane Hoffbauer, Waldo County Poultry Queen; Jacqueline Grant, Phi Sigma Pi Sweetheart.

Some of the Farmington Normal organizations and exercises had managed to hang on under the aegis of the FSTC, but nearly all of them gave up the ghost in the sixties. The Judiciary, after a thirty-year history, expired in 1963; the Modern Authors Club adjourned *sine die* before that, possibly to see their favorite television show; Arbor Day was made a part of the commencement week program in the mid-fifties, and then was dropped completely; the Newman Club, founded the first year of FSTC, carried on its religious activities, but the Christian Association, dating back to the Purington administration, finally concluded that its style and functions were outdated. (Established for religious reasons, it had become mainly a social organization whose folksy activities were discouraged by a more spohisticated as well as more impersonal college.) The demise of the CA was followed by the rise of the Christian Fellowship, a group far smaller than the CA but more devoted to the pursuit of religious experiences.

In 1965 when the FSTC became the FSC and the substantial expansion in numbers and facilities began, many of the FSTC organizations had to change. The rapid growth also affected the nature of some administrative positions. By the early sixties, the president could no longer involve himself in every area of college life. In 1958 Paul Judkins succeeded Mrs. Laurette Clukey as bursar; shortly thereafter, with the fast growth of the college, the necessity for a business manager was recognized, and Mr. Judkins was appointed to that office.* In 1963 Farmington engaged David White as its first director of admissions, a position which was combined with that of registrar during the first years of Mr. White's nine-year career. During normal school and some teachers college years, the principals and presidents selected new instructors without much, if any, advice and consent of the faculty. After their recognized legitimacy in 1965, department heads began to participate in this task. Now, with division heads and members of their departments** they frequently play the major role.

In 1966 Dr. Scott decided to retire from his responsibilities as head of the Farmington State College. It must have been with great satisfaction that he could point to the fact that in the year of his resignation the voice of the state college was being heard with increasing respect throughout the country. This gain in prestige was particularly marked in New England where, for so many years and decades, even the desirability of a state system of colleges was not accepted. The growth of the university system in Maine owed much

---

* In 1967 he was appointed administrative dean, but he never operated under that title because he left for a special training course at Harvard, after which he entered the employment of the Ford Foundation. Somewhere along the line the new title disappeared, for Roger Spear, the successor of Paul Judkins, was given back the title of business manager. Roger Spear has recently been made the administrative vice-president with the official title of Vice-Presidnt for Financing and Administration.

** In 1965 the faculty was officially divided into departments headed by department chairmen: education and psychology, Clayton Reed; Engglish, Eleanor Wood; geography, Myron Starbird; history, Gwilym R. Roberts; mathematics, Theodore Emery; science, John Mudge; health and physical education, Roger Wing.

The growth of UMF since 1965 has also resulted in an enormous expansion of secretarial and custodial groups as well as persons in other subsidiary services. In the 1930s Mrs. Rounds had handled all the official secretarial work, which meant, among other things, that she typed all the official correspondence not only for the principal but the deans and others. In the fall of 1973, thirty-two persons were performing secretarial functions and fourteen were in the offices of registrar, business manager, and bookstore. Three campus policemen patrol the grounds, a service that was the uncoveted prerogative of the Normal School principal. The number of custodians in the past twenty-five years has gone from five to sixty-three. The increase in this staff has made it unnecessary for the head of the college and his faculty to perform as emergency custodians, which they once did in preparation for such events as the Chapman concerts, teachers conventions, and commencements.

to Dr. Scott and his colleagues. It should be added that they took full advantage of the growing awareness in Maine that too small a percentage of its secondary school graduates were going to college.* On the eve of his retirement, President Scott assured his faculty that he was not leaving because of frustration or discouragement. Such assurance should hardly have been necessary in light of the institution's building program, increase in faculty salaries, and attainment of regional and provisional national accreditation.

---

* The Coles and Higher Education Planning Commission (HEP) reports set forth in detail the reasons for making a greater effort to enroll students in higher education. The HEP report included somewhat embarrassing statistics: "In 1963, Maine sent 31% of its high school graduates to college. In 1968, the proportion was 38%. Comparable figures for the United States are 51% in 1963 and 65% in 1968. Unfortunately, Maine was still lowest among all 50 states in 1968 in the rate of those going to college."

DR. MELVIN G. SCARLETT, President of Farmington State College, 1966–68.

III. THE SCARLETT AND OLSEN
ADMINISTRATIONS

From 1868 to 1870 Farmington Normal contributed many able teachers to Minnesota, especially to the Mankato Normal School. One of these was George M. Gage, second principal of Farmington Normal. He not only became the principal of Mankato Normal, but took with him several Maine teachers who were to make their contributions to Minnesota education. Hence, it was only right and just, in view of our past generosity to Minnesota, that in 1966, almost a hundred years later, a counter migration at least partially reduced the losses of the nineteenth century. Dr. Melvin G. Scarlett, who had been dean and then acting president of Mankato, replaced Dr. Scott in the fall of 1966. The new FSC dean of instruction in 1967 was Dr. Einar A. Olsen, also from Mankato.

Dr. Scarlett graduated from Catawba College in North Carolina, received an M.A. from the University of Florida, and an Ed.D. from Oklahoma State University. He was to stay in Farmington only two years, for in September 1968, he accepted an offer to head Middle Tennessee State. A controversial figure during much of his term as Farmington's president, Dr. Scarlett successfully led state college forces in opposing the first university merger bill, which was more unfavorable to Farmington than the law finally adopted. Dr. Scarlett was handicapped in that he was succeeding an unusually popular Farmington president. Whatever the reasons, he had frequent clashes with some members of his faculty. His plan for mass lectures in place of smaller class sections proved of limited usefulness, especially since it was soon to encounter protests against the impersonal attitude of many college lecturers. It should be added that such protests were nation-wide.

In 1966 the State Board of Education granted official permission to Farmington State College to train prospective high school teachers. Chester Willette, an experienced and successful high school principal, was selected to head the new Department of Secondary Education. FSC was to be the first of the former Maine teachers colleges to be entrusted with this responsibility. The popularity of the program was immediately apparent; 107 students enrolled in it in 1967, only the second year of the department's existence.

Such enlargements of the original mission of Farmington Normal were reflected in the jumps in registration. In 1966, FSC had 690 students as compared with 610 in 1965; in 1967 there were 881; and in 1968, 1,025. There were corresponding increases in the faculty. To avoid a further barrage of statistics, one more figure might be acceptable: in 1966, an unprecedented increase of the faculty took place when 16 instructors were added in order to maintain a proper student-faculty ratio. (For purposes of comparison it should be remembered that during the Second World War the entire faculty numbered 18 instructors.) A rather spectacular expansion of campus facilities was also necessary to take care of a student body which almost doubled from 1965 to 1968.

Such a rapid growth of the institution meant a further re-allocation of many administrative responsibilities. In November 1967, the president ceased to preside over faculty meetings; this function was handed to the dean of the college. This was a far cry indeed from the days when the principal announced policies that he had already decided upon, without any confusing help from a committee. In 1967 the faculty assumed new duties as they formed committees to establish policies in such areas as: instructional improvement, concert lectures, academic standards, scholarships and awards, admissions, and many more. Shortly after this faculty realignment, the students broke away from the faculty-student format of 1948 when the Coordinating Council had been formed. They decided to go it alone with the formation of a student senate. (The members of this student group observed the amenities by arranging for a faculty adviser. Such a person, however, soon learned that his prejudices were considered not only quaint, but passé and irrelevant.)

Other complicating developments accompanied the rapid growth of Farmington State College. In 1968 the institution became a part of the new university system and answerable to a chancellor and a board of trustees. This reorganization produced the new name for the college, the Farmington State College of the University of Maine. Inspired in 1968 by examples on other campuses, a rather small but highly vocal group began to step up its agitation and demands. These included parietal hours and liquor in the dormitories, uncensored and unedited articles for the college publications, and unlimited cuts in class attendance. It was not difficult for many of the older generations to accept exaggerated stories of youthful depravity as they became uneasy or outraged by the long hair and beards of the men as well as the shabby attire of the women. To top off these unsettling developments, the president's resignation in September was not the most convenient time to adjust to a presidential change. (A harbinger of troubled times had occurred early in the year when Professor Robert Bigelow missed his first class in twenty years of Farmington teaching.)

Fortunately, the successor of Dr. Scarlett, Dr. Einar A. Olsen, was accustomed to rough seas, having been born and brought up in Gloucester, Massachusetts. A member of the U.S. Navy in World War II, he earned B.S. and M.Ed. degrees from UMO and an Ed.D. from Boston University. Before becoming a faculty member at Mankato, where he was chairman of the Department of Health Education, he was an associate professor at Texas Western, and then taught at the University of New Mexico at Albuquerque. Co-author of a college health text, he was also co-author of two sports books for juveniles. More recently he has written four childrens' books on oceanography.

One of the continuing major problems that faced him as acting president was that of further expanding the campus facilities. (Another problem was whether or not he was to be the president. After a trial run of one year the Board of Trustees decided affirmatively.) In the early 1960s legislative appropriations for new buildings had coincided with the permanent stalling of the Mallett Fund Drive. A committee, headed by Dr. Dearborn, entertained many suggestions as to how the money could best be used, and the consensus seemed to point to a new president's house. (Dr. Scott and family were furnished a new house on the Byron Small lot, but many considered that it lacked proper space for entertaining.) In June 1970, at the Alumni Day banquet, Dr. Dearborn announced that the fund was to be used for the construction of a president's residence on the site of the old Abbott School gymnasium on High Street. A closer look at the spiraling building costs helped to rule out this plan, and several already-built houses were considered. Eventually President Olsen asked the Alumni Council to drop the effort to get a new house for the president and recommended, with the agreement of Dr. Dearborn, that the Memorial Fund be used to purchase an alumni house. Consequently, when the Jordan Tarbox house on the corner of South and Main streets became available in the spring of 1972, it was purchased and then renovated and refurnished. The second floor was refurbished for the public information and alumni relations office; the first floor was designed for alumni receptions, meetings, and archival purposes.

In 1967 Scott Hall was completed when a second half was added seven years after the construction of the original dormitory. At a cost of $700,000 it was possible to house 150 more students. The Helen Lockwood dormitory was available by September 1968, and two years later still another one, the Stella G. Dakin dormitory, was essential to provide housing for the continuing increase in numbers of students.

Another important expansion of the physical plant to take care of a bulging college was a new multimedia classroom building* (The Learning Center) completed in 1970. This enabled some of the fac-

---

* The siting of the Learning Center continued the southern expansion of the campus begun with the Dining Center, and provided for the acquisition of property long involved in Farmington's educational history. In the 1950s the old Kappa Delta Phi House, acquired in 1937 from the defunct Abbott School, was considered increasingly to be a fire hazard, to the extent that the fraternity found it advisable to post a fire watch at night. When an opportunity came to sell the property in 1961, the fraternity erected a new house at the end of Lincoln Street, to the east of the campus. The new owners of the Abbott grounds ran into difficulties in their plans for commercial use of the Abbott School site, and the property finally came into the possession of the college, unfortunately after "Little Blue" the artificial mountain which had symbolized the Abbott School, had been leveled by the developer. At about the same time, the college acquired former Abbott School property on High Street, including the old Abbott School gym.

DR. EINAR A. OLSEN, current president of the University of Maine at Farmington.

FARMINGTON FACULTY RETIREES (1974), front row, left to right: Alice Knowlton, a supervisor of student teachers; Clifford N. Oliver, professor of mathematics; Margaret Armstrong, associate librarian. Back row, left to right: Harland Abbott, dean of instruction and assistant to the president on retiring; Myron Starbird, professor of geography and head of the department, and Robert Bigelow, specialist in methods course in teaching science.

Left to right: Dick Rice, academic vice-president; Ross Fearon, head of the Division of Education; Gwilym Roberts, head of the Division of Arts and Humanities; Theodore Emery, head of the Division of Mathematics and Science.

ulty (a group which numbered 44 in 1965 and 96 five years later) to escape from their ghetto-like quarters in the crowded rooms of Merrill Hall. In this modern building, with its latest audio-visual equipment and individual offices for the faculty, life seemed positively sybaritic.

Early in Dr. Olsen's administration, a major change was made in the academic administration of the college with the creation in 1968 of two division heads. Dr. Dick C. Rice, whose experience was chiefly as a teacher and administrator in the public schools of Ohio, and who holds the Ph.D. degree from Ohio State, joined the faculty as head of the Division of Education, and Dr. Emery Dunfee was named head of the Division of Arts and Sciences, embracing all non-professional aspects of the academic program. Dr. Dunfee, long a teacher in Deering High School and a former member of the State Department of Education, had joined the Farmington faculty in 1964. In the academic year 1969–70, this division was split into two parts, with Dr. Dunfee remaining as head of the Division of Mathematics and Science and Professor Gwilym Roberts becoming head of the Division of Arts and Humanities. During the same academic year, Dr. Rice moved up to the newly-created position of academic vice-president. From 1970 to 1972, the education division head's position was filled by Dr. Robert Beynon, who came from Ohio to join the Farmington faculty. After an interim year in which Dr. Carlene Hillman and Professor Ross Fearon served as acting division heads, Professor Fearon was named education division head in September 1973. Upon Dr. Dunfee's retirement in 1972, Dr. Theodore Emery, returning from two years of graduate study, was named as his successor.

Some of the building projects seemed ill-fated; certainly the student union proposal had times when it did not appear to have been conceived under favorable auspices. From the late 1940s such a building was a high priority choice, and the need for it provided considerable motivation in raising money for the Memorial Building. It was not as essential, however, as either dormitories or classrooms, so it was unable to get to the very top of the priority lists. Just as it seemed likely in 1968–69 that the student center would finally have its turn, yet another setback was encountered when Maine voters turned down a bond issue that would have resulted in the construction of a student union. At that time the taxpayers, after experiencing sharp increases in their taxes, were re-examining educational needs and requests. All of this coincided with countrywide unrest on campuses, and although this had little disruptive effect in Farmington, the national malaise in higher education did nothing to popularize an educational bond issue. In 1972, however, the voters of Maine finally gave the go-ahead sign for this much-delayed building. And so, with the construction of the student center as part of an addition to the dining center, the dream of at least two decades was to become a reality.

When, in the late 1940s, President Errol L. Dearborn told a faculty meeting that he could foresee the day when the college might own nearly all of the block on which it was centered, most faculty members reacted with incredulity. With the purchase of the Whitney property for the library extension in 1966, the Vincent Davis residence on South Street for a health service center, the three Helen Davis residences surrounding Franklin Hall in 1970, and the Dill and Merrow residences in the center of the block in 1970 and 1971, the college had more than fulfilled Dr. Dearborn's prophecy. Through the purchase of fourteen different pieces of property, the college had become the owner of the whole block on which it was centered, with the exception of the public library, the Methodist church, and two residences. In addition, the purchase of six pieces of property west of Main Street had provided space for a large dormitory and parking lots, while eight purchases to the south provided a solid block of land for completed and planned structures. Four lots purchased to the east of the main campus had provided space for three dormitories.

To the one classroom building, one laboratory building, one gymnasium, and two dormitories which comprised the campus in 1948 had been added in the space of a quarter century, four dormitories, a dining center, two large classroom and faculty office buildings, a new gymnasium, a president's house, an alumni house, and a health center.

A review of over a century of struggling for adequate educational facilities at Farmington takes us back to the "majestic walls" that were so described by *The Farmington Chronicle* in 1864. These so-called majestic walls have been succeeded throughout the years by walls that would have amazed *The Chronicle* correspondent. Those who appreciate the importance of adequate physical plants for educational institutions can derive satisfaction in contemplating the faith and heroic persistence of the many Farmington planners from Principal Kelsey to President Olsen.

In 1968 it was again time for a committee of the New England Association of Colleges and Secondary Schools to visit and re-evaluate Farmington State College. (No national accreditation is possible without first obtaining regional accreditation.) This investigation was headed by the late Athern Daggett, professor of government and later acting president of Bowdoin. The results of it were, on the whole, gratifying. The chief criticism of FSC had to do with the continued absence of language instruction. The 1958 committee had said what the 1968 committee found appropriate to repeat: "Foreign language for the purpose of improved general education should be instituted in the near future." The 1968 committee extolled the "able direction and management" which John Burnham was giving the library, but pointed to the need for an expansion of library facilities. This action proved to be only one year away. It also stressed the need for the continued development of the collection in science and the humanities. The accreditation recommendations were again useful for those who valued the continued growth of the library.

The strengths of the institution were thought to outweigh the weaknesses. The committee described the student body as "serious, responsible, and attractive." It thought there was "a nucleus of committed and able faculty administrators," and it found other aspects of FSC to be commendable. Those specifically mentioned were: special education, home economics, and the geography department. Last, but by no means least, the committee commended "the devotion to teaching which seems to characterize the college." Despite these recognized strengths the regional accreditation of 1968 was only provisional, which meant that Farmington was due for both a regional and national investigation in 1971.

In that year Dr. Harland Abbott again alerted the faculty to organize their materials for an inspection. In 1969 the long-awaited return of modern languages had taken place, and this was to assist in clearing the way in 1971 for full and unqualified accreditation, both regional and national. Much had happened since 1954, the year Dr. Scott first tried for accreditation. The extent of the change in the nature of the instructional program can perhaps best be appreciated by comparing the faculty members of 1953–54 and their duties with those of twenty years later.

Top: Roger Wing, director of athletics. Middle: Dr. Robert Martin discusses a bat (?) with his biology class. Above: SEAM (Student Educational Association of Maine) with Dr. Anna Small.

In 1953–54 all science courses offered by the college were taught by two men who would still be serving on the faculty two decades later—Robert Bigelow and John Mudge. The latter also served for over a decade as dean of men. By 1973–74 these men had been joined by ten more scientists. Mr. Bigelow, by now specializing in the teaching of science, had been joined in the chemistry department by Dr. Harvey Aft (1969), department chairman and a specialist in the chemistry of wood fibers, Charles Chakoumakos (1965), specializing in environmental problems, and Dr. Albert McDaniel (1970). Dr. Mudge was by 1973 one of our biologists on campus, including Department Chairman Dr. Richard Robinson (1971), Vance Wells (1962), and Dr. Robert Martin (1966). The physicists included Chairman Donald Robinson (1967), Dr. Frank Doran (1970), and James Wolfe (1968). Dr. Archie W. Berry Jr. (1970) was the first member of the new Department of Geology. (The subject had been very popular in the nineteenth century Farmington Normal School, but after 1909, there was no one to teach it until the appearance of Dr. Berry.)

Mathematics had been taught for many years by Dr. Errol Dearborn, even after he assumed the college presidency. No mathematics instructor, at least willing to identify herself or himself as such, seems to have been serving on the faculty in the period between Dr. Dearborn's resignation and the beginning of Clyde Jones's eight-year term, starting in 1957. By 1973–74, the mathematics department consisted of six persons: Chairman James Couser (1966), Verne Byers (1966), Ernest Hannon (1969), Clifford Oliver (1969), Gail Lange (1972), and Dr. Theodore Emery (division head, teaching part-time).

In 1953 Albert J. Doran was teaching the history of civilization as well as serving as athletic director, and Librarian Agnes P. Mantor taught Maine history. All other offerings in the social science area were handled by Myron Starbird and Gwilym Roberts. During Roberts's absence for study in Wales in 1953–54, his courses were taught by Allen Pease, who also substituted for Starbird in 1954–55; Pease later served for many years as executive assistant to Maine's Governor Kenneth Curtis. During Roberts's absence for study at Columbia in 1959–60, his courses were taught by Ronald Banks, professor of history at Orono.

Professor Starbird taught all the geography courses and sociology; at other times he took on the responsibility for political science,

European history, and an education seminar. Professor Roberts taught British history, current history, several courses in American history, American government, political science, and economics. (In his earlier years at Farmington, Professor Roberts's schedule had also included at various times three courses in European history, physics, general science, mathematics, sociology, and education in the Junior High School, as well as brief stints at coaching varsity basketball and serving as adviser to the college newspaper.)

By 1973–74, Myron Starbird had been joined in the geography department by Albert Mitchell (1963) and Dr. Eldred Rolfe (1966). Dr. John Quinn III (1969) handled the work in government, including a program of field experiences in politics and state government. The history department, with Dr. Richard Condon (1965) as chairman, included Brian Lister (who had succeeded Albert Doran in 1968), Lawrence Warren (1965), and Dr. Robert Burch (1973), with Dr. John Bingley (1965) dividing his teaching between English and history, and Professor Roberts teaching one-quarter time while serving as division head. Charles Lawton had become the college's first full-time economist in 1970, which was also the year in which Dr. John Roman had succeeded Jane Asklof in sociology.

In 1953–54, two women handled most of the English courses. Eleanor Wood, in her seventh year of more than a quarter-century spent at Farmington, taught English and directed publications. Shasta Boynton, who would be at Farmington in 1973–74, was in her first year as a teacher of composition. Ruth Williams, in her fourth year of a twenty-two year tenure as dean of women, taught one course in English many semesters, and Dr. Julia Eaton (later Van Zanten) was in her fourth year of a twenty-year career as director of dramatics and professor of speech and literature. Ruby Blaine was starting her eighth year as director of all courses in music, and Elsie Grote (1951) handled all courses in art, as she would during most of her nineteen years at Farmington. In 1962, Miss Blaine was succeeded by Russell Jack, who remained at Farmington for eleven years.

By 1973–74, the five full-time faculty in English and fine arts had been succeeded by a staff of sixteen full-time faculty members. Miss Wood and Mrs. Boynton in English had been joined by departmental chairman Dr. Allen Flint, who had come from Illinois in 1970; Dr. Leonard Gilley (1968), a teacher of literature and creative writing whose poetry was widely published; Glenn Frankenfield (1965), a specialist in linguistics; Jay Hoar (1969); Priscilla Noddin (1965), who also supervised the student teaching of English majors; and Dr. Bruce Dean (1970), who taught courses in modern literature and in composition. Dr. John Bingley also offered courses in English on a half-time basis.

Work in drama, music, art, and speech had undergone a tremendous revival with the formation of the Department of Fine Arts in 1970 under the chairmanship of John Schneider, who had come from New Jersey in 1966. Herschel Bricker, who arrived on campus in 1970 after a distinguished career in the theater at Orono, soon produced a vigorous theater program, both in the classroom course and in well-received productions. He was assisted by Nicholas Scott (1973), from the University of Massachusetts, as set designer and director of some productions. Scott also assisted in the speech program led by Dr. Harry Kerr, who was heading the speech program at Harvard University when he came to Farmington in 1971. Dr. Kerr, who succeeded Mr. Schneider as chairman of the fine arts department in 1973, infused new life into the speech program and also founded a reader's theater. Jerry Owens, who arrived from Missouri in 1970 to take charge of the program in vocal music, organized "The Designed Xpression," a fourteen-student group featuring movement as well as singing, which was chosen by the USO for tours of Europe and the Caribbean during its first three years of existence. Dr. Colleen Norvish developed an active instrumental music program during the first few months after her arrival on campus in 1973, while Mr. Schneider was joined in an active visual arts and film program by John Scarcelli (1970) and William McCarthy (1972).

On the 1973–74 faculty, too, Raymond Legueux had been for four years providing instruction in French and German—an area lacking from 1904 to 1969.

Perhaps because of its earlier degree-granting status and its higher degree of specialization in 1953–54, the home economics area offered less contrast in faculty positions by 1973–74 than appeared in some other fields. An expanded area of early childhood education, emerging from the work of Martha Wasgatt (who retired in 1972 after nineteen years at Farmington) and featuring a new two-year program, now included Dorothy Sweatt (who joined the college faculty in 1966), Margaret Heath (1970), Shirley Allen (1972), and Richard

Original group in "The Designed Xpression" that went on a 13-week European performing tour sponsored by the USO and the National Music Council. Sitting, front, left to right: Bob Bragdon, Paula Groleau, Jim Bryson, and Linda Cote; rear, Aline Doran, John Rogers, Neil Flynn, Laura Jones, Judy Johnson, Tom Linder, Gail Poisson, Bill Curran, Robin Lisherness, and Bobbi Boghosian.

Kingsley (1973). (Mr. Kingsley's program in 1973–74 was chiefly in the course in human growth and development.)

The remainder of the home economics program allowed a much greater degree of student specialization and was handled by Dr. Carlene Hillman and six faculty members on campus, with two supervisors of field experience. Including Martha Wasgatt, mentioned above, five of the six home economics faculty members of 1953–54 served through most of the twenty-year period. Julia Ksionzyk taught for twenty-six years in the areas of clothing and family life, until her death in 1973. In 1973–74, clothing and textiles were handled by Virginia Morrill (1967), assisted by Bonnie Quigley (1973). Gladys Taylor also taught foods and nutrition for twenty-six years until her retirement in 1972; Margaret Butler, who had begun to teach on a part-time basis in 1969, was specializing in dietetics in 1973–74. Madeleine Parker, a specialist in home furnishing and housing, retired in 1969 after sixteen years of Farmington teaching; Mary Giboleau (1972) taught in these areas in 1973–74, as well as serving as director of the home management house, a function filled in 1953–54 by Evelyn M. Benjamin and later by Dr. Hillman, Alfreda Skillin, and Virginia Morrill. Elizabeth Marks (1969) was working in the areas of family-child relationships as well as teaching skills, assisted by Cathy Warner (1973) on campus and by Connie Winship (1973) and Ruth Putney (who had emerged from a 1973 retirement) in field supervision. As has been noted, Dr. Hillman had succeeded Mabel Hastie as chairman of the department in 1965, and in 1973–74 was serving as area supervisor in special education areas.

Aside from the home economics group, the Farmington faculty of 1953–54 listed only one full-time person in education—Clayton Reed, Director of Student Teaching. Julia Cox had completed in 1953 twenty-one years of work in the Mallett School, along with methodology courses and student-teaching supervision, and was soon succeeded by Geraldine Quint, who was followed by long-term faculty member Dr. Arlene Low in 1956. Methods courses in subjects such as art and music were taught in 1953–54 by faculty members primarily assigned to those fields, as in 1973–74. The only other offerings in education seem to have been Professor Starbird's education seminar, the education-oriented courses taught by Professor Stofan, and occasional part-courses taught by Mallett School faculty members who would come to the college classrooms for the purpose.

Above: 1973–74 Women's Basketball Team which won the Maine Intercollegiate Women's Basketball Championship. Front, left to right: Kathy Richard, Debbie Hardy, Val Williams, Katy Farrell, Bunny Amevor, Debbie Coombs, Paula Linder. Rear: Coach Stella McLean, Jackie Williams, Charlotte Linder, Claire Palmer, Teresa Campbell, Pam Swan, Kathy Verhille, Joy Duplessis, and ·   ?   . Below, Members of the 1972–73 men's ski team which compiled a 33–3 regular season record and was invited to the National NCAA Alpine Ski Championships at Wildcat Mt., New Hampshire. Left to right: Jeff Hawksley, Steve Hodgkins, Blaine Morse, Rick Hardy, Coach Tom Reynolds, Rod Lawrence, Jim Morrill, Jeff Hopkins, Mike Waddle and Mike Barnes.

By 1973–74, the resident staff in education and psychology (aside from the home economics group) numbered more than twenty, with five other persons directing student-teaching centers in the field. Although departmental lines were obscured by the massive program reorganization being carried out, Lawrence Stofan had been joined in the psychology area by Dr. Robert Fast in 1967 and by Dr. Bertram Jacobs in 1972. In elementary education, in addition to Dr. Low, were Dr. Margaret Cobban (1971), Dr. Grace Stiles (1969) a specialist in social studies methodology, and Dr. Peter Williams (1973), a specialist in the teaching of mathematics. In charge of student-teaching centers in the field were George Diplock (1969) and Alice Knowlton (1969), Leonard Brooks (1970), and Bryce Meldrum (1971); Mrs. Knowlton, Mr. Brooks and Mrs. Meldrum were all Farmington graduates. Retha Watson (1971), also a Farmington alumna, was supervisor of the reading clinic. Edmund Currie (1969), chairman of the education program revision, also served as a reading specialist.

In the secondary education area, Chester Willette, the previously mentioned original member of the department and its director, had been joined by Dr. Stephen Godomsky in 1970 and by Richard Handrahan in 1971. The special education department founded by Ross Fearon in 1961 now had seven members on campus and Diane Wilmot (1973) as liaison representative in the field. Dr. Edward Schultz (1972) was in charge of the area of emotional disturbance, Richard Glasser (1973) taught in the area of learning disabilities, Paulette Grondin (1972) specialized in the trainable mentally retarded, and Richard Holmes (1966) directed the speech and hearing clinic in which Donald Weatherbee (1969) assisted, along with Natalie Jones, speech therapist.

The unprecedented increase in student enrollment from 1965 to 1968 was reflected in both the men's and the women's athletic program. During the 1950s only one person, Rose Lambertson, was needed to take care of the physical education program for women. In fact it was not until the expansion of the mid-sixties that more than one person had ever been needed for the department. It now has three instructors: Hilda Barstow (1965), Estella McLean (1966), and Brenda Obert (1968). All of them are involved not only in a strong intramural athletic program, but a competitive athletic program with women from other Maine colleges. But it did take about a hundred years for Farmington women to break through the institution's walls to compete with other schools and colleges.

Skiing was introduced in Farmington as an intercollegiate sport in 1961–62. A student coached the team, and if any excitement was generated, it was usually confined to the participants. In 1966, however, a new skiing era was begun in Farmington when Tom Reynolds joined the coaching staff. This may not have been immediately apparent to the casual observer, because in 1966–67 FSTC was forced to submit to a two to seven record. However, since that rather doleful season, the Farmington Ski Team has captured the NESCAC northern division championship for five straight years. They placed second in the NESCAC championships, behind Johnson State College in 1967–68 and again in 1971–72. In seven years of competition, the UMF Ski Team has amassed an outstanding 174 to 42 record.

James Corriveau led the team during the early years (1967–69), winning the Ski Meister trophy during the 1967–68 and 1968–69 seasons. Rick Whittier was the Ski Meister in 1969 and 1970–71; in 1969 he was the EISA Division II Slalom champion and represented Farmington at the NCAA championships. Many believe that Rick Whittier was the most outstanding skiier ever to race for Farmington. Perhaps the best balanced team represented UMF during the 1972–73 season. A 33 to 3 record made them eligible to compete in the NCAA Alpine championships which were held at Wildcat and Cranmore mountains in New Hampshire. The team of Jeff Hawksley, Steve Hodgkins, Mike Waddle, Mike Barnes, and Jeff Hopkins was not far from the top in total points, as it placed third behind Dartmouth College and the University of Massachusetts.

In 1966, with the addition of a second male physical instructor, coaching assignments were changed, and Roger Wing, who had been coaching baseball, became the golf mentor. During the following year, fall golf was initiated to enable the college's linksters to prepare for the ECAC championships. Along with the program at the University of Maine at Portland, this was the first fall golf schedule to be played by a collegiate team in the State of Maine.

Three individuals have dominated Farmington's golf successes: Tom Allen, Tom Wentworth, and Wayne Nelson. From 1966 to 1968, Allen won 34 of 38 matches. He had the low season stroke average for the team in each of those years, and in 1967, had a perfect

10-0 record. Tom Wentworth (1967–70) holds the college record for matches won in a career, 36, and is tied for the record of total points won in a career—35½. Wayne Nelson (1969–72) is the co-holder of the college record for points won in a collegiate career. In his freshman year, when he accumulated an 11 to 1 individual match record, he scored an average of 75. Nelson competed in the ECAC championships in the fall of 1969, '70 and '71. He is the only State of Maine golfer ever to qualify for the ECAC fall championships and he did it three times in succession. In the spring of 1971, Nelson crowned his outstanding achievements by qualifying in the NCAA National Championship Tournament at Chico State College in California.

The baseball team, which was so successful during the last two years of the Scott administration, continued with its winning ways in 1967 by becoming co-champions of the New England State College Athletic Conference.

In 1970–71 Roy Gordon became the seventh baseball coach at Farmington in the twentieth century. (As has been noted, Farmington Normal students introduced baseball to this area in 1867. If there were any coaches then, they have been hidden under the accretions of time.) During the 1971–72 season, the college became the University of Maine at Farmington, and as a result of this, was accepted as a member of the Northeast College Conference. The Beavers celebrated their first season of competition in this league by winning the NCC championship. Lloyd Conners, Barry Peaco, and Paul Wintle were named to the All-Conference first team; Mark Burns, Barry Davis, and Ray DiPompo received second team honors.

The 1973 season marked the first time a UMF baseball team was invited to a post-season tournament. Finishing the regular season with a nine to four record, the Beavers were selected to play in the NAIA District North championship. They lost in the first round, one to zero, in eleven innings to the eventual champions, Husson College.

The basketball team, like the other athletic teams of recent years, excepting soccer, has a better than .500 average by a comfortable margin. Len McPhee's eight-year record shows 94 wins and 73 losses. In 1967–68 the FSC Beavers won 17 and lost 6. Their top performances were Ernie Metivier, Dick Meader, and Truman Libby. The two leading scorers in Farmington history have been Barry Peaco and

Steve Williams. This they accomplished despite the fact that recent teams at Farmington have lacked the size and rebound strength that usually is essential for high scoring.

In 1966, Roger Wing took over the coaching of soccer and continued in this role for four years. In 1968, the Beavers posted their best record ever, winning nine games while losing two and tying two. Although this was the third best record in the NAIA District 32, financial considerations forced the team to turn down a post-season tournament bid.

In 1970, Roy Gordon became the soccer coach. His enthusiastic squads were handicapped, as other UMF soccer teams have been, by the lack of experienced players. Soccer has been slow to develop in the Maine high schools, which has meant that UMF players have been taught the game in their college years. At present soccer is continually gaining popularity in Maine, which points to greater success in the future for UMF teams. Some of the names of the better UMF players have been: Tom Taylor, Peter Loughlin, Ray Winship, Peter Brown, Charlie Ulrickson, Gary Record, James Talbot, Barry Maguire, Colin Campbell, Ray DiPompo, Gerry Durgin, John Poulin, Peter Campbell, and Mike Berticelli.

Chairman Roger Wing, basketball coach Len McPhee, ski coach Tom Reynolds, and soccer and baseball coach Roy Gordon constitute a very competent athletic staff. They bear little resemblance to other coaches in the institution's history in that they are professionally dedicated to the world of competitive sports. Nearly all those who served as coaches at Farmington before 1961 were primarily interested in teaching academic subjects; none of them, as far as can be determined, had any illusions about their futures as coaches. The writer can attest to the fact that such modesty was frequently well-placed.

After UMF had been involved in a graduate program for some six years (1964–1970), the chancellor and UM trustees decided that graduate studies should be pursued only at UMO and UMPG. Consequently, the programs at Farmington that formerly led to advanced degrees began to be phased out as currently enrolled students completed their studies or transferred to Orono or Portland-Gorham. The erasure, however, of Farmington's graduate program was balanced by the addition of a liberal arts course of study. This development was encouraged when it was discovered that an increasing number of students were entering UMF without any intention of teaching. Some of these enrolled at the local college because it would enable them to obtain a college degree, which many in Franklin and neighboring counties had concluded was within their means only if they could commute to Farmington. In September 1971, the liberal arts offering became available in Farmington. Beginning with only those who wanted to transfer from the teacher-training sections, it was able to claim during its first year about 50 students. Its accelerating popularity exceeded the hopes of its strongest supporters. In September 1973, Professor Albert Mitchell, in charge of the program, announced that the number for the year 1973–74 was to be in excess of 200; a year later the number had jumped to nearly 300.

Public services such as the Health Education Resource Center (HERC) have highlighted the expanded mission of UMF as compared with FSTC. HERC has been involved since 1972 in a wide-ranging program to produce health education materials for schools, public and private health, medical and social service agencies. The Veteran's Early Education Program (VEEP) has been in operation since December 1972, and has served 132 veterans in two basic areas —a remedial refresher component and a basic education component in which students work toward attainment of their High School Equivalency Diploma from the State of Maine. (Federal funds, unknown to Farmington before the establishment of special education, have financed VEEP.*) The Program of Basic Studies (PBS) was organized in 1970 to assist students who lack academic background for regular college admission, or who have some physical handicap which requires special help through tutoring, counseling, and special classes. In addition, non-college children and adults received services, primarily through the PBS reading clinic, which had administered, as of the fall of 1973, diagnostic and remedial services to 107 referrals, and consulting services to 30 individual teachers as well as 12 schools. The Division of Continuing Education (CED), which also operates the UMF summer session, inaugurated two developments of significance. One was the combination of CED evening courses with regular daytime courses in which there was space to provide for house-

---

* In 1973–74 the federal government helped to finance UMF operations to the tune of $1,250,073. Of this total, $655,639 was allocated for student aid; the remainder, $594,434, went for program funding. In 1967–68 the federal government granted UMF a little over $100,000, so the difference over a six-year period was considerable.

THE 1973 CANDIDATES for Miss UMF. The subsequent winner, Carlene Quimby, second from right, went on to become Miss Maine. The candidates were, from left, Melinda Duval, Debbie Heath, Caron Coyne, Emily Doak, Rebecca Julewitz, Mary Beal, Miss Quimby, and Anne Hairsine.

UMF President Einar A. Olsen (left) with University of Maine Chancellor Donald R. McNeil.

wives, retirees, veterans, and other students with special scheduling needs. The other was the establishment of the summer-spring option for students with all the qualifications for admission to UMF but for whom there was no room for entrance in September. CED registration soared to 1,308 for 1972–73, plus 758 for the summer session.

After the overdue changes had been effected in dormitory regulations in the immediate postwar period, the lifestyle and rules of conduct at Farmington College underwent little change throughout the 1950s and the greater part of the 1960s. Reflecting the increase in enrollment, two new sororities were formed (Chi Delta Phi and Delta Rho) and two fraternities (Omega Sigma Beta and Phi Sigma Pi). These additions were somewhat contrary to the national trend, which showed a decrease in fraternities and the loss of influence and fervor in many of those which survived. (One national development was reflected locally when Kappa Delta Phi decided that their national affiliation was unjustifiably expensive. The fraternity became Kappa Delta Chi after it ceased to belong to a national organization.)

In the early 1950s, television made its first local appearance as the new major medium. It did not thrill, however, the student body as the radio had in the early 1920s. This was because its coming had been heralded for many years and its local installations lagged considerably behind those of the larger urban centers. Its impact on manners and morals, however, was probably even greater than that of the radio. Certainly it was the chief contributor to the further reduction of regional differences in dress, speech, and social attitudes.

The Farmington college, in these television years, has usually responded to national events in a fashion similar to the other academic communities, but there have been differences. Local collegians could appreciate, partly through the help of the paper and pulp industry, what the accelerating rate of technological change could do to the environment. Pollution of air and water was all too apparent to the senses. On the other hand, there were national developments that did not stir up the Maine student to any great extent. Unrest on the college campuses in 1970 did not affect UMF to any substantial degree. A few agitators were imported "to educate" the local undergraduates, but the results were minimal. The sparseness of Blacks in Maine tended to leave Farmington students unaware of, and indifferent to, the reasons for the change of Negro to Black, civil rights to Black Power, and the outmoding of moderates in favor of an El-dridge Cleaver. Pornography and the use of previously-rejected Anglo-Saxon words were accepted at Farmington, at least by those anxious to get into print. Supporters of communal living had few influential opponents, and those from Farmington who attended rock festivals looked, acted, and responded the same as those from any other section of the USA. The old Protestant ethic and WASP ideology, so completely dominant in normal school days, had not disappeared but had been badly riddled by a new brand of hedonism. The middle-aged and elderly were frequently appalled by some of the changes in mores, yet some of them found a great deal to admire in the new values and attitudes. Whatever reluctance some of the young, and more of the old, had in accepting the changes, there was the obvious fact that the last five years had brought about a vastly different college in Farmington.

There is of course no proper time to be smug, least of all in an educational institution where the learning process remains elusive and mysterious. There have been certain developments at Farmington, however, which have been satisfying to many, and may augur well for the future. The high standards of feminine pulchritude were upheld last year when Carlene F. Quimby was Miss Maine of 1973; the skiing team has been for years one of the best in the country, and the other sports teams have won more than their share of victories; a renascence has taken place in music and the theater, and the faculty has been argumentative without being mutinous. Both the social and natural sciences have appropriate specialists and not the overworked generalists of a former day, whose last-minute and desperate reading kept them one chapter ahead of the class. Both the English and mathematics departments, already noted in years past for their superior teaching, have been strengthened. If Maine salaries can continue to be competitive, Farmington should continue to prosper because of the most important part of any college—provocative and challenging teachers.

APPENDIX

NOTES

1. George C. Purington. *History of the Farmington State Normal School (1864–1889)*. (Farmington, 1889).

2. *History of Bowdoin College*. Nehemiah Cleaveland and Alpheus S. Packard (Boston, 1882), p. 260.

3. Ibid, p. 537.

4. George Purington. *Opus cit.*, p. 25.

5. *Public Laws of Maine, 1863*, Ch. 210, Sec. 9.

6. David P. Page. *Theory and Practice of Teaching* (1847).

7. James P. Wickersham. *Methods of Instruction* (1865).

8. Gage did the research on salaries quoted here in his 1866 report to the State Superintendent.

9. See letters in the D. C. Heath scrapbook in the Farmington Public Library.

10. Asa Gray. *The Flora of North America*.

11. George Purington. *Opus cit.*, p. 20.

12. After Gage's departure *The Maine Normal* was continued in Portland under the name of *The Maine Journal of Education*.

13. In the 1920s, William, one of the children of R. Woodbury, became a popular superintendent of schools in Farmington before he moved on to Skowhegan. On some Saturday mornings he would take one of his two sons and me to Lewiston for music lessons. One day he established a record for his Overland car by speeding to Lewiston in three hours. Another son, Nelson Woodbury, worked many years for the Maine Central and is now 99 years old.

14. See *The Chronicle*, Oct. 27, 1874.

15. N. T. True, M.D., became a professor of the natural sciences in the Normal Training School, Oswego, N.Y. He died in Bethel in 1887 after writing a history of the town.

J. B. Severy left the practice of medicine for that of law and was judge of the local municipal court until he moved to Colorado in 1882.

Robert Goodenow was county attorney for Kennebec County and was elected to the thirty-second Congress, being the last Whig member from the Second District. He was co-founder of the Franklin County Savings Bank and its treasurer from the day of its organization in 1868 until his death in 1874.

16. See *Chronicle*, Oct. 1, 1874.

17. *Public Laws of Maine 1875*, Ch. 114, Sec. 1.

18. See Purington's 1894 report to the Board of Trustees.

19. Constance M. Green. *Washington: Village and Capital* (Princeton, N.J., 1962), pp. 369–71.

20. George Purington. *Op. cit.*, p. 68.

21. A biographical sketch of Francis E. Stanley appeared in the *Dictionary of American Biography*, but none has appeared to honor his brother. The DAB article credited Francis with an earned diploma from FSNS, whereas it was actually honorary. The *American Heritage* magazine had an interesting article in a 1959 issue, and several popular books have been written about the late lamented Stanley Steamer. *The Farmington Chronicle* not only described Freelan's trips up Mt. Washington, but frequently took note of the time involved in the Stanley brothers' trips from Boston to Kingfield.

22. Two excellent sources for researching the Stevens story were: a series of 1906 articles in *The Outlook*, by John Foster Carr, and a pamphlet containing the remarks that were made before Stevens accepted the John Fritz Medal. Other books or articles were: *And the Mountains Will Move*, by Miles Duval (1947); *Russia Leaves the War*, by George Kennan (1956), and *The Decision to Intervene*, by George Kennan (1958), a 1963 speech by Secretary of the Army Ailes, which was put into the Congressional Record, pp. 1095–97; *The Panama Canal*, by Donald Chidsey (1970); an article by David G. McCullough in the *American Heritage* in June, 1971; and the article on John F. Stevens by Neal FitzSimons in the *Third Supplement of the DAB* (Volume 32, p. 326), the *National Cyclopedia of American Biography* (1971 Reprint).

23. William Harper had a daughter, Wilhemina, who wrote children's books as well as a series of school readers published by MacMillan. She became librarian of Redwood City in California.

24. Mark Sullivan in *Our Times*, Vol. II (New York and London, 1927), discussed the typical textbooks of this period. He found in them the origin of many of our less attractive traits: aggressive complacency, insularity, anti-foreign attitudes, and a ludicrous ignorance about other people and cultures. D. C. Heath, in his 1874 report as superintendent of schools for Farmington, came down hard on the inadequacies of the average textbook. A few years later, as a publisher, he was successful in improving the quality of such books.

25. *Maine Journal of Education* (1870), pp. 61–63.

26. *Maine Journal of Education* (1873), pp. 23–26.

27. One of the signers of the 1886 resolution was a future principal of the school, W. G. Mallett.

28. The Reverend Burr may have been recommended by Rounds. Both of the Rounds boys fitted for college at the Hallowell Academy, and later taught there for a short time.

29. High schools had received a stimulus in 1872 when the U.S. Supreme Court declared constitutional public expenditures for secondary education.

30. In 1883 appropriations did not permit more than four grades in the Model School.

31. *FSNS Catalogue and Circular, 1883.*

32. *Farmington Journal,* May 9, 1885.

33. The Mr. Butler of notable poundage was Amos Butler, a brother of Frank W. (class of 1887), Ernest (class of 1892), and a brother-in-law of Alice Smith Butler of the class of 1890.

34. Communication of J. W. Fairbanks to State Superintendent. *The Maine School Report, 1898.*

35. From a Lincoln article in *The Farmington Normal,* 1901.

36. *Everyday Pedagogy* (Boston, 1915); *Practical Projects* (Boston, 1924).

37. Two somewhat contradictory reports were picked up about Purington as a musician. W. R. Chapman, director and successful promoter of Maine music festivals, praised Purington extravagantly as a chorus director. A recent conversation with a musically gifted member of the 1905 class indicated that the principal had a tendency to flat as he neared the end of the Welsh folk song, "All Through the Night." Whatever the truth of this allegation, the principal of FSNS played an extraordinary number of flute solos in the 1880s and rendered continually, throughout his Normal School days, vocal solos. No social event at the school was complete without at least one vocal solo from Purington.

38. Quoted in Herbert Brown's *Sills of Bowdoin* (New York and London, 1964), pp. 186–87.

39. *Farmington Chronicle* (2\3\1909).

40. In 1907 Arthur D. Ingalls was appointed principal of the town school, a position he held until 1930. In that time there were two grade schools in Farmington; one was run by the Normal School, the other by the town. The Model School was a quasi private school in that pupils were selected or rejected by the principal, but no tuition was charged. In 1931 the two schools were amalgamated into one which in 1942 was named the Mallett School. Arthur D. Ingalls was the principal and Emma Mahoney and Julia Cox of the Normal faculty supervised the student teachers.

41. Before his death in 1913, Professor Chapman served for several years on a committee which had the responsibility of inspecting Farmington Normal. His colleagues on the committee were State Superintendent of Schools Payson Smith and Carl P. Merrill. Both George Purington and W. G. Mallett had a most harmonious relationship with him. The latter often said that the worst teaching he ever encountered was in college; however, he considered Henry L. Chapman and Franklin C. Robinson, Bowdoin professor of chemistry, to be the best teachers he ever had.

42. Edward Thompson was a blind classmate at Bowdoin of W. G. Mallett.

43. Principal Mallett's 1911 report to the trustees.

44. Marion C. Ricker left Farmington in 1918 for further study at Columbia. She later went to Pennslyvania State University where she was on the staff of the Home Economics Extension Service until her retirement in 1942. Her successor, Bernadine Cooney, was also state director of home economics as well as head of the FSNS department. She was to be the last to combine these two positions. Her successor, Helen E. Lockwood, took over the department in 1923 and would devote her entire time to FSNS. Another person would be employed to devote her entire time to being state director.

45. Marion Reed Kimball. *The Pilgrim Way* (Portland, Maine: House of Falmouth, 1962), p. 145.

PART TWO

1. Cited in *150 Years of Education*, by Kermit Nickerson (Augusta: State of Maine Department of Education, 1970), p. 45.

BIBLIOGRAPHY

GENERAL:
Abbott, Jacob. *The Teacher* (1836).
Abbott, Jacob. *Gentle Measures in the Training of the Young* (1872).
Bestor, Arthur E. *Restoration of Learning* (1955).
Butts, R. Freeman, and Lawrence A. Cremin. *A History of Education in American Culture* (1953).
Commager, Henry Steele. *The American Mind* (1950).
Cremin, Lawrence A. *The Transformation of the School: Progressivism in American Education 1876–1957* (1961).
Curti, Merle. *The Social Ideas of American Educators* (1935).
Good, Harry G. *A History of American Education* (1962).
Hofstadter, Richard, and C. DeWitt Hardy. *The Development and Scope of Higher Education in the United States* (1952).
Rogers, Dorothy. *Oswego: Fountainhead of Teacher Education* (1961). Of all the countless normal school histories perused, this was the best. It was particularly applicable to my study of Farmington Normal because the two institutions had an exchange of ideas and personnel.
Smith, Mortimer. *The Diminished Mind* (1954).
Sullivan, Mark. *Our Times*, Vol. II (1927).
Woodring, Paul. *Let's Talk Sense About Our Schools* (1953).
Woodring, Paul. *The Higher Learning in America: A Reassessment* (1968).

BOOKS ON FARMINGTON AND MAINE EDUCATION:
Brown, Herbert R. *Sills of Bowdoin* (1964).
Butler, F. G. *History of Farmington* (1885).
Chadbourne, Ava. *A History of Education in Maine* (1936).
Cleaveland, Nehemiah, and Alpheus S. Packard. *History of Bowdoin College* (1882).
Fernald, M. C. *History of Maine State College and the University of Maine* (1916).
Hall, Edward W. *History of Higher Education in Maine* (1903).
Hatch, Louis C. *A History of Bowdoin College* (1927).
Hatch, Louis C. *A History of Maine* (Reprint 1974).

Marriner, E. C. *The History of Colby College* (1963).
Nickerson, Kermit S. *150 Years of Maine Education* (1970).
Purington, George C. *Farmington State Normal School* (1864–1889).

LOCAL SOURCES:
The Farmington Chronicle (1863–1920); *The Franklin Journal* (1881–1886, 1912–1974). The FJ, for lack of financial support, folded in 1886 but was revived in 1912. In 1920 the FJ absorbed *The Chronicle*. Both of these local newspapers were rich sources for Farmington Normal news. The editors approved of the school and both newspapers usually had a column devoted to school happenings.

Principal George M. Gage started the first FSNS magazine, *The Maine Normal*, in December 1866, and it continued until December 1868. With the departure of Gage for Minnesota, the publication was converted to a state-wide educational vehicle and was renamed *The Maine Journal of Education*. The first issue appeared in January 1869, and the last one in December 1874. Two of the several editors were C. C. Rounds and his first assistant, Roliston Woodbury.

The Farmington Normal issued an annual catalogue and circular from 1867–1924. This made it possible to follow the curriculum changes as they took place throughout the years.

In 1889 George C. Purington decided to recognize the 25th Anniversary of Farmington State Normal School by issuing a history of the institution. He sent questionnaires to all the graduates whose replies told of their post-school life and accomplishments. This constituted the greater part of the book but the first several pages gave valuable documented information concerning the events leading up to the founding of the school.

In 1901 George C. Purington started a school magazine, *The Farmington Normal*. It was to expire for lack of reader interest in 1904. During its brief lifetime it provided a means for some of the faculty to expound their educational views. W. G. Mallett set forth what he considered the legitimate duties of the school superintendent; Lillian I. Lincoln wrote about the teaching of history and geography as well as providing bibliographies for these subjects. George C. Purington and Hortense Merrill described their trips to western Europe. The only contributions from the students were selected class parts.

The Farmington Normal reappeared in 1914, but was somewhat different from its 1901–1904 predecessor in that nearly all the articles were written by the students. It had three or four issues a year and lasted until 1922 when it was replaced by the first FSNS yearbook. This was called *Effesseness* and it lasted with this name throughout its normal school life. From 1946 to 1965, the teachers college period, it was known as *Effesteco*. In 1966, when the Farmington State Teachers College had become the Farmington State College, the yearbook title was changed again; this time to *Dirigo*. No matter what the changes in titles have been, they have all yielded much appreciated information. Yearbooks and the Graduate Catalogue of 1957 have been my major help in identifying graduates, hopefully with the correct spelling.

The Mirror, founded in 1931 and carefully edited by faculty advisers, finally gave way to a publication mainly unedited and unexpurgated, *The Baked Apple*. The changeover was in 1970, and the new student publication is of limited help to the historian for it specializes in expressing opinions rather than recapping campus news and gossip.

Since 1954 the periodic reports of the Farmington college released to the New England and national accreditation teams have been helpful.

In the office of the State Commissioner of Education I was allowed to scan the minutes of the meetings of the Normal School trustees. The annual reports of the normal school principals to the State Superintendent of Schools contained considerable unique information.

Other sources were the Farmington Normal address and handbooks which helped to guide me through the decades of changes in the school rules and regulations; the scrapbooks, kept by both the library and individuals, yielded some amusing tidbits, and the letters and diaries (1916–1941) of W. G. Mallett revealed some secrets out of school.

INDEX